⟨ THE ⟩
SENSATIONAL PAST

THE SENSATIONAL PAST

How the Enlightenment Changed

the Way We Use Our Senses

CAROLYN PURNELL

W. W. Norton & Company

INDEPENDENT PUBLISHERS SINCE 1923

New York | London

For information about permission to reproduce
selections from this book, write to Permissions,
W. W. Norton & Company, Inc.,
500 Fifth Avenue, New York, NY 10110

For information about special discounts for bulk purchases,
please contact W. W. Norton Special Sales at
specialsales@wwnorton.com or 800-233-4830

Manufacturing by Quad Graphics, Fairfield
Book design by Brooke Koven
Production manager: Louise Mattarelliano

Library of Congress Cataloging-in-Publication Data
Names: Purnell, Carolyn, author.
Title: The sensational past : how the Enlightenment changed
the way we use our senses / Carolyn Purnell.
Description: First Edition. | New York : W. W. Norton & Company, 2017. |
Includes bibliographical references and index.
Identifiers: LCCN 2016031574 | ISBN 9780393249378 (hardcover)
Subjects: LCSH: Senses and sensation—History—18th century. |
Enlightenment—Influence.
Classification: LCC BF233 .P87 2017 | DDC 152.109/033—dc23 LC record
available at https://lccn.loc.gov/2016031574

W. W. Norton & Company, Inc.
500 Fifth Avenue, New York, N.Y. 10110
www.wwnorton.com

W. W. Norton & Company Ltd.
15 Carlisle Street, London W1D 3BS

1 2 3 4 5 6 7 8 9 0

To Betty, Johnny, Linda, and Albert.

The most fundamental things I know about feeling,
I learned from you.

We are amazed by thought, but sensation
is just as remarkable.

—Voltaire,
Philosophical Dictionary

CONTENTS

INTRODUCTION

A CCORDING TO THE eighteenth-century French writer Voltaire, oysters had two, moles had four, and other animals—men included—had five. "Some people recognize a sixth," he stated, referring to sex, but when it came down to it, they were just plain wrong. Five is our lot, Voltaire assured his readers, and "it is impossible for us to imagine or to want more."[1]

Given the subtitle of this book, you may have picked up on the identity of the mysterious things that Voltaire was counting, but even if you guessed correctly—the senses—Voltaire's claims might still seem a few sandwiches short of a picnic. Who really cares how many senses oysters have?[2] Why does it matter that moles are blind? And while it might make kindergarten education more interesting, who nowadays would argue that sex is a sixth sense? What's more, lest you think Voltaire's logic stopped there, he went on to speculate about the sensory abilities of aliens. Dreaming of far-off planets and peoples, he wrote: "It's possible that on other planets, they have senses of which we have no idea. It may be that the number of senses increases from planet to planet, and a being with innumerable and perfect senses is the ultimate goal."[3] To hear Voltaire talk, it seems like the truth is out there, but even Scully and Mulder from *X-Files* would have had their work cut out with this one.

Let's not be too quick to dismiss Voltaire, though. Famous for his wit, satire, and highly caffeinated social interactions—he allegedly consumed about forty cups of coffee per day—Voltaire was far from being a crackpot. Nor was he rambling aimlessly about topics that were of no interest to his readers. In fact, he was riding the tide of a major conversational and intellectual trend of the day, and readers would have gobbled up his speculations with zeal. In the eighteenth century, which for this book's purposes is the period between roughly 1690 and 1830, writing and talking about the senses were frequent practices. Authors, artists, philosophers, doctors, politicians, naturalists, and common people were fascinated by the topic, and debates about the senses, the effects of sensory experience, and the links between the mind and body filled the period's letters, literature, and thought.

Here's one quick but important example. Between 1751 and 1772, the writer Denis Diderot and the mathematician Jean Le Rond d'Alembert undertook a massive project that subsequently has been considered indicative of the Enlightenment's optimism, rationality, and innovative spirit. They chased the modest aim "to collect all the knowledge that now lies scattered over the face of the earth, to make known its general structure to the men among whom we live, and to transmit it to those who will come after us."[4] This exhaustive collection of knowledge, to be known as the *Encyclopédie*, filled seventeen volumes of text and eleven volumes of plates before all was said and done, and it featured articles written by more than 130 contributors, including Voltaire, Baron de Montesquieu, and Jean-Jacques Rousseau, all of whom you will come to learn more about in these pages. The whole project kicked off with d'Alembert's bold assertion, "All our direct knowledge can be reduced to the ideas that we get from our senses. . . . Nothing is more indisputable than the existence of our sensations."[5]

This respected mathematician was far from alone in his sentiments. Talk of the senses and sensation seemed to be everywhere in the long eighteenth century, popping up in every genre imaginable. As d'Alembert suggested, just about everyone seemed to agree that the senses were the key to knowledge and meaningful conversation. Novelists and poets dove headfirst into the emotional world of sensory feeling through the concept of sensibility, which you may know from Jane Austen's novel *Sense and Sensibility*. New theories of the brain and nervous system abounded in this era, replacing older ideas of sensation and perception, and physicians were increasingly fascinated with the relationship between physical stimuli and mental processes. Inventors and naturalists used theories of the senses to create delightful new machines like the perfume organ. And let's not forget all the sensory changes that were occurring in daily life: the invention of new pigments and dyes, which radically expanded the color palette for clothes, homes, and art; the spread of new foods, spices, and drugs, thanks to larger trade networks and colonial expansion; and the creation of new perfumery techniques, fragrances, and hygienic routines. All told, the eighteenth century was a period fixated on the processes of all types of perception, making it a rich era for the people of the time and the sensory historian.

This book will delve into the sensory worlds of the eighteenth century, exposing how people in the past thought about the senses, what cultural values they attached to different sensations, the various ways that they used their senses, how they perceived new sensory experiences, and how they tried to manipulate the senses through science and medicine. Each of the ten chapters presents a different "episode" in sensory history in the eighteenth or early nineteenth century. In these pages, you will encounter the tobacco enema, the fad for wearing "prince poo," and a dinner party that took place in the belly of an iguanodon. You'll learn why, in the 1860s, British cats were eating salted elephant meat while their owners ate rotten panther. In short, you're going to encounter some interesting characters, quirky practices, and what might seem like deeply weird beliefs. But, as you will see, they were all completely reasonable for their time. You might even say that they made perfect sense. . . .

Part of the joy of history is trying to figure out how and why the worlds of the past were different from our own, but one also finds elements that seem quite familiar. Some eighteenth-century educational reforms sound remarkably like reforms circulating today. Eighteenth-century perspectives on disability will also resonate deeply with modern initiatives, and indeed, may even furnish valuable new insight on how to think about physical and sensorial differences. Certain elements of consumer culture, the prevalence of dietary fads, and certain medical trends also bear a direct relationship to our current culture. The past may be a foreign country, but it is not a wholly different world.

While the importance of the senses did seem to be indisputable in the eighteenth century, suffice it to say that everything else was highly disputable. *Philosophes*, in particular, were always ready to debate, argue, and critique. The *philosophe* was a key cultural figure of the era, and while I will often refer to *philosophes* in this book as "philosophers," it's a term that doesn't quite do them justice. In the eighteenth century, philosophy was more about a general approach to living than the development of a set of esoteric, heady principles. To be a *philosophe*, it was important to engage, critique, and to be part of a never-tiring intellectual public. Alternately called the "Republic of Letters," the Enlightenment social world was connected through publications, oral debates, and correspondences read aloud. *Philosophes* would, from time to time, indulge in deep ruminations on the nature of time, being, and life, but they would just as often perform music, publish novels, write plays, and perform scientific experiments. They attended salon discussions, led by intelligent and charming women, and they had conversations about everything from the price of grain to the atomic composition of matter.[6] In the eighteenth century, the separation between intellectual disciplines and genres was much looser than it is today, and the fluidity of such boundaries—or truly, their nonexistence—meant that the *philosophe* resembled a Renaissance man much more than he resembled a modern-day philosophy professor. Denis Diderot might have been one of the founders of the *Encyclopédie*, but he also wrote treatises on medicine and science, critiques of art, a novel that involved sadomasochistic nuns, a deeply philosophical set of dialogues that involved wet dreams and spiders, and an allegorical novel about a sultan who owned a magic ring that could make women's genitals talk. That's quite an ambitious intellectual range.

Peter Gay, one of the most noted historians of the Enlightenment, has called the *philosophes* "a loose, informal, wholly unorganized coalition of cultural critics, religious skeptics, and political reformers from Edinburgh to Naples, Paris to Berlin, Boston to Philadelphia," who made up a "stormy family" and a "clamorous chorus."[7] These turbulent *philosophes* thought of themselves as being part of a major historical shift, which they affectionately dubbed "the Enlightenment," a moniker they coined as a way of contrasting themselves with the ignorance of the "Dark Ages."[8] Nowadays, the Enlightenment is frequently associated with intellectual changes, such as the valorization of science and reason, a movement away from traditional religious structures, and an emphasis on values like intellectual freedom, equitable laws, and better education. While I don't deny that any of these themes appear in Enlightenment writing, I tend to think of the period as much more complicated. Conservative and radical philosophical perspectives coexisted, and neither was more or less "enlightened" than the other. In salons, coffee shops, and other social spaces, religious figures met with deists, and Catholic natural philosophers met with atheists. Nobles who dedicated their downtime to literary pursuits joined the fray of Enlightenment print culture alongside down-and-out journalists, and common folk had the chance to rub elbows with hoity-toity spectators at public science demonstrations on the streets of Paris. Even though ideas were freely communicated across national borders, the "common sense" approach of the Scottish Enlightenment had rather a different tenor than the Enlightenment principles in the *Nakaz*, a law code published by Catherine II of Russia in 1767. In short, groups of all religious, scientific, philosophical, and social ilk came together under the banner of Enlightenment, and while the debates could get quite ugly, there was a widespread sense among proponents of the cause that open conversation was the first step toward truth. Yet if this "little flock," as Gay descriptively called them, agreed on three points—that they were living in a transformative historical moment, that debate was the only way to learn, and that the senses were an important part of human nature—they tended to agree unanimously on little else.

The traditional view of the Enlightenment as an "Age of Reason" gives only a partial snapshot of the movement's full scope. The Enlightenment was much more than a purely intellectual affair or an appeal to cold, objective reason. Just as John V. Fleming has shown in his recent book *The Dark Side of the Enlightenment,* our modern notions of "reason" are far too restrictive when compared to its eighteenth-century counterpart. Passion, emotion, and feeling were crucial to the Enlightenment, and public intellectuals and social reformers had just as much to say about the body as about the mind.

My focus on the eighteenth and nineteenth centuries certainly doesn't imply that earlier periods had no sensory history or that ancient, medieval, and Renaissance writers had nothing of interest to say about sensation. Nothing could be falser. But the Enlightenment is of particular interest for readers today because it's an era in which the world came to resemble our own in a number of significant ways. This is the time period that historians identify as the beginning of the modern era, and it was a time in which social structures, politics, culture, and science shifted radically. The spread of capitalism, industrialization, and the rise of consumer society went hand in hand, significantly altering the ways that people thought about money, identity, and the possibilities of commerce. Politically, America and France moved away from aristocratic structures to democratic and representative governments, and cultural life flourished. The novel, a new literary form, exploded in popularity, filling the hearts and heads of many ladies. (While most novelists were men, the novel was considered a lady's genre for quite some time, even before the reign of Harlequin romances.) The restaurant, the coffee shop, and the public opera house were all relatively new social spaces, and the newspaper, fashion magazine, and literary journal were all new forms of media.

Given their centrality to our daily lives and their close relationship to biology, it might seem odd to think about the senses as having a history. While we understand that subjective tastes may differ, we still intuitively believe that there's something universal about the way our senses take in the world. But throughout time, the ways that humans have categorized the senses, described their sensory experience, or put their senses to use have significantly varied. Perception is not dependent on the body alone. Technology, medicine, culture, and society all play a significant role in the way that we experience the world around us, and the ways that we use our senses, consider our senses, or perceive sensations are just as historically and geographically specific as the clothes we wear or the food we eat. In light of this fact, you won't find modern scientific information about the senses here. My goal is not to contest modern scientific claims or to deny their importance, since I'm happy to live in a time and place where survival is common enough that I don't feel compelled to celebrate the anniversary of my surgeries.[9] But instead of relying on modern understandings of how the body works, I'm going to take eighteenth-century ideas on their own terms.

There's a lot to be gained by doing so. Traditionally, it is the responsibility of history to chart the major changes that have occurred over time. Extraordinary people and events leap out from the page, and the ideas that fundamentally altered the world take front and center. But humans are not just minds, buffeted by the tides of great change. People have daily lives. They have aches, joys, fears, and feelings. These quiet moments are rarely remarked upon by history, but they are important nonetheless. If you were to look back on your life, you would probably remember events of larger historical value (e.g., 9/11) or ideas that changed you in a fundamental way (e.g., religious teachings or political ideologies), but you would also remember the slow burn of a skinned knee, the pleasure of summer tomatoes, and the way you felt when you first saw a shooting star. Mundane though they may be, the aspects of life that aren't centered on large-scale change, revolutions in thought, or radical transformations in behavior still matter a great deal.

Due to a lack of sources, it's not always possible to get to this granular level of analysis or to move fully away from the "great figures" type of history, but by trying to reorient the discussion to bodily considerations and the importance of the every-day, we become more aware of the value of all those emotional moments, the intensity of physical feelings, and the power of the things that tend to stay the same across time. Sensory history can teach us how to question long-standing assumptions and how our mental concepts of the world connect to the ways that we behave in it.

Plus, it's undeniable that the smallest moments are usually inextricable from larger, "more important" issues. For instance, the fact that it's possible to eat strawberries in Chicago in February has a sensory dimension, but it also relates directly to economics, environmental issues, legal restrictions, and political notions on trade. Sensory history is a powerful tool for connecting everyday experiences and common modes of perception to macrolevel structures and concerns. To use the more eloquent language of the Abbé de Condillac, writing in 1746, "Whether we raise ourselves, so to speak metaphorically, into the heavens or descend into the abyss, we do not go beyond ourselves."[10] Regardless of whether a thing is grand or minute, Condillac insisted, it always comes back to experience. By focusing on the senses, it's possible to link the self and questions of identity to broader external, collective, and social factors.

So that may all be well and good, but what does a history of the senses even look like? There are as many ways to write about the senses as there are to use them, and as you might imagine, this leaves the door wide open for some creative history-writing. But generally speaking, the field can be approached from four main angles, all of which you will experience over the course of this book. For one, it is possible to consider how the ideas that we have about the senses have changed over time. For instance, we tend to assume that there are five senses, but not all cultures have followed this line of thinking. As you'll learn in Chapter One, many eighteenth-century writers maintained that imagination, memory, and reason were "internal senses" that had every right to the title of "sense," and as you'll see in Chapter Six, many also wanted to add sex to the roster. Chapter Seven will focus on some nontraditional musical systems to show different historical ideas about the relationship between the senses. (This is where a fantastical instrument called the cat piano comes in.) These chapters will focus on how ideas about the senses have changed over time, but throughout the book, you will be introduced to other common sensory tropes that are more historical than our intuition would lead us to believe. For example, we're taught early on that "seeing is believing," and modern science tends to rely on observation to verify the truth of claims. Yet in the eighteenth century, sight was not considered to be as dominant or objective as we may deem it today. Indeed, in the Enlightenment, touch was frequently considered to be the most truthful of the senses, since the eyes could easily deceive.

A second way to approach sensory history is to consider changes in the way that we use our senses. In Chapter Three, you'll be swept back to eighteenth-century Parisian nights, which were pitch-black before the spread of streetlamps. Amid the inky shadows, there was a vibrant commercial culture where customers and vendors relied more on their ears than on their eyes. In the eighteenth century, smell was an important part of a physician's repertoire, and as you'll see in Chapter Five, it would not have been unusual for them to take a whiff of urine or feces to figure out what ailed a patient. We would never dare go to the Metropolitan Museum of Art and run our hands over the paintings or try to lick a mummy, but as Chapter Ten will show, nineteenth-century British museums actually invited these behaviors, suggesting that visitors make use of all their senses when engaging with artifacts. These chapters show that as technology, manners, and cultural norms change, so do the ways that we interact with the world.

A third approach, and the one that is most popular among scholars, is to think about the relationship between social structures and sensory perception. This technique is not quite as obvious as the others, but it reveals a great deal about how people relate to one another. The sociologist Pierre Bourdieu has written about a concept called "habitus," which can be defined as the deep-seated practices, sensibilities, tastes, and habits that define the self, most of which don't get articulated. These tendencies often develop in response to class, education, and environment. For instance, the fact that I speak with a particular accent, feel comfortable eating squirrel, and walk a certain way probably stems from my upbringing in rural Texas. This habitus has been subsequently altered by the education I've received and the other places I've lived, but ultimately, my preferences and bodily habits are influenced on a deep level by the experiences that I've had. This concept is important for sensory historians because there are many ways that we experience the world that we don't explicitly articulate but that still significantly alter our behavior and feelings. In his book *How Race Is Made: Slavery, Segregation, and the Senses,* Mark M. Smith shows how people in positions of power often used sensory prejudices to reinforce their dominance. For example, white smells were the "good" and "normal" odors, whereas those associated with African-American culture were often labeled as stinky or foul.

In the rapidly shifting economic, political, and cultural world of the eighteenth century, sensory prejudices similarly carried a great deal of power, although the primary debates often centered on refinement as much as race. Chapter Four focuses on how blindness became intricately bound up in eighteenth-century debates about economic status and social utility, and in Chapter

Eight, you will see how something as simple as the color of a person's clothing could trigger assumptions about his or her political affiliations and social status. Similarly, Chapter Nine reveals how spectacular visual displays and strict etiquette at the dinner table were thought to reflect diners' deepest character.

Finally, it is possible to consider the changes in sensation that have occurred over time. Why might a woman in the seventeenth century have preferred to use a perfume scented with a deer's anal glands instead of one laced with flowers? How, Chapter Two asks, did European culture change once stimulants like tea, tobacco, and coffee were introduced? This book is peppered with such questions, showing just how historically contingent our perception of "desirable" or "undesirable" stimuli is. Transformations in sensory environments can reveal a great deal about the daily life of people in the past and about the role that experience plays in the formation of identity.

Obviously, there is a lot of theory out there about how to approach sensory history, and while some of these concepts will appear here, the goal of this book is not to give you a crash course in historians' practices. Instead, my intent is to give you a solid understanding of the eighteenth century through an unexpected and unfamiliar historical lens: how people experienced their senses in daily life. If you learn a little or laugh a little, then I consider my job to be done. Generally speaking, I do harbor a deeper wish, though it is my ultimate hope that we might rekindle the eighteenth-century fascination with the senses. Much of our daily life revolves around the corporeal habits of eating, sleeping, bathing, breathing, and exercising, and our bodies enable us to feel the rich textures of life. The senses give solidity to experience, and, evanescent or lingering, the scents, sights, tastes, sounds, and feelings of day-to-day existence help us process the world and make sense of our place in it. By looking at the sensory worlds of the past, I hope to inspire you to think more about the sensory environments we inhabit. What assumptions do we make? What unusual things do we take for granted? In what ways have our senses improved our lives, and in what ways might we benefit from taking the practices of the past to heart? So with all that in mind, grab a coffee (or forty), sit back, and relax. The doctor will smell you shortly.

THE SENSATIONAL PAST

⟫ 1 ⟪

The Self-Made Man:
Creating Genius in the Enlightenment

TODAY, MOST OF US have heard tales of people who have "pulled themselves up by their bootstraps," and we've learned that we should be the sorts of people who make lemonade out of life's lemons. In many ways, this trope of the self-made man emerged during the Enlightenment. At the end of the seventeenth century, the philosopher John Locke announced that humans should be "equal amongst one another without subordination or subjection," and in 1776, the American Declaration of Independence stressed "that all men are created equal."[1] Obviously, this did not mean that all inequalities disappeared, but with the Enlightenment ideal of self-improvement, inequalities came to be seen, not as the natural distinctions of birth, but as the product of education, industry, and discipline.

But there's another version of the self-made man that was highly prevalent in the eighteenth century that is not commonly known today. This "self-made man" was engineered, not through the diligence of his character, but through sensory experiences and physical manipulations. Inhaling the grassy tang of a freshly cut fern, touching the fur of a particularly soft cat, or experiencing the sharp piquancy of vinegar—in the eighteenth century, these and all other sensory experiences, no matter how minute, had the power to dramatically alter a person, remaking her body, emotions, and social skills in an instant. In other words, self-improvement was a physical and sensory process just as much as it was an intellectual or moral one. This perspective was informed by a number of intertwined cultural assumptions, intellectual beliefs, and scientific findings, all of which stressed the prominent role that sensation played in the development of individual character.

In the eighteenth century, people trusted that the body and mind were in a close, mutual relationship. In fact, it was virtually impossible in the eighteenth century to think about the mind and body as being separate. Everything that affected the body would also have an effect on the mind, and whatever affected the mind would also affect the body. Today we would consider imagination, memory, reason, will, attention, and emotions to be affairs of the mind. They are a part of our intellect, and while they may be informed by the experience of our bodies, many of us tend to think of them as mental faculties. But for many Enlightenment writers, there was, strictly speaking, no difference between the mental and physical. Imagination, memory, and all of their companions fell not into the category of "mental faculties," but into that of "internal senses." The internal senses were those inspired from within the body, which, in addition to emotions and mental faculties, included hunger, thirst, the need to urinate, and other such sensations. The internal senses were thought to have just as much of a physical basis as the external senses. Claude-Adrien Helvétius, the author of the atheistic *On the Mind* (1758), was so convinced of the physicality of the mind that he went so far as to claim, "All judgment is nothing more than a sensation."[2] In *Sys-*

tem of Nature (1770), the equally radical Baron d'Holbach treated "perception" and "idea" as "terms that designate nothing more than the changes produced in [the brain]" when objects interact with the body and cause sensations.³ And lest these two examples give the wrong idea, atheists weren't the only ones to focus on the mutuality of the mind and body. The Christian *philosophe* Charles Bonnet argued, "There are no ideas except through the intervention of the senses."⁴

It's easy enough to say that the mind and body are linked, but it's not as easy to explain how they work together to create functional human beings. Enlightenment philosophers eagerly took up this task, writing treatise after treatise on epistemology, a branch of philosophy that investigates the limits of knowledge and how humans come to know things. The dominant Enlightenment epistemology was called "sensationalism," with other terms being sensationism, sensualism, or sensism. The theory held that humans acquire all knowledge through their senses. In this line of thought, every human experience is mediated through the senses, and sensory experience is the main way we develop and exercise our mental faculties.⁵

The English philosopher John Locke is often considered the father of Enlightenment sensationalism. In 1690, Locke set out to explain how humans learn, reason, and develop in *An Essay Concerning Human Understanding*. Locke called the *Essay* "the diversion of some of [his] idle and heavy hours," and going on length alone—750 pages—he must have been in need of a great deal of diversion.⁶ Locke studied medicine at Oxford and worked with some of the greatest scientific men of the seventeenth century—Robert Boyle, Robert Hooke, and Thomas Willis, to name a few—and as much as he protested that he was not concerned with the "Physical Consideration of the Mind," his philosophy was greatly influenced by his medical training.⁷

Locke was dissatisfied with the notion that humans are born with innate ideas. Chief among the philosophers with such a notion, Descartes had argued in the 1640s that we "come to know [innate truths] by the power of our own native intelligence, without any sensory experience. . . . Our knowledge of God is of this sort."[8] Locke, on the contrary, argued that humans have no innate knowledge and are instead born with minds like blank slates. There are two main sources of ideas that fill in this blank slate: sensation and reflection, or, in other words, the external and internal senses. The external senses yielded what Locke called "simple ideas." These are things like the taste of sugar, the yellow of the rose, and the coldness of ice. Simple ideas were stored in the mind, and by reflecting on them, individuals could come up with complex ideas. These ideas included abstractions like "loyalty" or "infinity," ideas of relation like "bigger" and "smaller," and compound ideas like "fish ice cream" (where I know what fish is and what ice cream is and can therefore form a concept of the two together—and then hopefully banish it from my mind forever). According to Locke, nothing that humans can conceive was beyond the realm of sense experience and reflection. In other words, I can only imagine an alpaca flying in a helicopter while listening to Rachmaninoff because I have preexisting concepts of all the component elements. Locke's philosophy met resounding success, and across Europe, "experience" was the word on everyone's lips.

Naturally, the French like to take everything one step further, and the French cleric Étienne Bonnot de Condillac took it upon himself to give Locke's ideas a slightly different turn. Born in Grenoble, Condillac moved to Paris in his late teens to study philosophy, physics, mathematics, and theology. He became a priest in 1741, but Condillac was never particularly invested in churchly duties or theological debates. Instead, he hobnobbed with the who's who at the salon of Madame de Tencin. By the mid-1750s, he had gained an international reputation as a philosopher, and his *Treatise on Sensations* was generally well regarded when it appeared in 1754.

In this treatise, Condillac argued against Locke's two categories of reflection and sensation, insisting that our ideas come only from a single source: sensation. "Judgment, reflection, the passions, all the operations of the soul are, in a word, nothing more than sensation itself, converted differently," he asserted.[9] In order to walk his readers through this claim, Condillac offered an offbeat coming-of-age narrative. Because it was impossible to have an experimental human subject who truly was a blank slate, Condillac asked his readers to imagine a statue whose internal organization was human-like but whose exterior was marble, such that he could not use any of his senses. Condillac then had the statue introduced to the senses one at a time.

The statue first gained the sense of smell, which Condillac considered to be the sense that contributed the least to human knowledge. The statue, standing stock-still, had no sense of shape, color, sound, taste, or feeling, but when he was presented with a rose, he began to form impressions, and his whole being was taken up with the scent. Condillac described this capacity to be consumed by a sensation as "attention," and once the statue was able to pay attention to sensations, he began to experience joy and suffering. If his attention were turned to the pleasant smell of the rose, then he would be filled with pleasure, but if his attention were turned to a disagreeable odor, then he would experience nothing but pain. According to Condillac, these feelings were preservational mechanisms: "Nature gave us organs to alert us, through pleasure, to those things that we should seek out and through pain those that we should flee."[10] By this reckoning, everything that is good for us will give us pleasure and vice versa.

But the more that philosophers thought about the implications of these ideas for morality, the trickier it got. By the 1790s, philosophers like the Marquis de Sade tested the limits of these claims by arguing that some people could find pleasure in destructive behaviors, like swallowing live snakes.

But I digress. You'll have to wait a few chapters to hear about the dear marquis. For now, we have a statue, capable only of smelling, who is reveling in the pure bliss of his rose. But what would happen if you were to take away the flower that occupied all of his attention? According to Condillac, the statue's attention would be redirected to his internal senses, and he would begin to think about the sensation of the rose, even though it was no longer present. *Voilà!* Memory is born. If, in addition to the rose, the statue were offered a different kind of flower, he could begin comparing sensations, and by determining that the other flower's odor was distinct from that of the rose, the statue's faculty of judgment and reason would be born. If the statue took his experience of the rose and mentally combined it with that of the other flower in order to come up with a new, hybrid scent, then he would be learning to exercise his faculty of imagination. As the statue gained more and more senses, he was subjected to more and more sensory impressions, and his judgment, imagination, and memory developed in increasingly complex ways. Through the statue, Condillac showed that understanding, as intricate as it is, is nothing more than modified sensations and that the self is nothing more than a complex collection of sensory impressions.

Condillac's friend and fellow *philosophe* Jean-Jacques Rousseau took up, in fictional form, many of the same questions that Condillac raised in his *Treatise*. In April 1740, Rousseau took a post as the tutor to two of Condillac's nephews, but, by his own admission, he was given to "periodic outbursts of rage" at the children, he fell in love with the sons' mother, and he was caught pilfering wine from the family's cellar.[11] Needless to say, he left the post quickly. Nevertheless, a few years later, Rousseau struck up a friendship with Condillac, and the two became quite close. The friendly pair soon formed a trio with the *Encyclopédie* co-creator Denis Diderot, and they would meet once a week for dinner and a walk.[12] (This tradition gave way after Rousseau picked fights with many of his friends in the 1750s, earning him a reputation among the *Encyclopédistes* as an ungrateful cad.) In 1762, Rousseau published *Émile*, a controversial book that, along with his *Social Contract* (also published in 1762), was condemned throughout Europe. *Émile* traced the development of a fictional boy, and Rousseau sought to show that good character comes not from book learning, but from sensory experience.

In a riff on Condillac's statue, Rousseau offered a hypothetical scenario that he trusted would prove the importance of sensory learning: "Suppose a child born with the size and strength of manhood, entering upon life full grown . . . such a child-man would be a perfect idiot, an automaton, a statue without motion and almost without feeling."[13] According to Rousseau, a human's identity didn't depend on size, physical development, or innate ideas. Instead, "In the dawn of life, when memory and imagination have not begun to function, the child only attends to what affects its senses. His sense experiences are the raw material of thought; they should, therefore, be presented to him in fitting order so that memory may at a future time present them in the same order to his understanding."[14] Rousseau, following a sensationalist model, explained how Émile followed his curiosity, trusted his own will, and relied on firsthand sensory experience. As a result, Émile turned into a gracious, intelligent, loving, and honest young man who had little time for artificial social niceties (much like Rousseau himself).

The fact that Rousseau was a terrible tutor to the Mably children is not the only irony surrounding *Émile*. I should also point out that Rousseau's mistress gave birth to five children, all of whom the couple gave up for adoption, so Rousseau had no empirical basis for his pedagogical methods. Some of these methods do seem to be sound—for example, Rousseau was a key advocate for having mothers breastfeed their own children instead of having the children sent to wet nurses—but in its extreme aspects, Rousseau's freedom-loving pedagogy yielded some terrible results. Richard Lovell Edgeworth, the father of the novelist Maria Edgeworth, raised his son Richard Jr. (born in 1765) with Rousseauean techniques. As a result, Richard Jr. had stunted social skills, a stubborn disposition, and a penchant for disobedience. He left home at the age of fifteen to become a sailor and ended up leading a dissipated life in South Carolina. Jane Austen modeled the eldest Musgrove son in *Persuasion* (1816) on Richard Jr., and her depiction was not favorable, consisting of descriptors like "thick-headed," "stupid and unmanageable," "unfeeling," "seldom heard of, and scarcely at all regretted."[15]

Real-life problems aside, *Émile*'s sensationalist pedagogy showed just how intricately tangled the mind, emotions, and body were in the eighteenth-century sensory system. In fact, medical science also maintained that scents, tastes, sounds, sights, and tactile impressions could deeply affect identity. At the center of eighteenth-century medicine was the "animal fiber." It was considered to be the basic unit of bodily matter, much like how we think of the cell as being the basic unit today. These fibers were thought to be microscopic, hollow tubes that interlaced with one another to form sensory organs, muscle tissue, nerves, and vessels. The first image in the diagram shows a fiber in its basic state. Whenever the body encountered a sensory stimulus, these fibers supposedly filled with fluid and swelled, as you can see in the differences between F2 and F3. Because of the fibers' proximity to one another, doctors argued that a change in one

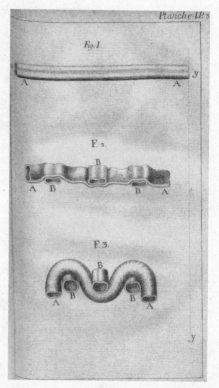

In eighteenth-century medicine, animal fibers were the smallest physical unit. Here you see an individual fiber; limp, interconnected fibers; and swollen, tightly interwoven fibers.

fiber necessarily affected the fibers around it. The fibers would weave together to form complex arrangements, and if one fiber filled with fluid, it would push against the connecting fibers, creating a chain reaction throughout the body.

These tiny, imperceptible fiber movements were the key to the whole process of sensation. The vibrations passed through the body until they reached the *sensorium commune*, the place in the brain where the nerves, which were made up of bundles of fibers, were thought to originate. This was also where, according to a number of anatomists, the body, mind, and soul met. Once the sensations reached this area in the brain, the brain (or soul, depending on the particular writer's religious or philosophical inclinations) reg-

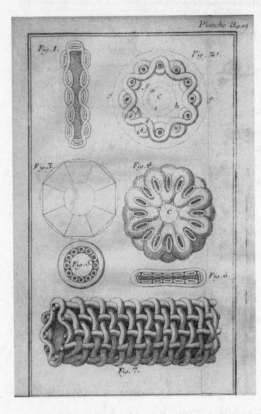

Even though they may look more like Spirograph designs than pieces of the human body, these images represent the complex ways that fibers came together to form muscles, tissue, nerves, and various other important body parts.

istered the sensation. This chain reaction would happen instantaneously, so a person would never consciously register the fibers' actions. Instead, she would only get the "immediate" sensation (e.g., heat from a fire, sweetness from candy) that registered in the *sensorium.*

Because every person's body is different, eighteenth-century doctors recognized that everyone's fibers were also different. Each fiber had a "spring" or "elastic virtue" that determined how receptive it was to stimuli. Doctors cared a great deal about this "elastic virtue." If a person's fibers were overly springy, then the smallest sensation would set off a violent reaction, overwhelming both the body and the brain. The French physician Victor de Sèze, writing in 1786, described how a young woman went to a Parisian perfumer and spent the day in a closed-off room, deeply inhaling roses. The scent worked too strongly on her olfactory nerves, causing them to vibrate violently, and these vibrations sent shockwaves through her entire nervous system. As a result, the girl became hysterical and died.[16] Moral of the story: if you are a sensitive person, maybe you shouldn't take the time to stop and smell the roses.

If, on the other hand, a person's fibers were too rigid, it would take a lot of stimulation to make the fibers swell and transmit the signal to the brain. This underreactivity could cause listlessness, apathy, or a loss of memory. De Sèze, in addition to fretting over sensitive young ladies, was a thoroughgoing ageist and argued that the fibers of the elderly were too dull and rigid to experience proper vibrations. Consequently, the only passions that old people could experience were fear, jealousy, dull lust, sadness, and suffering.[17] Unfortunately for de Sèze, he lived to the ripe age of seventy-six.

In order to ensure that the fibers were in peak condition and that the right impressions were being sent to the brain, it was necessary to carefully monitor every sensory stimulus. Some doctors warned that eating too much red meat could overexcite the fibers, leading to intense rage and in extreme cases, murder. Benjamin Franklin, an exemplar of the self-made man, may not have gone so far, but he nonetheless spoke out against what, in twenty-first-century parlance, we call the "meat sweats." Eating beef or bacon would lead to "low spirits," and the resultant sweating under the bedcovers would pervert "the order of nature" by making the mind uneasy.[18]

Given that sensory experiences could have such sweeping effects, it's unsurprising that a number of Enlightenment writers tried to figure out how best to manipulate sensory stimulation. Not content only to eradicate meat sweats, many came up with plans to improve society through sensory manipulation. One such writer was the Parisian doctor and medical professor Antoine Le Camus, who wrote a lengthy book called *Medicine of the Mind* (1753). In this book, Le Camus wanted to pinpoint the ways that the body could be manipulated in order to create genius. The Enlightenment concept of genius was different than ours and more wide-ranging. It derived from the classical concept of a "genius," which referred to the guiding spirit of a person, family, or place. As such, genii (the plural form of genius) defined the particular character of someone or something. The genius of my dog, it seems, is to bop my other dog on the nose. My other dog's genius is to take it. Another common meaning, closer to our own, referred to an individual's particular talents, but it did not demand singularity, great intellect, or immense creativity. According to this definition, a person with genius was able to do something easily and naturally, but not necessarily exceptionally, and it applied to a broad grouping of skills. One could have a genius for candle-making, raising children, or teaching as readily as one could have a genius for science, art, or music.

In *Medicine of the Mind*, Le Camus explained how these different types of genius emerge, how to manage and improve them, and how to turn anyone whose "genius" was lacking into someone with ample skills. Like John Locke, Le Camus claimed that people were born blank slates, but the difference between a simpleton and an intellectual powerhouse emerged quickly. He argued that this gap was not the result of education, wealth, or resources. Instead, it was the effect of climate, "which can be regarded as one of the first causes of the difference between minds, talents, manners, customs, and laws."[19] Le Camus was far from the only Enlightenment writer to adhere to climate-based psychological theories. In fact, one of the most well-respected books of the eighteenth century, the Baron de Montesquieu's *Spirit of the*

Laws (1748), included a large section on the relationship between a nation's laws and its climate. In colder climates, he maintained, the air contracted the fibers, making people stronger, braver, and better at weathering the hardships of battle. In warmer climates, the air relaxed the fibers and diminished their elasticity, making people more delicate and attuned to pleasure. Montesquieu provided a meteorological, biological reason for the stereotypes of the hot-blooded Latin lover and the quick-to-anger Sicilian, and he explained that the English were "so distempered by the climate" that they had a "disrelish of everything, nay even of life."[20] Needless to say, there were a number of negative racial and ethnic stereotypes that were reinforced by climatological thinking, and such theories contributed to essentialist assumptions about entire groups of peoples, which had significant and long-lasting effects.

For Le Camus, climate was the first determinant of temperament, but it was not the only one. Through the strategic manipulation of sensory experience, he argued, any aspect of one's "particular genius" could be modified, corrected, or amplified, and anybody (or any body), no matter how coarse, uneducated, or dull, could be molded and shaped into a person with genius.[21] Because of the idea that the smallest sensory elements had wide-ranging effects, physicians like Le Camus paid increasing attention to what they called the "non-naturals," or things that had significant effects on the fibers. These included 1) air, 2) food and drink, 3) motion and rest, 4) sleep and waking, 5) bodily retentions and evacuations, and 6) the passions of the soul.[22] To manage all these variables, Le Camus prescribed a strict "Regimen of Living" that would keep the fibers vibrating properly. Le Camus was not being figurative when he described this course of action as a "regimen." His program was a strict one with little allowance for deviation.

If a person wanted to create "a work that would go down in history," Le Camus argued, "imagination is the most fecund between March and October. This is the time when nature is richest, when we feel a greater number of sensations, and when we consequently have the greatest number of ideas. From October to March, the senses are calmer. This is the time when we can return to our ideas, compare them, and draw conclusions from them."[23] (Given that much of this book was composed during a Chicago winter, it seems that I'm destined for greatness.) Le Camus also asserted that night was the ideal time to work because its absolute silence offered the prospect of a distraction-free work environment.[24] Le Camus required people to eat particular types of food, based on their ability to establish "mental advantages"; he stipulated that they regulate their sleep according to age, sex, temperament, season, and occupation; he recommended candles with specific scents and ideal forms of exercise. His lists went on and on, covering baths, medicines, drinks, foods, skin creams, clothing, temperature, drugs, sexual habits, and any number of other types of stimuli. Much of his advice may not seem that stringent to a modern reader, but it was quite novel in its day, and taken together, these prescriptions led to an extremely programmatic existence. Becoming a genius, it turns out, was hard.

He may have been talking about what foods a person should eat and how often one should have sex—Le Camus waxed poetic about how a man with an ideal sperm count "enjoys all the vigor of his nature; his body is firm and robust, his mind is bold and prompt in its operations"—but his prescriptions weren't just about improving the individual body.[25] Le Camus summed up, "Carefully handling these diverse physical elements . . . is in the interest of each citizen as well as that of the whole state."[26] As this conclusion shows, his ultimate goal was to improve society at large. Many other French philosophers and physicians shared LeCamus' idea that sensation was intimately connected to larger political processes. The *philosophe* Claude-Adrien Helvétius traced the lineage of justice back to sensationalist origins. He argued in 1758 that sensation was the "source of human virtues," and "without sensibility to physical pleasure and pain," men would be without desires, emotions, and personal interest, and they would not be able to assemble in society, make laws, and establish concepts of general interest.[27] Basically, these philosophers thought that sensation was the key to all social and political change.

The Marquis de Condorcet, a French philosopher, mathematician, and political scientist, echoed this sentiment in his *Sketch for a Historical Picture of the Progress of the Human Spirit* (1795). Condorcet, an acquaintance of many of the usual Enlightenment suspects—d'Alembert, Benjamin Franklin, Voltaire, and the *salonnière* Julie de Lespinasse, among many others—was a prominent member of the Royal Academy of Sciences and, for a time, the inspector general of the Paris Mint. During the French Revolution, he served as a representative in the National Assembly, and in addition to championing women's rights and serving as a vocal opponent of slavery, he helped draft a new French constitution (although it was never put to a vote). Because Condorcet spoke out against the execution of the king, a warrant was issued for his arrest. He hid for a while in the house of a friend, and it was at this point that he wrote the *Sketch*. Condorcet tried to flee Paris in 1794, but was arrested. Two days later, he was found dead in his jail cell. While the cause of his death was uncertain, the most widely accepted theory is that a friend helped him die by aid of poison, to avoid being executed publicly.

The *Sketch* was published posthumously, and it is one of the key articulations of Enlightenment notions of progress. It follows the history of human development, which Condorcet divided into ten main periods. He charted the cumulative progress of the human race across these eras, focusing on key moments like the development of agriculture, the invention of the printing press, and the rise of Enlightenment philosophy. Condorcet's narrative, however, began on what should be, by now, a familiar note: human life derives from sensory experiences of pleasure or pain.[28] From the building blocks of sensation, Condorcet traced humans' continual progress toward a utopian existence.

In the tenth stage, Condorcet predicted some of the developments in store for humankind in the future. Because humans could continually improve their bodies and intellectual faculties, "the good morals of man, the necessary result of his organization, are like all other faculties, susceptible to indefinite perfection."[29] He argued that social evils were simply the result of ignorance, and in time, the growth of science, reason, and improved sensory experience would render prejudices, vices, and errors obsolete. Inequalities between individuals would be eradicated, thanks to the development of new moral and political sciences. Excellent education would overcome any intellectual inequalities, and government-sponsored solutions would help overcome financial disparity. For example, Condorcet suggested that when minors came of age, the government should give them the necessary capital to develop their work skills. Through measures like these, industry would be improved, and philosophy would become so advanced that superstition and errors of judgment would disappear. Laws would be perfected, as would language, and the sexes would exist in perfect equality. Humans' physical faculties, strength, and sensory finesse could also be improved upon, and while humans could never become truly immortal, medicine could improve to the point that, barring any severe accidents or illness, life would seem infinite. This was Enlightenment optimism at its finest.

Faith in perfectibility is one of the lasting legacies of the Enlightenment, and it came from a highly particular concept of how human beings adapt, learn, and socialize. This concept was rooted as much in the body as in the mind, and sensation, too, was at the heart of it. Candles, baths, and moderate exercise sound like a recipe for a perfectly good date night, but they probably don't strike you as things that could cure the world's ills. Yet in the eighteenth century, they were precisely that. Eighteenth-century social reformers, philosophers, and men of science considered social perfection not just possible, but exceedingly attainable through sensory manipulation. It's like they heard the phrase "Don't sweat the small stuff," and decided to do just that. The small stuff was what mattered. The Enlightenment emphasis on hygiene, preventative medicine, public education, and public health came from the idea that humans could re-create and improve themselves through the sensory stimuli they experienced.

Lest you think that the Enlightenment was filled only with confetti-strewn tales of sunshine and life everlasting, there were some pessimistic takes on this whole sensory situation. Among the crankiest commentators was the Swiss physician Samuel-Auguste Tissot, who wrote an immensely popular book called *On the Health of Men of Letters* (Latin, 1766; French, 1768). Like Rousseau, Le Camus, and Condorcet, Tissot believed that paying attention to sensation was crucial, but instead of focusing on human perfection, he focused on human degeneration. Pitched as an investigation of the "reciprocal dependence between the science of morals and that of health," his work is a thorough screed against the academic way of life. Tissot argued that when the mind is occupied with thought, the brain fibers remain in a state of tension, and the rest of the bodily fibers fall into disuse. As a result, scholars had ravaged stomachs, improperly functioning bowels, and melancholic dispositions, and their sedentary lives affected their respiration, generated bladder stones, and caused infertility. Thinkers' nervous systems weakened, making them cowardly, afraid, and sad. "Everyday, men of letters have to give up their cherished books," Tissot chronicled. "Their nerves, being so weakened, make them incapable of attention. They lose their memory; their ideas become more obscure . . . the fear of sudden death makes the pen fall from their hands."[30] And these were among the least of academics' worries. Tissot offered cautionary tales that painted the most horrific portraits of intellectual life possible. He described how the Tuscan painter Spinello dedicated such a huge amount of energy to painting a hideous demon that he was seized by intense terror. Spinello began to imagine that the demon visited him regularly to complain about the ugly depiction. Tissot reported that Blaise Pascal's deep meditations had wounded his brain, forcing the mathematician to believe that he was always on the edge of a fiery pit. And the Swiss doctor also recounted the plight of the orator, poet, and doctor Gaspard Barloeus, whose excessive studies weakened his brain so much that he believed that his body was made of butter. Evidently, Barloeus studiously avoided fire, but he was so plagued by terror of melting that he killed himself by jumping into a well.[31]

According to Tissot, the only positive way to lead an intellectual life was to do so moderately. To keep the fibers in optimal condition, he suggested avoiding fatty foods, eating plenty of vegetables, exercising, drinking lots of water, avoiding too much wine, living in a temperate climate, avoiding cold feet, stopping tobacco use, taking cold baths, and giving oneself "frictions" each morning to improve circulation. (Frictions involved lying on one's back with the knees slightly elevated, while rubbing the belly with a piece of flannel.) Tissot may have used medicine to rail against certain aspects of society, but he still shared a worldview with his more optimistic colleagues. Pessimists or perfectionists, Enlightenment writers tended to stress that sensory management was the key to mental, emotional, and social well-being.

Recent philosophical studies have returned to this Enlightenment theory. In the words of Mark Johnson and George Lakoff, the

authors of *Philosophy in the Flesh,* "Reason is not disembodied, as the
tradition has largely held, but arises from the nature of our brains,
bodies, and bodily experience. This is not just the innocuous and
obvious claim that we need a body to reason; rather, it is the striking
claim that the very structure of reason itself comes from the details
of our embodiment."[32] I'm a wholehearted advocate of this concept,
and I'll be the first to say that our bodies and minds are more deeply
connected than most of us probably credit them to be.

Lakoff and Johnson are right that a host of philosophical and
cultural traditions have taught us that we should value ideas more
than the body or that we think, therefore we are. But we also
shouldn't overstate the degree to which reason, historically, has
been seen as disembodied. By acknowledging the interconnectedness of the mind and body, we aren't stepping into unknown
territory. The eighteenth century gives us plenty of precedent for
a more integrated perspective on the relationship between the
various parts of our being. Enlightenment writers suggested that
the true way to a rational, reasonable society was to slow down,
think about the value of daily experience, and consider the way
that the world around us affects our deepest emotions, relationships, and expectations. They asserted that our world is much
more complex than a simple, mind-focused perspective would
suggest, and that theory and practice should never be considered
apart from one another. They have offered us a different way of
thinking about identity and society, and we could benefit from
taking more seriously the connection between our sensory experiences and the "larger" concerns of the world. The things that we
experience have the power to shape us in profound ways. If we
openly acknowledged that power and sought to make the most of
it, there's no telling what kinds of feelings, ideas, and perspectives
might be within our grasp.

2

Drinking Your Way to a New You: Self-Medication, Sensibility, and Sociability at the Café

I F ENLIGHTENMENT PHILOSOPHY was born out of a critical spirit, a love of ideas, and a fascination with self-creation, the café was its cradle. Coffee shops gave new ideas a safe place to flourish and provided a comfortable atmosphere where creative types could freely express themselves, compare thoughts, and indulge in a warm beverage. Although it was only introduced to Europe and America in the seventeenth century, coffee quickly became a cultural standard. Americans now consume 400 million cups of the divine nectar daily, and we're no less devoted to the places that provide our fix, with over 55,000 coffee shops dotting our nation's landscape. Today, the café is viewed as a place to socialize, people-watch, work, or unwind, and it's hard to imagine a coffeeless world with no cafés.

In seventeenth-century France, there was no shortage of places where one could get a drink. Taverns, cabarets, inns, and *guinguettes* (drinking establishments outside the city's walls) dotted the urban landscape, offering alcoholic refreshment to patrons of all types. Paris alone boasted an estimated 5,000 cabarets and taverns, all with full support of the crown, thanks to the significant tax revenue that these businesses brought in.[1] Yet as the century progressed, many of these establishments became associated with violent behavior, gambling, and prostitution. In the 1630s, new ordinances passed that regulated the hours of operation, limited the types of activities (no more card-playing or chess), and forbade certain clientele (no more "debauched" women, soldiers, vagabonds, beggars, or swindlers).[2] If the seventeenth century taught us anything, it's that nothing attracts more drunken brawls and ladies of the night than a heated chess game. In 1647, a new series of regulations was issued that limited the types of beverages that could be sold in these places. All wine merchants, hotel owners, and cabaret owners were forbidden to sell beer, cider, pear cider, and liquor.[3] They could sell only wine, and all the vagabonds and swindlers seeking a tankard of ale or a shot of rotgut were left out in the cold.[4]

But just as the options for refreshment diminished, the king's court was becoming increasingly infatuated with exotic liqueurs. Over the course of the sixteenth and seventeenth centuries, a vast array of new products had flooded the French market, and the elite embraced the new sensory delights that poured in from colonial territories. Botanicals from Asia, sugar from the Atlantic colonies, coffee and spices from the Middle East, and new vegetables from America thrilled the palates of the elite, creating a variety of new sensations, tastes, and experiences. For the first time, consumers could experience the stimulating effects of caffeine, the spicy tongue-tingles of peppers, and the deep, bitter richness of cocoa. For the most part, these commodities were quite expensive, and the tradesmen who catered to these new tastes drew customers from the highest social echelons.

As the taste for these stimulating beverages grew, high-end cabarets began breaking the law in order to sell the fashionable drinks. Liqueurs and sweets were the order of the day, and while their grungier, seedier neighbors were left serving wine under police surveillance, it was rare that these upscale places were taken to task for subverting the rules. Because of the illustriousness of the clientele, these shops earned a reputation for elegance, refinement, and civility. Wanting to distinguish themselves even further, these upscale proprietors formed a separate guild in 1673, which the king formally recognized in 1676. They called themselves the *limonadiers*, or "lemonaders," and their shops' status as refined spaces, as opposed to those owned by vendors of other alcoholic beverages, was widely recognized. Louis-Sébastien Mercier, an eighteenth-century cultural critic, wrote, "Put a wine merchant side-by-side with a lemonade merchant; the difference is immense. The first is dirty and libertine; the second has the air of being on the verge of good company."[5]

The first *limonadiers'* shops were luxurious spaces, dripping with crystal, mirrors, and architectural embellishments. Liqueurs were served in gleaming glassware, candied nuts were dished out in fine porcelain, and coffee was poured from silver pots by men in fur-trimmed hats and Armenian caftans.[6] Fashionable sorts flocked to the *limonadiers'* shops, and the demand for these new wares and spaces seemed almost insatiable. By the middle of the eighteenth century, there were an estimated 1,800 *limonadiers*, and by 1780 there were 2,800 *limonadiers'* shops in the capital, as opposed to only 2,000 wine shops.[7] In a matter of decades, the *limonadiers* became one of the richest guilds in France. Our snide friend Mercier explained that because "liquor and sugar [were] at their discretion," even apprentice *limonadiers* slept and ate in a manner equivalent to princes.[8] Clearly, there was money and power in these goods.

As the popularity of *limonadiers'* shops grew, so did general access to the goods sold there. Exotic fruits and spices that had been impossibly expensive in the sixteenth and seventeenth centuries became much more affordable in the eighteenth as they began to be cultivated on a larger scale. Changes in international competition also favored broader commercialization, and investors weren't content to let potential profits pass them by. Thanks to their colonies in the East Indies, the Dutch controlled a large portion of the spice trade throughout the seventeenth century. But in the 1750s and 1760s, the French horticulturist Pierre Poivre decided to take matters into his own hands, and he managed to smuggle some valuable plants out of the clutches of the Dutch. He introduced these botanicals—including nutmeg and cloves— to the French colonies of Mauritius and Réunion, initiating the first real European competition for these commodities.[9] Similarly, the French started cultivating coffee in their colonial territories, cutting off their heavy reliance on Arabian supplies. Products that began as luxuries became increasingly common, and thanks to a general trend in agricultural productivity and an increased quality of life, the middle and lower classes were newly able to consume goods that had previously been only within the purchasing power of elites. The expansion of the market meant that even more money was at stake, and certainly, the *limonadiers* weren't the only ones who recognized it.

Being a part of a guild in the eighteenth century was no trivial matter. Guild members had the exclusive right to produce certain products, essentially guaranteeing a corner on the market. When popular goods were at stake, this meant a significant economic advantage, and guilds were eager to defend their privileges at all costs. The regulations surrounding guild membership were highly specific and often controversial. For instance, when the modern folding umbrella was invented in 1705 by the Parisian purse-maker Marius, fights broke out between multiple guilds that wanted the right to produce this rainy-day item. The turners' guild argued that umbrella handles had to be turned on a lathe like all their other products, which meant that the product fell firmly within their purview. Purse-makers argued that attaching umbrella fabric to its frame was similar to lining a purse, and the comb-makers and inlayers threw their hat into the ring for no discernible reason.[10] A series of court battles determined the victor, who oddly enough, turned out to be the enterprising and litigious comb-makers.[11]

The privileges of the *limonadiers* were no less specific than those of the turners, purse-makers, or the umbrella-loving comb-makers. Lemonade was a potent liqueur that one drank in relatively small doses, much like limoncello. Along with the basic lemonade, *limonadiers* had the right to produce all flavored lemonades, including those flavored with ambergris. Known for its sweet, earthy, "animal" scent, ambergris was a popular addition to a number of eighteenth-century drinks, and apothecaries claimed that it could fortify the stomach and aid digestion.

The *limonadiers* also had the exclusive privilege to produce all "refreshing beverages," which included drinks made with tea, chocolate, and vanilla, eaux-de-vie (fruit-based brandy), Spanish wines, Muscat wines, malmsey (a fortified, extremely sweet Madeira wine), rossoly (a brandy-based liquor), populo (a liquor similar to rossoly), and all wines categorized as "liquorous wines." They were also permitted to produce jellies, fruity and floral ices, sorbet, anise and cinnamon liqueurs, frangipane (an almond paste), bitter cedar, candied fruits, candied nuts, and sugared almonds. And finally, rounding out their roster, they could sell "coffee in beans, powder, and as a drink."[12] (It was the immense popularity of this latter beverage that led customers to call *limonadiers'* shops by the more familiar term "café.") In essence, the *limonadiers'* goods encompassed all the trendy new items that were hitting the French market, and unsurprisingly, a number of other guilds wanted in on the action.

Given that the limits of the guilds were so clearly laid out by law, you might think that it would have been easy to keep the boundaries firm. The above descriptions are not at all vague about the scope of the *limonadiers'* trade, and similar regulations guided every guild. But in practice, these boundaries were much more fluid. For one reason, as in the case of the umbrella, new technologies, processes, and products did not always fit neatly into one category. And secondly, there were already long-standing crossovers between foodstuffs, perfume, and medicine, which meant that many of the same products and processes were available to different guilds. Once the *limonadiers* came to the fore with their sexy new spaces and their delicious new drinks, other guilds who had access to the same materials and methods started to take notice. The potential for profit was just too tempting. Customers desired new sensations, and guild masters were all too eager to try to satisfy these cravings. According to the nineteenth-century distillation guru Pierre Duplais, "*Eau-de-vie*, employed at the beginning of the eighteenth century as medication, seamlessly passed to the table and soon became the favorite drink of the people."[13] This transition may have been seamless to customers, but it does not seem to have been as simple for producers. The novelty of food-related sensory experiences, minor though it may seem on the surface, actually drove significant commercial changes and challenged the status quo in economic, medical, and social contexts.

Such was the case in the 1749 scandal over the Oil of Venus. This sensuously titled liqueur, so named because of its resemblance to olive oil, was initially developed as a medicine. Its creator, the military physician Bouez de Sigogne, claimed that the oil could settle the stomachs of invalids, help old people digest their food, regulate menstruation, fortify the brain, ease difficult births, stop seasickness, prevent scurvy, and soothe smallpox.[14]

Taking after its namesake Venus, who was the goddess of love, beauty, sex, fertility, and prosperity, this was one multifunctional beverage. The cure-all oil was vastly popular medically, and because of its superior taste, fine texture, and the fact that it had "a name that displeased no one," it also experienced success as a recreational beverage.[15]

In 1749, the distillers' guild initiated a lawsuit against Sigogne, claiming that he was violating their production rights by producing a liqueur. Rather than being deterred, Sigogne stashed a number of the bottles in a friend's house, but unfortunately the police discovered them. The police placed the oil under lock and key, reporting to the distillers that the merchandise was now safe "under the hand of justice," but apparently that hand didn't have a tight enough grasp. On the morning of July 4, Sigogne, his lawyer, and another friend snuck into the locked room through a window and absconded with many of the bottles. It seems that the defense had successfully found its window of opportunity.[16] The battle over the Oil of Venus raged for over twenty years with the Paris Faculty of Medicine, the French Parlement, and the king's First Physician entering the fray. Sigogne and his nephew finally got the privilege to produce the Oil of Venus, but by this time, the drink was widely sold by distillers, who continued to make a significant profit off their Oil-loving customers.

The case of the Oil of Venus is only one of many battles that took place over new beverages in the eighteenth century, and it demonstrates just how easily the lines between medical consumption, luxury consumption, and mass consumption blurred. Beverages whose contents previously belonged to the world of the apothecary now cropped up in the *limonadier*'s shop with regularity. These drinks did not lose their medical status, but entrepreneurs with no connection to medicine, seeing the potential profit, now laid claim to the right to sell them. The sensory delights of exotic goods soon became inseparable from their salutary effects. And from the consumers' perspective, what was the difference between buying lemon syrup at an apothecary's shop and buying an identical syrup at a *limonadier*'s shop?

Very little, it turned out, and *limonadiers* made the most of the blurred lines between their wares and those recommended by physicians. Medically marketed beverages were frequent among the *limonadiers*' repertoire. In 1779, the distiller François-René-André Dubuisson published *The Art of the Distiller and Liquor-Seller, Considered as Medicinal Foods,* in which he argued that liquor could keep the body agile, able, and vigorous.[17] The distiller Onfroy advertised a "liquor for teeth" in a Parisian newspaper, and at the famous Café Procope, the impossibly fashionable hangout of Voltaire, customers could partake in a beverage called "The Water of the Queen of Spain" that was widely known to cure the nausea of pregnant women.[18] Indeed, Jean-Baptiste and Michel Procope, the sons of the famous *limonadier* Francesco Procopio dei Coltelli, both became physicians, and a number of writers remarked on the close link between the Procopes' professions.

Debates about *limonadiers*' goods clearly draw attention to the ways in which eighteenth-century ideas about the power of sensory experience differed from our own. In the last chapter, you read about the sensationalists, who claimed that all our knowledge and personal characteristics come from sensation. While high-minded philosophers were the people who most clearly explained such beliefs, they weren't the only ones who held them. People at all social levels believed that sensation had a great deal of mental and emotional power. This power was aptly summed up in the concept of "sensibility." You may be familiar with this term thanks to Jane Austen's *Sense and Sensibility.* Elinor Dashwood, the reserved, pragmatic heroine, best represents "sense," often placing the welfare of her family above her own emotions.

Her sister, Marianne Dashwood, was characterized by "sensibility," demonstrated by the fact that Marianne's "sorrows [and] joys could have no moderation."[19] In the nineteenth century, women who had an excess of sensibility were often seen as being easily conquered by their emotions. Swooning and fainting, which were frequent symptoms of such women, were so common that fainting couches and fainting rooms became popular features of Victorian homes. In Austen's novel, Marianne and her mother were frequently overpowered by "the agony of grief."[20] In this context, "sense" and "sensibility" were opposites, where the latter marked a woman who thrived on being overemotional.

This use of "sensibility" was a distinct offshoot of its eighteenth-century predecessor. Where the term most frequently referred to hysterical ladies in the nineteenth century, the eighteenth-century version was more complex. In the Enlightenment, everyone had sensibility, and the term referred to the knotty relationship between a person's body, emotions, and intellect. While it sometimes manifested as fainting and tears, it could equally manifest as artistic refinement, stupidity, or confusion. Both an opera-loving socialite and an art-loathing yokel had sensibility, albeit one was thought to have a much more refined sensibility than the other.

As you can tell from the examples of Le Camus and Tissot from the last chapter, popular medicine and science held that the best way to refine one's sensibility was—you guessed it—to sense things. This meant that drinking a cup of coffee didn't just mean taking pleasure in the morning. It also meant an opportunity to improve one's sensibility. Both the producers of the beverages sold in *limonadiers'* shops and the people who consumed them were well aware of sensibility and its power to connect their sensory experience to mental and emotional states, and they consumed beverages with these principles in mind. The anonymous author of the article "Café" in the *Encyclopédie* described *limonadiers'* shops as "manufactories of mind, as much good as bad," and he was not speaking figuratively.[21] Thanks to the concept of sensibility, the mind was considered to be a direct product of sensory experience. In other words, drinking coffee or lemonade would directly contribute to one's intellect, imagination, or madness.

Certain beverages created strong sensations and others were well suited to slowing down an overeager temperament. For example, tea was thought to ease the brain and strengthen the memory, while lemon had the power to soothe a wounded imagination (whether that means a slow, uncreative imagination or one fixated on naughty ideas is unclear).[22] Eighteenth-century consumers used sensory stimulation not only to experience pleasure, but as a means of self-improvement. For instance, imagine that you are a university student about to take an exam. You might ask for a dish made with basil because basil is good for strengthening the brain. If you're sluggish, you might want red meat since it will heat your blood. The type of food that you choose to eat, from this perspective, may have very little to do with its flavor.

So, if certain types of consumption were more about the food's inherent properties than its taste, can these discussions tell us anything about the senses? Absolutely! Nowadays, we frequently think about the relationship between the food we eat and our health, but in the eighteenth century, people went a step further, thinking about food as the bearer not only of physical well-being, but of emotional and mental well-being as well. This is a strikingly different concept of the power of sensory experience. For Enlightenment consumers, a delicious food or beverage had more than just the power of giving a person pleasure or making him momentarily happy. It had the power to affect her personality on a deeper level, altering her emotions, intelligence, and identity in one fell swoop. Through food, an introvert could become an extrovert, a bumpkin could become urbane, or a mild-mannered person could become brash. There were no limits to the changes that new sensations could bring.

Long-standing convergences between medicine and food meant that consumers in the eighteenth century were accustomed to eating according to their specific bodily constitutions. Physicians in the eighteenth century believed that there were six main elements in the body: air, fire, water, earth, salt, and oil. Fire was among the most important of these elements, since it was the element that caused motion, vibration, and sensation. For example, if you ate something that was thought to have a lot of elemental fire—like, let's say, a piece of vanilla- or nutmeg-spiced cake— the fire would quicken your blood, vibrate your fibers, and stimulate you. The elemental composition of a food didn't necessarily have anything to do with what it tasted like, although the properties often correlated. Alcohol burned one's throat because of the elemental fire inside it. Lettuces cooled the body because of their dominant water element. Many of these medical associations would have been in common circulation, and consumers would have been familiar with the medical properties of exotic beverages like coffee, tea, fruit liqueurs, etc. What was new was sensibility, which meant that all these "hot" and "cold" effects would operate on the mind and emotions as much as on the body.

Consumers did not blindly wander into a *limonadier*'s shop without having some knowledge of the link between food and medicine. In 1685, Philippe Sylvestre Dufour, a merchant who composed a lengthy treatise on coffee, tea, and chocolate, argued that knowledge about the properties of certain foods required very little expertise, and even the most ignorant individual could discern whether an item was hot or cold: "It's not necessary to be an [expert] to know that *eau-de-vie*, pepper, wine, and spices heat us up, and that to the contrary, chicory, lettuce, water, and a simple herbal tea refresh us."[23] Similarly, the accounts of the German traveler Joachim Christophe Nemeitz show that consumers were well aware of beverages' properties. He described coffee's power to "chase away melancholy:" "According to a certain Lady (it is claimed that this was an Illustrious Duchess from *Paris*, whose name I won't divulge here out of respect) who, learning that her husband was killed in a battle, cried: *Ah! How unhappy I am! Quick, quick, someone bring me Coffee!*"[24] While it seems implausible that any beverage could wrench one from the pit of despair, such stories reveal that, to some extent, eighteenth-century drinkers saw their purchases at the *limonadier*'s shop as a means of self-medicating. Through the beverages they drank, consumers revealed the qualities they desired, the social traits they admired, and the things about themselves they hoped to fix.

This is not to say that every single sip was a self-conscious medical act. Certainly, taste had its own dictates, and it didn't always match up with medical advice. But just as modern eaters may pay attention to the presence of animal by-products, gluten, or carbohydrates in the foods they choose, many consumers at eighteenth-century *limonadiers'* shops were at least somewhat aware of the composition of the substances they ingested, and they thought about the effects that these substances could have on their bodies. In contrast to modern practices, though, eighteenth-century concepts of ingestion carried direct and far-reaching implications for individual morality and society. A poor diet did not simply mean the propensity for diabetes, obesity, or high cholesterol, as it might today. Because of the strong belief in the mind-body link, bad eating habits could also signify immorality or madness. A "healthy" diet, on the other hand, could directly benefit society. By selecting beverages conducive to one's temperament, one could become more quick-witted, happy, and friendly.

More than any other element, it was fire that garnered public attention. One needed a certain amount of fire element in order to live, and in limited quantities it could have truly beneficial effects. It would quicken the vibration of fibers, making a person more alert and better able to sense the world around her. Passion, creativity, sensation, and desire were all products of fire, which moved the body and soul and sent heat cascading through one's entire being. Alcohol, coffee, and chocolate—among the most popular products at the café—were all thought to contain a large degree of elemental fire.

Generally speaking, liquors were the fieriest of substances, and their intense heat would loosen one's fibers. This looseness made the fibers vibrate more readily in response to stimulation, and thanks to sensibility, this helped the mind forge new, creative links. In a drunken stupor, reason went out the window, and the imagination was permitted to run free. In Voltaire's 1746 short story "The One-Eyed Porter," a character reported after a particularly bacchanalian evening that he "drank a great quantity of *eau-de-vie* the day before, which had made his senses drowsy and heated his imagination."[25] And it was suggested by the playwright Charles-Antoine-Guillaume Pigault-Lebrun that drinking alcoholic beverages was an excellent way to find creative solutions to problems. Robert, one of the main characters in Pigault-Lebrun's play *The Empiricists,* decides that what he needed was a night helped by "blazing *eau-de-vie*, which increases imagination.... The best idea is found at the bottom of the jar."[26] For artists, philosophers, and other creative types looking to expand their horizons, liqueur was an easy way to heat the blood and stir the soul, provided it was taken judiciously, of course.

The flavors of these liqueurs ranged widely, including herbal concoctions with thyme or chervil; fruit liqueurs with cherry, pear, or lime; and the more provocatively and mysteriously named drinks like the Water of the Queen of Hungary, a rosemary-based liquid. Because of the medicinal properties attributed to the various ingredients in these liqueurs, each concoction was supposed to have different effects. For example, rosemary was helpful in counteracting lethargy, sluggish blood, and paralysis, and orange-flower water was considered especially effective in healing hysteria, stomach weakness, and "delayed menstruation" (possibly indicating that it was helpful in getting rid of an unwanted pregnancy).[27] While many of these ingredients could also be found in nonalcoholic versions, the heating properties of the liqueur were thought to aid the circulation of these medicinal substances, making them even more effective.

The Water of Carmes, a liqueur made with citronella and created by Carmelite monks, reportedly stimulated memory and got rid of unpleasant fantasies. While we may know it best for its power to keep mosquitoes at bay, apparently citronella also has the power to bring people together. This drink improved both the health and the personality thanks to its ability to get rid of sadness, loneliness, and the antisocial tendencies of any "extravagant and bizarre men."[28] According to medical experts, the Water of Carmes accomplished this task by redirecting the imagination so that it fixated on pleasant sensations. This broke the feedback loop of social anxiety and worry, ensuring that melancholics were no longer self-conscious and overly introspective. In the case of the Water of Carmes, latching onto the "socially lubricating" properties of alcohol was a perfectly reasonable way to become a more personable human being.

Of course, it was not always best to stay at the bottom of the glass. Fire was also highly dangerous if one consumed it too readily. A diet consisting of too many "hot" foods and liquids could lead to a person's complete physical, mental, and moral degeneration. According to the cleric Moreau de Saint-Elier (brother of the reputed philosopher and man of science Pierre-Louis Moreau de Maupertuis), if a person consumed too many fiery substances, she would develop a false appetite, making her eat more than was necessary. This ravenousness would be followed by indigestion or drunkenness, and her fibers would get used to being overstimulated. In order to elicit a sensation from these overworked fibers, she would have to give them increasingly intense stimulation, which would lead to "bizarre and depraved tastes."[29] Certainly, in the eyes of his contemporaries, the outrageous Marquis de Sade, who was known for his love of hot chocolate, fell victim to this pattern. The doctor Claude-Nicolas Le Cat affirmed this assessment, describing the plight of a delicate young man who consumed too much coffee and liquor. The boy took a substance intended to induce vomiting, but it didn't work, and his gastrointestinal distress continued. With his insides boiling, the young man became incurably mad and subject to frequent hallucinations. And, as if insanity weren't bad enough, in the worst-case scenario, doctors warned that an excess of heat could even lead to spontaneous combustion. The fire in the blood could literally ignite, turning an alcoholic into little more than a heap of ash.[30]

If one did temporarily lose control, all was not lost. There was another beverage that could restore one's wits. In the words of a popular eighteenth-century song, "[Alcohol] puts reason to sleep. Coffee awakens it."[31] Liqueurs may have been popular, but coffee was the triumphant beverage of the Age of Enlightenment. By the late eighteenth century, the chemist Antoine-Laurent de Lavoisier had calculated the annual coffee consumption at an impressive 110 pounds per person.[32] Coffee's rise to the top of the heap was, in large part, due to the properties that it was supposed to bestow on its consumers. It's no surprise to modern readers that coffee has the power to stimulate. In a 2011 study, 54 percent of coffee drinkers reported that coffee makes them feel more like themselves.[33] Eighteenth-century writers widely recognized coffee's power to keep a person awake, but they also credited the magical brew with inspiring creativity, sociability, happiness, and intellect. The delightful beverage would stimulate the fibers, sending all kinds of pleasant and invigorating feelings up to the *sensorium commune.* The Scottish philosopher Sir James Mackintosh claimed that "the powers of a man's mind are directly proportioned to the quantity of coffee he drinks," and given his alleged forty-cup-a-day habit, Voltaire seemed to have been in agreement.[34]

Jules Michelet, a nineteenth-century historian who had a way with words, described coffee as "the sober liquor, powerfully cerebral, which, contrary to spirits, augments clarity and lucidity—coffee which erases the vague and heavy poetry of the clouds of imagination, which, from reality truly seen, makes the spark and flash of truth pour forth."[35] It's a pretty highfalutin description, but Michelet tapped into a significant reason that coffee became such a popular beverage with the eighteenth-century intellectual crowd: it's a "sober liquor," which meant that it could heat the blood and stimulate creativity without causing inebriation. In fact, in the eighteenth century, coffee and alcohol were often consumed in the same sitting. After being taken upon drunken flights of fancy by the various liqueurs in a *limonadier's* shop, customers would frequently indulge in coffee to bring themselves back to their wits. Coffee, when appropriately combined with liqueur, could produce the longed-for "just right" state of sensibility. Doctors argued that the chemical makeup of coffee allowed it to "reanimate the idle spirits in the brain to excite them to waking," meaning that in a sober person, it could increase the capacity for wit, and in a drunk person, it could restore sobriety.[36] Thanks to coffee, it was possible to be transported by imagination without fear of being drawn too deeply into its perils. Coffee was one's tether to the rational world.

It was also considered the perfect antidote to sadness. A song written in praise of coffee promised, "If you want to live easily, live in good health seven days a week, drink good coffee. Will it protect you from all illnesses? Its good qualities will chase migraines and melancholy away."[37] According to doctors, depression was the product of a cold temperament, and coffee, as a fiery beverage, had the power to heat the blood and bring someone out of a sad, lonely, solitary mood. To drink coffee was to become friendly and happy. By this logic, Voltaire must have been a walking, talking Disney World.

The chatty, creative intellectual created by coffee was an ideal match for the spaces run by *limonadiers*. When we think of a café, we think of a social spot or a study hangout, a place where one could just as easily sit alone with a book as a place where one could catch up with friends. But in the eighteenth century, one went to a café to socialize. Men sat at long, communal tables (or at least, mostly men; certain cafés were acceptable for respectable women to visit, but many were not), and they debated ideas hotly, circulated news and gossip, read papers aloud, and held philosophical conversations. Philosophers, social reformers, artists, and writers all flocked to cafés, and these spaces were part of a new public world, where the price of a drink could buy you hours of entertainment. Coffee, as a beverage endowed with the traits of sober rationality, facilitated creativity and social commerce without leading drinkers astray, and it was the commodity that most closely embodied the intellectual and social traits desired by lemonade-shop patrons. It was probably this precise fit between the properties of coffee and the ideals of the space that caused consumers to give the name "café" to these new establishments by the early eighteenth century.

But the fires of coffee's inspiration and the fires of alcohol were not appropriate to all bodies, and chocolate, with its unique elemental properties, was also a sought-after item. In the eighteenth century, chocolate was almost always consumed in liquid form. Workers would make a paste from cocoa beans, which they would mix with additives like vanilla, cinnamon, cloves, and everyone's favorite animal secretions, ambergris and musk. The paste was then formed into small tablets and left on a wrapper to dry. These dried tablets were sold to consumers, who were advised to keep them away from heat and humidity. Prepared this way, it was believed that chocolate could keep for up to thirty or forty years.[38] To make the beverage, they added boiling water, milk, and possibly wine or eggs, mixing everything together well and drinking it while it was hot. The texture of the beverage would have been thick and viscous, more closely resembling the center of a lava cake than a modern hot cocoa.

When it was first introduced, physicians considered chocolate to be a cold material because of the fatigue, heaviness, and difficult digestion that some consumers reported after drinking it. Heating spices like cloves, vanilla, and cinnamon were added in order to warm it up, making it a stimulating beverage, both in terms of sensory and psychological experience.[39] But by the mid eighteenth century, physicians, naturalists, and pharmacists believed that chocolate did have the power to impart heat, and consumers were advised against making it with wine or adding too many aromatic spices, which would make the beverage too fiery.[40] Tablets of chocolate without any heating additives were called "health chocolate," and as its name suggests, by mid-century, this was the form in which it was considered to be the most salutary. Any potential heaviness or difficulty in digestion began to be attributed not to the elemental coldness of chocolate, but to the manner in which it was prepared. For instance, doctors warned that using milk as the foundation for chocolate could be nourishing, but it could also be too heavy, which would make digestion much more difficult. Eating bread or any other kind of food with chocolate could also be injurious to one's health because chocolate formed an unctuous and thick liquid in the stomach that would inhibit digestion.[41] The biggest culprit for bad digestion, though, was the quality of the chocolate. The popularity of chocolate meant that the market was quickly flooded with inferior versions, and newspaper articles told people how to choose high-quality chocolate. In the chemistry section of the newspaper *Journal de Paris,* Antoine-Augustin Parmentier explained to readers the sensory attributes of the ideal chocolate: it should have no gravelly qualities, it should spread a coolness throughout the mouth, and when cooked, its consistency should be halfway between liquid and solid.[42]

Chocolate was originally trendy among wealthy Catholics, who drank it during ritual fasts as a way of keeping themselves full and nourished.[43] But as it became more readily available, social reformers started considering the power of chocolate to sustain not only religious aristocrats, but also workers in need of quick, cheap, and effective nutrition. Reformers encouraged workers to start their day with a cup of hot chocolate instead of bread or other foods.[44] Chocolate, which was believed to have more nourishment in a single ounce than could be found in a pound of beef, was also thought to be well suited to the lifestyle of military men, travelers, sailors, and artisans. The Swedish naturalist Linnaeus suggested that "chocolate therapy" was particularly good for people who were overly thin or wasting away. (He also recommended chocolate as an aphrodisiac and as a treatment for hypochondria and hemorrhoids.)[45] D. De Quélus, a French doctor who spent fifteen years in America, wrote eagerly of an elderly patient who, for the last thirty years of his life, "lived on nothing but chocolate and biscuit." Apparently, this old fellow was so nourished by his diet of chocolate that, "at fourscore and five, he could get on horseback without stirrups."[46]

In addition to its nourishing properties, chocolate shared

many of the sensibility-related properties of coffee. It was able to cure melancholy, enhance sociability, fortify the stomach and the brain, fight off the "fumes of wine," and "excite vigor."[47] Unlike coffee, though, chocolate contained a great deal of oil, which prevented the dehydration of fibers that could sometimes result from coffee-drinking.[48] Its heat was less forceful, and its effects were "more delicate and longer-lasting than that of coffee; because chocolate, being fattier and more viscous, imprints itself longer on the spot that it touches."[49] Chocolate may have been less inspiring than coffee, but its mental effects were much more suitable for people with delicate fibers, like convalescents, women, and the elderly. Because of its benefit to these delicate individuals, chocolate quickly became known as "the milk of the elderly."[50]

Chocolate, as a soft and durable form of heat that could gently excite fibers, was an optimal means of warding off the ravages of time. More than any other beverage, chocolate was "capable of prolonging the days of the elderly, giving to their dried-out and almost entirely hardened fibers, the suppleness so necessary for maintaining health and life."[51] An apple a day may keep the doctor away, but a sip of chocolate will keep the grim reaper at bay. A popular song about the effects of chocolate affirmed that old people would be the greatest beneficiaries of the mental stimulation offered by the beverage: "You in whom the burden of years makes nature languish, this drink is sure to heat up your senses a bit. Also, minds as cold as an ice cube . . . serve yourselves this drink; it will be divine for you."[52]

Women, whose delicate fibers needed the stability offered by the unctuous consistency of chocolate, were also encouraged to drink it. This is not to say that women never drank coffee, but much more frequently, chocolate was seen as a woman's beverage. In the words of one songwriter, "[Coffee] excites bile, and its activity, makes woman indocile."[53] Men's bodies were thought to contain a great deal of "the oily principle," so their fibers were naturally firm and supple, but women's bodies supposedly contained more water than oil. The doctor Jean-Claude de La Métherie assured his readers that a lady's body couldn't reach the oily perfection of a man's, but by ingesting chocolate, she would be able to add some necessary oomph to her fibers. The beverage could also be restorative in instances when women needed physical strength, like when they were giving birth. Chocolate was also a good bulwark against nervous maladies like hysteria, which were thought to occur when the sensory fibers were too loose and vibrated too readily. Chocolate was, all told, a beverage whose gentleness matched that of its intended consumers.

Today, we think of our consumption practices as part of our process of self-definition. For instance, I might buy organic foods because of a particular ethical stance, or I might wear a certain type of clothes because I want to project a certain image. We can create and re-create ourselves through the stuff we buy, changing our personae as easily as we change the color of our hair or the types of beer we drink. But how many of us truly think that these choices alter us in a fundamental way? Does choosing a croissant over a cookie change who we are; does it transform the very essence of one's being, or does it instantly affect one's body?

With food, it's possible to argue that these effects are tangible. Drinking coffee can make you feel less sluggish. Eating greens instead of a giant hunk of cake will probably make your body feel better. And if you're anything like me, if you let yourself go hungry, then woe betide all who dare to come near. We still recognize some kind of implicit link between our bodies, our emotional states, and the things that we consume. But I would wager that our concept of this link is nowhere near as strong or direct as the one that informed eighteenth-century ideas about consumption. Thanks to the concept of sensibility, people in that era trusted that every decision, sensation, purchase, touch, sight, scent, taste, and experience had the power to transform the mind, body, and personality. An overpronounced taste for meat could lead to a taste for murder; mint enlivened the heart and the brain, giving fresh vigor to those in need of a boost; sweet, fresh foods could produce a sweet, fresh-faced child. Any sensory experience entailed emotional and intellectual effects, and one had to pay close attention to the types of sensations in which one indulged.

On one hand, it may be easy to dismiss this as a ridiculously oversimplified version of cause and effect, and on another, it may just seem like a pessimistic theory that negates free will and makes a person the helpless agent of her bodily condition. And yet, I find something admirable in this conception of self. It recognizes how deeply connected our daily experience is with the person that we become, and it also recognizes that change, evolution, and growth are necessary elements of the human condition. We still rely on the market, money, and consumption to define ourselves, but to a large extent, we've lost faith in their power to actually elicit deep change. From a modern perspective, the objects we buy may define us, but they don't necessarily make us who we are. Yet in the eighteenth century, for better or for worse, sensory experience was much more than a process of redefinition. It was a constant process of transformation, with each experience fundamentally altering a person's relationship to the world. Consuming was a chance to actually recreate yourself, a means of designing and building yourself into the person that you wanted to be. And there was a deep, resounding belief in the idea that it was possible to become better with each passing moment.

❊ 3 ❊

Living in a World of Sound:
The Pitch-Black Markets of Paris

P ARISIAN CAFÉS MAY have been filled with the glints of crystal and the rumble of polite conversation, but as coffee's popularity spread to workaday men and women, the beverage moved to more humble settings. As the elite of Paris slept warm in their beds, the early morning marked the start of the day for the city's many artisans, workers, and poor. At 6 A.M., coffee-women already would have congregated on street corners, their backs weighed down with tin urns. They sold the bitter nectar—lightly sugared and laced with milk—in earthenware cups for a penny, and workmen, sleepy in the frail light of morning, would gulp it down as a substitute for breakfast.[1]

The writer Louis-Sébastien Mercier vividly described Parisian life in his massive *Tableau de Paris* (written 1781–1788), and there's no better source for getting a sense of daily life in Paris during the eighteenth century. Mercier was born to a working-class family but, despite his origins, received a good education and was exposed to theater and literature from an early age. Neither a "have" nor a "have-not," Mercier was able to observe the lives of every echelon of Parisian society, and his colorful descriptions give voice to a rich, busy city full of paradoxes and pleasure. In more than one thousand chapters, Mercier revealed the many contrasts of eighteenth-century Paris. He uncovered a world of filth and luxury and commented on the propensity of the "sybarites of Paris . . . to lie abed till noon" while the unprivileged sorts labored amid the clangs of metalwork, the stink of leather and varnish, and the penetrating tolls of church bells.[2] The tone of the *Tableau* was often disapproving, and Mercier was unafraid to criticize the corruption that he believed permeated all classes of Parisian society. Yet he also saw hope, light, and possibility in the dense contradictions of urban life, and he represented, perhaps better than any other Enlightenment writer, the sensory worlds of average people.

In one of his most memorable pieces, called "The Hours of the Day," Mercier outlined the timetable of the city, describing how artisans took to their tasks after morning coffee, and at 9 A.M., other businesses began to come to life. Barbers, wig whiteners, and waiters rushed to and fro, followed at 10 A.M. by the "black cloud of legal practitioners" that descended on the courts in the center of Paris. (Mercier never missed a chance for a joke, noting, "You should always take three bags into court; one for your money, one for your brief, and one to stow your patience in.")[3] Noon brought out the stockbrokers, financiers, and idlers, and at 2 P.M., those with dinner invitations set out, "powdered, adjusted, and walking on tiptoe not to soil their stockings."[4] Calm reigned for a few hours while everyone was indoors, but at 5:15 all hell broke loose as throngs flooded gardens, cafés, and other public spaces. At nightfall, workmen headed to their humble homes, leaving "white footprints from the plaster on their shoes, a trail that any eye can follow." At 9 P.M., fine men and women set out for the theater, and prostitutes populated the streets. By 11 P.M., silence was renewed as people sat down to supper, cafés closed, and prostitutes hid from police patrols. While card-players, johns, and truly avid pleasure-seekers kept going until about 6 A.M., a few carriages took the sleepy elite back to their homes just after midnight. Mercier remarked that the thunder of the carriages' wheels woke tradesmen, who would then turn to their wives who were "by no means unwilling."[5] As a consequence of those noisy wheels, he claimed, the Parisian birth rate rose regularly.

At 1 A.M., one particular section of the city sprang into life, and it stayed crowded, noisy, and hectic until 7 A.M. This area, called Les Halles (pronounced "lay all"), was the city's central wholesale market, and in the 1780s, over 6,000 peasants came to ply their wares each night. If you're lucky enough to have spent any time in Paris, you may recognize the name of the large area in the 1st *arrondissement* that is now home to an underground shopping mall, kiosks hawking touristy goods, and throngs of pedestrians. This is the same site Les Halles market was on, and all told, the market had a pretty good run, since it was founded in 1183 and was only dismantled in 1971, when it was relocated to the suburb of Rungis. The nineteenth-century novelist Émile Zola gave Les Halles the nickname, "the Belly of Paris," for each morning, it swelled with food, people, and money. It was possible to find almost anything and everything at Les Halles: saltfish, fresh seafood, meat, wool, cloth, flour, butter, candles, corn, grain, rope, leather, wine, secondhand clothing, and the goods and services of many tradesmen like shoemakers, bakers, and bankers. As a wholesale market, Les Halles was the source for the other markets of Paris, and in the wee hours, vendors would select wares to cart back to their own stores and stalls. The choices were immense, given that regional producers united at Les Halles to provision the urban population. In 1770, Jean-Aymar Piganiol de la Force, a spectator besotted with the immensity of the market, noted, "Les Halles of Paris is undoubtedly the richest Market in the world, because you can find everything necessary or pleasurable there that the air, earth, and water produce."[6]

Nestled in the center of the city and at the edges of dreams, Les Halles was a realm of organized chaos. Food, politics, money, and the messy richness of life flooded its streets. Florent, the main character of Zola's novel *The Belly of Paris*, marveled at "the eternal trail of carts and horses" that formed the disorienting sea of Les Halles. Astounded at its vast scope, he likened the market to "a huge central organ [of Paris], furiously pulsating and pumping the blood of life through the city's veins."[7] Energy and exchange united to form the vital force of the city, and for quite some time, that force made its home in the unlit expanses of the early morning.

This was an era before reliable street lighting, and vendors' wheelings-and-dealings took place in the dark, or at best, in the wan light of the moon. Les Halles came alive at night, a time that, in popular imagination both then and now, is populated by dreams, dark deeds, and shadows. The wholesale market of Paris was a black market in the truest sense. According to Mercier, "there is hardly a light to be seen; most of the deals are done in the dark, as though these were people of a different race, hiding in their caverns from the light of the sun. The fish salesmen, who are the first comers, apparently never see daylight, and go home as the street lamps start to flicker, just before dawn; but if eyes are no use, ears take their place; everyone bawls his loudest, and you must know their jargon, to be able to catch what your own vendor shouts in this bedlam of sound."[8] This "different race" of people, according to Mercier, was so sensorially distinct that they may as well have been biologically distinct.

Natural light governed the lives of most craftsmen. They would rise with the sun, work until dusk, and sleep in the thick blanket of night. The high price of candles significantly limited their use, even among bourgeois families. But for those who worked in the interstices of moonlight and morning, eyesight provided only the barest information. Baker-boys were nicknamed "bats" since they worked in unlit basements, and in those crafts where lighting was permitted, workers paid fines if they let the candles burn too long.[9] If a trade required long hours or early mornings, then one simply had to adjust to performing tasks with the assistance of muscle memory, hearing, or other sensory aids. In the darkness of the market, sound, smell, and touch became even more important senses of discrimination. To choose the best produce, someone would have to smell the fruit and vegetables, searching for hints of rot, or touch it, seeking out tender spots. The colors of vegetables or their shapely appearances would have had much less of a bearing on whether that person picked quality products. In fact, darkness could even work to vendors' advantage, as was perhaps the case with the secondhand clothes dealers whose stalls were "ill-lit on purpose, that stains may be less noticeable, and colors deceive the eye; thus the suit of solemn black, bought and paid for, is transformed before your eyes, by the mere light of day, to purple or green, and spotted at that."[10] At Les Halles, appearances were deceiving, and the visual inspection of goods could easily fall short.

As a consequence, the trust relationships that developed between vendor and buyer at Les Halles had a different tenor than the ones that we experience today. At its core, every commercial transaction requires trust: trust in the quality of the goods, trust in the fairness of the price, trust in the ability of the consumer to pay, and so on. But today, it is rare that these commercial transactions are based on an individual, personal level of trust. I don't have to know my grocer to trust that my apples will be fresh, nor do I have to know who made my dress to know that I'm not getting ripped off. Because of companies like Visa and Mastercard, vendors can trust that they will be paid, and because of return policies, consumers can trust that they can get their money back if they are dissatisfied with their products. Trust is a huge part of the commercial system, but often, it doesn't rely on trust in a single, specific individual. The commercial situation in the eighteenth century was somewhat different. Two Dutch travelers, writing about their experiences in Paris, insisted that one should buy secondhand goods only if "you are really familiar with [the sellers]."[11] Eighteenth-century France was a credit-based society, where most goods circulated without any cash changing hands, and if a consumer went to the market "with empty pockets, he or she had no choice but to rely upon familiar shopkeepers."[12] With wholesalers, interpersonal connections were sometimes looser thanks to more complex networks of exchange, but by and large, eighteenth-century networks of credit were highly personal, and they created powerful social obligations. People tended to buy from people that they trusted. Given the shortage of specie in the period, sellers were obliged to extend credit to customers, and like buyers, they also relied on familiarity.[13] Vendors and customers engaged in mutual, repeated acts of trust, and these invisible links were a crucial part of navigating the shadowy lanes of the market. The sensory verification of goods may have been made more difficult by the darkness, but as a result, the social bonds between marketgoers necessarily remained tight.

Of course, in an era called the "Enlightenment," darkness may have been the reality, but it wasn't the dream. Over the course of the eighteenth century, reformers, men of science, and politicos collaborated to develop the technology that would allow them to do away with such expansive darkness. To some extent, street lighting did exist before the eighteenth century, but its use was highly regulated and sporadic. Introduced by royal decree in

1667, lighting was intended to make the urban space safer and more orderly, and it was under the control of the street police. Initially, 2,700 lanterns were installed across Paris, each one consisting of a glass box strung across the road, containing a single candle. This figure grew to 5,000 by 1700 and between 7,000 and 8,000 by the 1780s.[14] These lanterns dotted the city with faint patches of light, but to a large extent, public lighting was still governed by the times and tides of nature. In order to save money, the police usually did not light the lamps in the summer or on nights when the moon was out, and once the daily allotment of candle had burned out, it was not replaced until the following day. Given the paltry candle length or oil supply, many of the lanterns were already out by ten P.M., meaning that the workers at Les Halles wouldn't have seen their welcoming glow.[15] At night, citizens could hire a lantern-man to walk them to their doors, and these lantern-men were known to be good protection since they often worked as police informers. And in times of deep fog, people would hire a blind guide for a day, take hold of his coat, and set off behind him, in the confidence that he could lead them around the city without the need to see.[16]

In 1763, the light grew brighter, thanks to the invention of the reflector lantern, which won a contest sponsored by the Academy of Sciences for "a better manner to light up the streets at night." The police chief Antoine de Sartine footed the bill for the 2,000-livre prize, which was not too shabby, considering that this was about ten times the annual wage for an average worker.[17] Our friend Mercier praised the "steady, clear, and lasting" light of the reflector lamps, which he considered far superior to their "feeble and wavering" predecessors.[18] The steadiness rapidly improved in the following two decades, and in the 1770s, the chemist Antoine-Laurent Lavoisier developed a theory of combustion that recognized the importance of oxygen in the air. This theory encouraged the development of lamps with better air supplies for the flame. Using Lavoisier's theories, the chemist François Ami Argand revealed a new lamp design in 1783 that revolutionized modern lighting, thanks to its "extraordinary bright, lively and almost dazzling light" and lack of smoke.[19] It remained in wide use even after gaslight became popular in the nineteenth century. From our perspective, late-eighteenth-century lighting would be scanty at best, but for people who had never had readily available lighting at night, the lanterns were a brilliant beacon of Enlightenment: the power of reason, order, and progress, all in a small glass box. The symbolic importance of the lamps shone much brighter than their actual light.

As these lighting developments became more ubiquitous, they had massive social effects. Artificial lighting meant that human rhythms no longer had to abide by natural cycles. Nighttime safety increased, and public spaces were made more accessible. People could freely go out when they previously had been forced to choose between the safety of their homes and the uncertainty of the night. According to the historian Wolfgang Schivelbusch, the eighteenth century gave birth to nightlife, which has become a feature of modern urban existence.[20] The positive effects of these technological developments are clear; mobility, safety, and freedom are assets that we cherish. But a number of critical theorists have argued that they had a number of negative effects as well, which we may not think of as readily.

For one, artificial lighting made the labor requirements of industrial capitalism possible. In the words of Schivelbusch, "To light up a cotton mill with hundreds or even thousands of candles in the eighteenth century would have cost as much as the festive illumination of a medium-sized chateau."[21] Economically, the cost-benefit ratio of such an endeavor would not have been favorable, but once more efficient means of artificial lighting emerged in the nineteenth century, employers could feasibly introduce longer working hours, which would be dictated by the clock rather than the sun. In a newly boundaryless cycle of production, the grueling labor ethics of the Industrial Revolution became possible.

Increased production is usually accompanied by increased consumption, and the rise of consumer society meant new forms of marketing and the creation of new types of desire. Elaborate window displays, brilliantly lit at night, encouraged visitors to sight-see and to take in the marvelous new spectacles that greeted the eyes. New store policies oriented toward consumers who just wanted to look led to the gradual development of a specifically modern form of consumption, which, in the words of the scholar Rachel Bowlby, "is a matter not of basic items bought for definite needs, but of visual fascination and remarkable sights."[22] According to Guy Debord, a critical theorist writing in the 1960s, this link between visuality and capitalism is so deep now that we take it for granted. He claimed, "In societies where modern conditions of production prevail, all of life presents itself as an immense accumulation of spectacles." He argued that these spectacles dominate all social life and that all interactions are defined by appearances.[23] From this perspective, the duo of capitalism and spectacle led to a superficial existence in which people no longer connect to life as fully sensual beings. The "sense of having" replaces a true engagement with objects. In other words, we get obsessed with acquiring, with labels, and with appearances, instead of connecting to the objects that we own or use.

It was for this reason that Karl Marx wrote in 1844, that in order to "emancipate the senses," it was necessary to move beyond capitalism. To his mind, people had to deeply engage with objects in order to cultivate "the richness of subjective *human* sensibility (a musical ear, an eye for beauty of form—in short, *senses* capable of human gratification, senses affirming themselves as essential powers of *man*)." Ownership, he argued, was not the same as appreciation. Human sensibility required a process of social development that was encouraged through the deep, learned appreciation of objects and experiences. According to Marx, this did not just apply to the physical senses. It also applied to "the so-called mental senses, the practical senses (will, love, etc.), in a word, *human* sense." All our emotional and sensory lives would benefit from experience rather than ownership, he argued, and only by moving away from the allure of profit, possession, and consumerism, could we experience true satisfaction with the people and things in our lives. Looking back to reflect on how capitalism had developed and looking forward to the desired state, he boldly proclaimed, "The *forming* of the five senses is a labour of the entire history of the world down to the present."[24] Regardless of whether you agree with these condemnations of modern life, it is undeniable that illumination dramatically changed the ways that humans engaged with one another and with the world around them. In the eighteenth century, even the rock-solid contours of day and night, which had seemed immutable for thousands of years, began to shift.

But for the majority of the eighteenth century, Les Halles was still steeped in darkness, and shoppers relied heavily on their sense of touch when weaving through the crowds and narrow lanes of the market. Studies of modern visual impairment have emphasized the importance of routes, spatial relations, distance, rhythm, landmarks, and kinetic memory in navigating urban spaces.[25] Individuals who frequented the "black" markets of Les Halles would also have used many of these methods. They would have navigated the market by "feeling" the space and focusing on patterns, cognitive memories, and muscle memory. What may seem like an odd and difficult endeavor to many of us—shopping and selling in the dark—would have required different modes of using the body and a different level of comfort with trusting the nonvisual senses.

Some forms of touch were more benign than others: the silky feeling of fake flowers, the gentle jostle of a neighbor at a vegetable stall, or the wet squelch of feet on damp soil. But other tactile experiences were not quite as simple. In the market, everything was packed into close quarters. Feet could easily be crushed under carts, and one had to be ever-vigilant about pickpockets, since the lanes were tight and required frequent contact with strangers. What was said about London's Smithfield Market could have been said about Les Halles: "Through the filthy lanes and alleys no one could pass without being butted with the dripping end of a quarter of beef, or smeared by the greasy carcasse of a newly-slain sheep."[26]

As with any belly that becomes overstuffed, indigestion was a potential problem for "the Belly of Paris," and Les Halles was frequently described as an area that had been overtaken with the bloat of rotten human produce. Piganiol de la Force, who had waxed about the bounty of the market, added, "It is also the most vile and filthy quarter in Paris."[27] Dark streets may have necessitated a reliance on touch, but the touching was not always of a sort that would have found the sanction of "good" company. Prostitution had quite the presence around Les Halles—indeed, it still does—and the names of streets in the quarter reflected the ill repute of their inhabitants, e.g., rues Tire-Boudin ("Pull-Sausage"), Trousse-Nonain ("Nun Humping"), Pute-y-Muse ("Idling Whore"), Poil-au-Con ("Pussy Hair"), Petit Cul ("Small Ass"), Gros-Cul ("Large Ass"), and Gratte-Cul ("Scratch-Ass").[28] Nineteenth-century reformers did away with these bawdy names, favoring slightly more pleasant ones like Beaubourg ("pretty village") and Petit-Muse ("little muse"), but Les Halles' reputation for illicit dealings carried on.

Eighteenth-century literature also made it clear that probity had no place in the dark walkways of Les Halles. The marketplace was famous for its high population of *poissards* (a slang word for "thieves"), and these rascals were so much the talk of the town that they inspired their own literary genre. *Poissards* (of the literary sort) were filled with the colorful misdeeds of the gutter. Plays like *The Sheller-Woman of the Market* depicted the drunken exploits of market folk and mixed raunchy humor with vaudeville and dancing. Writers fascinated by the darker side of humanity found plenty of inspiration between the shadowy stalls. One such author, Nicolas-Edme Restif [alternatively Rétif] de la Bretonne, traipsed about town, calling himself "the nocturnal spectator."[29] His accounts of the time he spent among the *poissards* and ne'er-do-wells earned him the illustrious nickname "Jean-Jacques des Halles" (a moniker that played on the fact that both Rousseau and Restif de la Bretonne loved to take solitary walks and write *ad nauseum* about their own experiences). Describing an evening spent in the wine shops near the market, the nocturnal spectator observed, "I expected to find some fascinating sights there, but I saw nothing but debauchery, people smoking, or sleeping; lewd women with billiard or card sharks, brawling and swearing at one another; a few sad rakes who had come there looking for amusement and who were bored instead."[30] I'm not sure what fascinating sights he hoped to see at a wine shop in the middle of the night, but that's beside the point. All in all, it seems that Les Halles' moral makeup left something to be desired.[31]

Sellers' manners were repeatedly described as coarse and untrustworthy, and writers warned shoppers to be wary about their purchases. Two young Dutchmen wrote about their experience with secondhand dealers at Les Halles in 1657: "The huge quantity of clothing and furniture that they have is unbelievable: you can see some beautiful things, but, for fear of being swindled, it's dangerous to buy unless you know the trade well, because they have marvelous skill in restoring and patching up old things so that they seem like new."[32] These complaints persisted a century later, and in 1758, Henry de Lécluse (the pseudonym of a man who was both an actor at the Opéra comique and the official dentist of the King of Poland) used a highly original writing device to show that vendors could not be trusted. He composed a satirical list of the curiosities that could be purchased at Les Halles, which included "a philosopher's stone that becomes invisible when you want to use it"; "plumes taken from Jupiter's eagle"; "a throat lining that can be used by gluttons who eat their soup too hot"; "an Arabian flute without holes, which can be played without moving your fingers"; and "a whip used on Matthew's buttock" (apparently Jesus's disciple needed corporal punishment at some point).[33]

But it was not only the vendors' ethics that were questioned. They were also brought to task for their incessant noisiness. One traveler noted, "At all hours, one is bothered by their continual cries."[34] Mercier was amazed at Les Halles' early morning escapades, writing, "There is never any silence, any rest, any intermission. . . . Millions of eggs are piled in baskets that move up, down, and around, and yet, miraculously, not a single one is ever broken. Then the brandy flows in great floods in the taverns. . . . There is constant buzzing."[35] Mercier called the ruckus of the halls "stunning" and "so appalling that only the most superhuman voice can pierce it."[36] And in another chapter, he complained at length about the racket: "Cries make a Babel of our mean streets, cries raucous, or toneless, or shrill. . . . Add to all these the voices of the used-clothes men, the umbrella-sellers, used-iron vendors, and water-sellers; men screaming like women, women shouting like men. The din never ceases." Utterly exasperated, Mercier finished, "No words can give any idea of the abomination of this piteous vocal torment when all the cries meet and mingle."[37]

Clearly, the author of the *Tableau* had a concept of noise pollution well before the term existed. Authors like Voltaire and the abbé Barruel referred to the speech of common people as "the language of Les Halles," and female vendors, who were not uncommon, had a reputation for being especially crass.[38] The term for fishwife, *harengère,* also meant a "loud-mouthed woman," and from depictions of these women, I'd imagine that a herring-selling *harengère* knew how to harangue with the best of them. A satirical song called "The Pleasures of the Halls and Markets of Paris" (set to the tune of another diddy called "Shut Up, Shut Up Françoise") had a verse dedicated to the fishwives, praising the way that they "slip *bons mots*" into their conversations: "Listen to these gossips/ Everything stinking of mackerel/ All rotten, they say/ The vegetables too."[39] Jean-Jacques Rousseau did give the women of Les Halles a bit of credit, noting that they had a tendency to break up fights. But that credit immediately went out the window, since he then used that fact to support his claim that compassion is inherent in humans since even the coarsest people (i.e., the fishwives) had some.[40] This jaded perspective surely contributed to adages like, "One can buy anything in the market but silent prudence and honor."[41]

I'm sure that the market was far from an elegant, glistening bastion of manners, but despite these various testimonies, one should also be careful about writing it off as a wholly horrid place. There were plenty of practical reasons for the din of the market. In the darkness, where directional signs would have been of little aid, sound became an important geographical marker. Sellers would bark their wares, giving information about prices and condition, in an attempt to attract buyers. Customers would listen for bargains and navigate to their favorite vendors based on these cries. In a market filled with 6,000 people, it would have been the most epic version of the game Marco Polo imaginable.

And yet to those involved, it was perfectly natural. Sound, interminable though it was, was a necessary part of market life.

Much of the judgment against Les Halles had to do with the fact that the poorer sorts congregated there, and privileged writers often passed quick judgments on these folk. Mercier, for all his criticisms of the nobility, also stereotyped the poor: "The lower classes are naturally excessive bawlers; they raise their voices in jarring cacophonies. You hear these raucous, sharp, deaf shouts from all sides. . . . Chimney-sweeps and fishsellers even make these horrible cries in their sleep, given that they have become second nature."[42] To his mind, lower-class individuals had no control over their own bodies, to the point that they could not even force themselves to stop screaming. The auditory assault perpetrated by such people correlated to their rough manner of living, coarse character, and lower-class manners. In eighteenth-century terms, this makes some sense. Recall that in the Enlightenment, thanks to the concept of sensibility, the mind, body, and morals corresponded, so for Mercier, it would have been only natural to assume that a filthy environment would have an effect on the manners of the people there, and vice versa.

But sensory historians and sociologists have theorized another, less Enlightenment-specific aspect of claims like Mercier's, where rough manners, loud noises, bad smells, coarse skin, poor taste, and other unpleasant sensations are linked to certain groups of people. According to these theorists, sensory prejudices are one way that people (often unconsciously) reinforce social hierarchies. People tend to accept others with whom they share sensory attributes. For example, if someone who smells like lavender is at a party where two people smell like fish and ten others smell like lavender, then that person will probably gravitate toward her fellow lavender-smellers, wrinkling her nose at the fishy odor. Conversely, people often attribute sensory offenses to folks that they consider to be of a lower social status. If that same partygoer attends a *fête* where there are ten celebrities, all of whom smell like fish, and four waiters, all of whom smell like lavender, she might change her opinion of the "goodness" of the lavender smell and decide to compliment Angelina Jolie's *eau de* herring. As a means of raising her own status, the next time the fictitious partier appeared in public, she might wear her own *soupçon* of *poisson*.

These prejudices are around us to such an extent that we aren't usually aware of them or don't think of them as prejudices. They simply seem like natural reactions. A more realistic example would be the snap judgment a person makes when they hear someone's accent. If you met a person for the first time, and she spoke with a slow Southern drawl, you would make different assumptions about her than if she spoke with a Boston accent. (And of course, where you grew up would affect what these accents meant to you in the first place.) For better or worse, stereotypes are shorthand ways that humans categorize others, and these types of social assumptions aren't always bad. For instance, you may notice someone reading *The New Yorker* and assume that they might like other magazines that you like. Or, if you self-identify with a particular group, you may dress in a similar way so that you can feel more integrated into the community. But there are other instances—as with race, gender, or sexuality—when social assumptions can be divisive and harmful.

In general, the things that a dominant social group finds appealing tend to become the standards of "good" taste. For example, wine, literary fiction, and classical music tend to fall under the rubric of "good taste," and those who want to be part of the elite might try to develop an appreciation for these things. By gaining cultural capital, one gains social standing. But it's not just people who want to fit in who use ideas of "good" and "bad" taste to their advantage. Even people who aren't part of the dominant social group (or don't aspire to be) use sensory prejudices to define their own social position. For example, remember the brouhaha that broke out in 2007 when Barack Obama asked Iowa voters about the price of arugula? The president's love for spicy greens suddenly became a stand-in for "elitism" and "out-of-touch politics." For many pundits, an appreciation for arugula was tantamount to a political statement. In the midst of the scandal, many of Obama's critics spoke out in favor of iceberg lettuce, which, I suppose, is the lettuce of the people. Lettuce may not seem like a big deal, but the social groups that dictate the terms of "good" and "bad" taste have a great deal of power.

Unfortunately, this power often comes at the expense of people lower on the social totem pole. George Orwell perhaps explained this best in his 1937 *The Road to Wigan Pier*. Recruited to write a report on the living conditions among the unemployed and lower classes, Orwell argued that the "the real secret of class distinctions in the West . . . is summed up in four frightful words. . . . *The lower classes smell*." He continued, explaining why this was such a powerful aspect of class formation: "Here, obviously, you are at an impassable barrier. For no feeling of like or dislike is quite so fundamental as a *physical feeling*. . . . It may not matter greatly if the average middle-class person is brought up to believe that the working classes are ignorant, lazy, drunken, boorish, and dishonest; it is when he is brought up to believe that they are dirty that the harm is done."[43] The senses, given their physical basis, provide stereotypes a visceral foundation; they become a gut reaction, born from a deep-seated part of the body that no longer relies on reason. Because we think of these reactions as "natural," it makes our prejudices seem objective, as if they are located outside of ourselves and are beyond our capacity to change.

In his book *How Race Is Made,* Mark M. Smith has shown just how strong sensory prejudices can be. He argues that during

American slavery, when visual distinctions between white skin and black skin failed (as in the case of mixed-race children), other sensory prejudices came into play that ensured slaveholders' social superiority. Chief among these sensory prejudices were claims about the "bad" odor of slaves. In the mid eighteenth century, Mark Catesby, an English naturalist who focused on the natural history of certain American regions, used odor to frame his experiences with two nonwhite populations: "[Native Americans] are naturally a very sweet People, their Bodies emitting nothing of that Rankness that is so remarkable in *Negres* [sic]."[44] Aroma, couched as a biological, "natural" attribute, gave people like Catesby license to treat other people as higher or lower on the Great Chain of Being.

In the thicket of darkness that surrounded Les Halles, eyesight was not a readily available tool for discernment. In its absence, the other senses stepped in to play an important role, and often they were used to reinforce social hierarchies. Attributes like odor, noise, and calloused skin became important tells for deeper issues of character and status.[45] In a market setting, complaints about noise certainly may have had some basis in truth, but it doesn't mean that sellers' loud voices were a sign of coarse character or dishonorable behavior.

Given the open-air nature of the market, sensory stimuli would have mixed freely. The thick aroma of fish might have mingled with sweet touches of hyacinth and lily from the flower stalls, while the noise of patrons at the wine stalls mingled with the cries of children accompanying their vegetable-selling mothers. Les Halles was a bustling, swirling, confusing place, filled with both the finest and roughest elements of life. In the pale light of the moon, shadows played freely, and specters danced among the frenetic, determined movements of people in need of earning a living. Chaos and order found expression in the solidity of objects and the intangible bonds of faith that existed between people. Sounds, smells, tastes, and touches combined to form a kinetic world, unbound by distinct impressions of form, shape, and color. The nonvisual senses were essential to anyone who wanted to try to make sense of this ever-changing tableau.

By 1873, when Zola wrote *The Belly of Paris,* street lighting had become more predictable, and yet, he still preferred to portray the market as a force that rumbled in the depths of the black morning hours. He described how his character Florent spent several cold, weakly lit hours among cabbages, listening to the discordant symphony of the market: "To the right, to the left, everywhere, the shrill cries sent the treble notes of a flute into the bass rumble of the crowd. It was the sound of seafood, butter, poultry, and meat being sold. The pealing of bells sent added vibrations through the noisy market." Only as dawn began to break did a new world emerge: "All around Florent, sunlight set vegetables on fire with color. The pale watercolor he had seen at dawn had vanished. The ample hearts of lettuce were aflame. The hues of the greenery had turned brilliant, the carrots flowed bloodred, the turnips turned incandescent in the triumphal sunlight."[46] Freshly peddled, the wholesale goods of Les Halles found their way to daylight in smaller shops, food establishments, and the plates of Parisians. What began in the dark continued in the stark light of day, sunshine spreading color over what had, only a few hours before, been a world composed of touch, scent, and sound.

4

Becoming Useful Citizens:
The Talents of Blind
(and Blindfolded) Children

JUST OVER A MILE AWAY from Les Halles, Saint Ovid's Fair was held in the Place Louis XV (now Place de la Concorde). Filled with boutiques boasting jewels, exotic printed cloths, and the latest fashions, the fair also played host to a number of arresting spectacles, including a marionette theater, menageries, and tightrope walkers. Among the most popular of these spectacles were the performances given by a blind orchestra at a local café during the August and September of 1771. The fair's almanac described the scene vividly, reporting that the eight members of the orchestra were dressed in long red robes, clogs, and pointy bonnets. Their conductor, whose cap sported donkey ears, floated above the orchestra on a stuffed peacock while he beat out of time. Each blind person had a sheet of music and a lighted candle in front of him, regardless of the fact that he had no need of these objects. According to the almanac's author, "The throngs of people who came to see this joke were often so large that it was necessary to put riflemen at the door of the café and to have the so-called musicians step down from time to time." In fact,

GRAND CONCERT   EXTRA·ORDINAIRE
Exécuté par un Détachement des   *Quinze vingt au Caffé des*
à l'Hôpital des Foire Saint Ovide au   *Mois de Septembre 1771*

Patrons found it "lovely to hear these blind people sing," at the concert given by blind musicians at Saint Ovid's Fair in September 1771. Notice that emblems of light surround the musicians: candles, a chandelier, and a mirror. They all "read" sheet music, and one violinist even wears spectacles.

the spectacle was so popular, rival cafés tried to imitate it, and an engraved caricature of the event became a bestseller.[1] A "Café of the Blind" (so named because of the nightly performances of blind musicians) was even established in the basement of the Palais-Royal, although its shadowy ambiance quickly gave the café an unsavory reputation.

While blindness had been on the cultural radar for centuries, there were a number of reasons it became such a popular topic in the Enlightenment. Before easy access to corrective lenses, blindness and visual impairment were fairly common occurrences. In addition to congenital blindness and visual degeneration, a number of diseases afflicted the fragile sense of sight. One of the major culprits of blindness in the early modern world was venereal disease. Syphilis, allegedly a disease brought back to Europe by explorers to the New World in the 1490s, hit epidemic levels in the sixteenth century. Also known as "the French Pox," "the Great Pox," the "evil of Naples," and "the clap," the illness was commonly considered God's punishment for lewd behavior, and many doctors refused to treat the afflicted sinners.[2] Obviously, this did little to curb the spread of the disease, and by the eighteenth century, there was a full-on war against it. In English newspapers, remedies for sexually transmitted diseases were among the most prolifically advertised products, and charlatans had a field day with desperate clientele.[3] Untreated syphilis had a great number of adverse effects, with blindness figuring prominently among them.

Because of its association with venereal disease (and the fact that it was also considered a side effect of overenthusiastic masturbation), blindness often carried with it the taint of immorality. The Jean-Jacques of the marketplace, Restif de la Bretonne, penned a rather long song whose fifty-fourth verse was dedicated to Edmond, an immoral character afflicted with the pox:

Oh! Who could count the suffering
Of poor and unhappy Edmond!
Covered all over with unhealthy red spots,
Blind, and full of infection!
God prolonged his life
So that he would suffer longer.[4]

However, syphilis was not an affliction content to affect only promiscuous offenders. It also had congenital effects, and children born of syphilitic mothers often had physical handicaps, including blindness and deafness. In both eighteenth-century England and France, reformers were anxious about the high population of syphilitic children, and they speculated that the disease was destroying both the "present race" and the future of the nation.[5] It probably didn't help matters that the most common treatment for syphilis was mercury. Eighteenth-century doctors didn't know that one possible side effect of mercury poisoning is visual impairment or blindness.[6] If the disease didn't get you, the cure would.

Smallpox, another disease that ran rampant in the early modern world, also contributed to the prevalence of blindness. Smallpox epidemics struck cities with particular force. In London, there were eleven peak years between 1700 and 1800, each of which resulted in over 3,000 deaths.[7] Individuals who survived smallpox were left with scars, disfigurements, and, in many instances, blindness, and at the end of the eighteenth century, the disease caused an estimated one-third of all cases of blindness.[8] During the early part of the century, reports of Turkish and Chinese inoculation procedures captured the attention of European doctors, and in 1721, Lady Mary Wortley Montagu, the wife of the English ambassador to Turkey, requested that her daughter be inoculated. This high-profile endorsement, as well as reports about the successful use of inoculation during an outbreak in Boston, encouraged the practice in England. Yet because of its complexity and cost, as well as furious debates about its efficacy, inoculation was mostly an elite practice for another thirty years.[9]

Despite the prevalence of blindness and other disabilities, handicapped individuals had long been considered to be separate from society, and in many cases, they were actually kept in separate housing. In the Middle Ages, blindness was treated as the result of parents' transgressions or a fault of character, and medieval literature often portrayed the blind beggar as a dim-witted individual who could be laughed at relentlessly.[10] The disabled were often the object of derision, portrayed as being "nothing but a piece of shit" (in the less-than-delicate words of one medieval play), and popular theater portrayed the blind as humorous buffoons with no real talent. A blind person's only possible career path, if it could be called such, was to become a beggar, meaning that blindness also became associated with laziness, torpor, and vice.

In the thirteenth century, Louis XI established a hospice for three hundred poor blind people from the city of Paris, which came to be known as Quinze-Vingts, or "Fifteen Twenties."[11] This charitable enterprise recognized the humanity of its residents by providing for their basic needs and by establishing a confraternity of individuals with similar conditions. Yet in order to earn their keep, residents of Quinze-Vingts had to collect money and bread. While begging, they wore an outfit with the king's *fleur-de-lis* insignia, and at night, they would return to the hospice and divvy up their earnings. This system meant that the blind had a highly public presence, but because of their separated housing and lack of occupational options, they were still kept on the social fringes.

This neither-nor position fascinated Enlightenment philoso-

phers, and blindness became a popular conundrum in intellectual circles. One of the hot-button philosophical debates was the
"Molyneux problem," a brain-teaser named after the philosopher
William Molyneux, whose wife had become blind after an illness.
The Molyneux problem went something like this: Let's say a man
is born blind, and he learns to distinguish between a sphere and
a cube by touch. If he were suddenly able to see, would he be able
to identify these same shapes by sight alone? Uneventful as the
question might seem to you and me, pretty much any and every
Enlightenment thinker had a horse in this race. Molyneux and
his friend John Locke both agreed that the blind man would not
be able to tell the difference. In 1709, the Anglo-Irish philosopher
George Berkeley argued that there was no necessary connection
between the sensations of touch and sight and that experience
alone could be the blind man's guide.[12] In the mid eighteenth century, others joined the debate: Condillac argued, contra Locke,
that the tactile experience of space could translate to visual
impressions; the Comte de Buffon sided with Locke, based on
his belief that individuals initially see the world as inverted, dou-
bled, and without distance until they learn to interpret their sight
alongside spatial experience; and the philosopher Julien Offray
de La Mettrie argued that a blind man would be able to discern
the shapes since his visual experience would conform to whatever
tactile impression the imagination had "engraved on the brain."[13]

Given the close connection between sensation and emotion in
the eighteenth century, questions about the blind's abilities seg-
ued into questions about the emotional effects of a lack of eyesight. Some, like Antoine Le Camus, had a less-than-favorable
impression of the blind. He claimed, "Knowing neither light nor
colors, [a blind person] is a creature inferior to man." Le Camus
also compared the blind to prisoners trapped in dungeons and
remarked that for such people, "Death is a consolation."[14] The

philosopher Denis Diderot, drawing on the idea that the mind
and morals are built out of sensory experience, toyed with the
idea that a person lacking one of her senses may have an idiosyncratic sense of morality. In his *Letter on the Blind*, he asked
the rather colorful question, "What difference is there, for a blind
man, between a urinating man and one who bleeds without complaining?"[15] The blind man, unable to see the pain of the bleed-
ing man, would be unable to experience appropriate levels of pity.
Diderot also suggested that in a community where men were
blind, wife-swapping would have to be acceptable since it would
be so easy for wives to sneak around behind their husbands'
backs. Basically, Diderot was interested in the way that different
sensory configurations led to different sorts of moral expectations
and social expectations, and he suggested that the morality of the
blind would not necessarily conform to the mandates of polite
eighteenth-century French society. (As an ardent Diderot lover,
I have to point out that unlike Le Camus, he didn't despise the
blind. In fact, in the *Letter on the Blind*, Diderot praised the blind
mathematician Nicholas Saunderson and several other blind men
who, "with one less sense, seem so far elevated above the rest of
mankind."[16] Furthermore, Diderot retracted his claims about
the morality of blind individuals in a 1782 addition that he wrote
to the *Letter*, describing his encounter with a precocious blind
woman of the highest moral character.)

While some writers addressed the potentially negative aspects
of blindness, many others tended to stress its great social potential. In some cases, the traits that had excluded the blind from
society came to be seen as positive attributes. One particularly
zealous reformer was Jean-Bernard Mérian, who argued that
blindness should be seen as a social boon rather than an impairment. After writing seven short pieces on the Molyneux problem
that summed up the arguments of other philosophers, Mérian

dedicated an eighth to his own observations. He presented these ideas to the Prussian Academy of Sciences in 1782, standing before some of the most illustrious naturalists in Europe. Mérian proposed to take poor children "from the cradle and to raise them in profound darkness."[17] He helpfully added that doctors would need to develop a special blindfold to ensure that the children's sight would be completely checked.[18] Mérian thought that the darkness would help the children develop better manual skills or intellectual powers. Sight, he claimed, causes a great number of distractions, and if students were "disencumbered of sight . . . [their] touch would acquire the most exquisite finesse . . . their fingers would be like microscopes."[19] In other words, the loss of one sense would allow the children's other senses to grow more adept. (In today's parlance, this is called "sensory vicariance.")

Mérian's claims relied on a particular notion of attention, which he drew from sensationalist philosophers like Condillac. He treated attention like a zero-sum game, assuming that there is a limited amount available, which is constantly divided into lesser and greater parts. According to Condillac, humans register the sensations that strike the animal fibers most vigorously and therefore command the greatest amount of attention. For example, if I were to listen to a podcast while chopping vegetables, my attention would be divided between several stimuli. But if I sliced into my finger, that pain would draw my attention, and I'm sorry to say, poor Ira Glass would no longer occupy my mind. A zero-sum concept of attention meant that there was a limited amount of possible focus, and by depriving children of their eyesight, Mérian was trying to cut down on the stimuli that competed for their attention.

With their newly reconfigured attention, the blinded students would fall into two camps. Those whose attention redirected to the sense of touch would have improved manual skills, making them ideal "mechanics, sculptors, artists of all kinds." They would be able to create masterful objects that would be the envy of all other European nations. With its bevy of blind workers, France could become the leading manufacturer of artisanal products, and the country would be flooded with money from international trade. The second group of students, whose attention redirected to the internal senses, would have improved their powers of reflection, and they would become "physicists, naturalists, geometers of the first order, and above all philosophers exempt from the thousand prejudices that we suckle from our birth."[20]

Mérian wasn't totally out of touch with the ways of the world, and he realized that there would be people who would object, most notably the mothers of these blindfolded children. But he argued that the public benefits outweighed the "popular prejudice" of tradition, and mothers should be able to recognize that this philosophical education would be best. Mérian longed to "ask most of these tender mothers who shudder at my proposition and who would be inconsolable if their children were blind up to a certain age: how, then, will you spend this precious time in their favor? Alas, to blind their mind and to spoil their heart!" Keeping children near the family home could only keep them closer to destitution. He railed, "Look at these objects of disgust and pity, these half-naked children, barely covered with miserable rags, prey to vermin, raised in laziness and dishonesty, these baleful cripples, often rendered blind without even returning to the monsters that they call parents."[21] Surely, Mérian opined, good mothers would understand, nay *be grateful*, for the chance for their children to become productive, talented, and contributing members of the French state. The children's lives would have more purpose, and they would not be confined to a life of skill-less poverty.

While there are many shocking elements of this proposal, one of the most striking is the way in which Mérian stressed the positive side of blindness, arguing that this "disability" was not a disability at all. Having different sensory abilities and different bodies was, to his mind, a social asset. "I have proved that there would be infinitely more to gain than to lose for the children who would be raised in this manner," he wrote. "We have always looked at those who are born blind indifferently: [but] never understood what true advantage could come to them from their [different] senses."[22]

This perspective on sensory education was certainly not idiosyncratic to Mérian. Many philosophers thought this was precisely what was needed. Fictional accounts of the "ideal education" took sensationalist pedagogy seriously and described how specific sensory stimuli could aid childhood development. You've already encountered the most well-known of these accounts: Jean-Jacques Rousseau's *Émile*. Unlike Mérian's hypothetical pupils, Émile was not permanently blinded, but Rousseau did stress the importance of keeping him in the dark. Émile was encouraged to play in the middle of the night so that he could learn to judge objects by touch. According to Rousseau, most people rely on vision and neglect the development of touch. As you can probably guess, this tendency was among the litany of things that got Rousseau's goat. Touch, he argued, was the sense that most directly connects us to the world, and it needed to be more valued.[23] Jean-Jacques admired that "the blind have a surer and more delicate sense of touch," and he proclaimed, "I had rather Emile's eyes were in his finger tips than in the chandler's shop."[24] The blind, he argued, were always self-possessed, and they never feared the onset of night, whereas sighted people are helpless half the time. If you overlook its reputation as a sordid place, Les Halles might have made the perfect playground for the fictional Émile.

Similarly, Gaspard Guillard de Beaurieu wrote a novel called *The Student of Nature* (1763) where the student in question began his life in a dark, skyless cage where he was supplied with meat, bread, fruits, and water "by means which [he] could not discern."[25] In 1765, the Abbé Dulaurens wrote a novel called *Imirce, or Nature's Daughter,* where the eponymous heroine was purchased as a baby and kept in a cellar. This coming-of-age novel followed the "natural" development of Imirce, who grew into sexual and intellectual maturity thanks to the company of a boy named Emilor and a series of sensory objects strategically presented to her by her master.[26] During her confinement, Imirce was blindfolded and allowed to see only when her master permitted.[27]

Not all social reformers were zealous about creating blind citizens, but many did see the benefit of helping those who were already blind. Valentin Haüy, a skilled linguist and interpreter to the king, made it his mission to help the blind. Haüy saw the blind orchestra at St. Ovid's Fair, but instead of laughing along with the crowd, "an entirely different sentiment seized our souls," he wrote. "From that moment, we came up with the possibility of improving [the lives] of these Unfortunates."[28] As close as he was to the king, Haüy did not tend to speak of himself with the "Royal We." Instead, the "we" in question was the Société Philanthropique, a charitable society of which Haüy was a part, which had been founded in 1780. The society was considered "the most respectable of all those that exist in Paris," and it had an impressive lineup of contributors, including Benjamin Franklin, the chemist Antoine Lavoisier, and the Marquis de Lafayette (of American revolutionary fame).[29] In the late eighteenth century, thanks in large part to growing secularization, philanthropic societies became a popular alternative to church-based charity. Privately funded, many of these groups focused on how to incorporate beggars into a working population so that they could be useful members of society. For instance, in 1777, the Academy of Châlons-sur-Marne proposed an essay competition to figure out

"the means of destroying mendicancy in France by making beggars useful to the state without making them unhappy."[30] As part
of this tide of philanthropic feeling, Haüy came up with a plan
that would save the blind from the "idleness that they did not
think they could ever escape," and he presented his idea for an
Institute for Blind Youth in 1783.[31] With the financial support of
the Society, Haüy was able to take in twelve blind children who
were the offspring of poor workers.

There were several reasons for targeting youth, aside from
the commonplace idea that the youth of today are the leaders
of tomorrow. For one, the French government had been trying
since the mid eighteenth century to clear the streets of orphans.[32]
The government and the police maintained the opinion that public order depended on finding work for the growing number of
beggars, and Haüy's school was one option for ensuring that disabled children had a place to go. This emphasis on youth also fit
with the second prerogative: to teach the blind skills at an early
age that would "make these unfortunates useful to society while
assuring them a means of subsistence."[33] While Quinze-Vingts
had successfully furnished a home and support system for a number of blind citizens, it had not made them socially productive.
The Institute for Blind Youth, on the other hand, placed skill-ori-
ented instruction front and center.

True to eighteenth-century norms, Haüy thought that the
blind had excellent manual and tactile capacities, and it was
through these skills that Haüy sought to incorporate his students
into a sight-dominant society. Haüy reported success in teaching his students bushel-making, knitting, sewing, bookbinding,
and above all, printing. In fact, Haüy established a printing shop
at the Institute's headquarters, and several high-profile printers
and booksellers oversaw the students' work. Haüy also believed
that the blind had "natural dispositions" for music because of

their improved dexterity and hearing. He encouraged many of his students to take up instruments, although he continued to frown upon the mockery of the blind concerts described above. Thanks to the idea of sensory vicariance, in the late eighteenth century the blind were integrated into a program of national, social improvement. They became an important part of society instead of staying in the neither-nor space that they had occupied for centuries as beggars. To make the blind feel even more included, the Institute emphasized French history, which would give students "an inviolable attachment to their king," and geography, which would permit them to distinguish different kingdoms and provinces.[34] To achieve these goals, Haüy decided to use the blind's tactile talents in a totally new way: he decided to teach them to read with their fingers. Using raised characters, students could overcome the limitations of their eyes. This system of raised printing was a direct precursor of Braille, which was developed in 1824 by Louis Braille, one of the Institute's later residents.

Haüy was a born marketer and made the Institute a success. Every Wednesday and Saturday at noon, a who's who of Paris would travel to the Institute to watch public demonstrations of the blind students' skills.[35] Haüy also presented his students to the king, queen, and all the courtly kith and kin at Versailles; the Academy of Sciences; the Royal Academy of Music; and literary salons. François-Joseph Gossec, a wsell-known contemporary composer, wrote songs for Haüy's blind chorus, and the students performed concerts in various churches and marched in parades. In 1789, Haüy even managed to get a prestigious spot for the blind orchestra in the king's chapel.[36]

The blind were no longer being mocked, but they were still on display, and it's legitimate to ask why Haüy didn't just train his students, set them up with jobs, and leave it at that. Why the need for spectacle? There are a few good reasons, one of which had to do with eighteenth-century standards for scientific proof. In an era before rigorous experimental methods, advanced laboratories, or specialized scientific professions (the term "scientist" wasn't even coined until 1833), there were different standards for what constituted scientific "fact." Demonstration was central to this process, and within the scientific community, eyewitness proof was the key to establishing whether someone's claims were true. As the historian Patricia Fara has argued, "seeing was closely allied with knowing," and by seeing the blind students in action, potential donors and other men of science could be assured of the success of Haüy's educational program.[37] Having audiences of illustrious, intelligent people (like the king, high-ranking nobles, and the members of the Academy of Sciences) ensured the legitimacy of the enterprise.

But it wasn't just men of science who saw these demonstrations. The performances were open to the public, and people from all walks of life watched them eagerly. One of the major Enlightenment goals was to spread knowledge to new groups of people, and when it came to eighteenth-century science, there was no better way to draw in audiences than with awe-inspiring spectacles. The Enlightenment was not spread by philosophy alone; its proponents filled stages, seats, and streets as well as books, and they successfully reached new audiences through laughter, spectacle, and wonder. By making the blind more interesting to the public, Haüy's demonstrations allowed disabled individuals to have a strong, positive cultural presence. A skeptic could argue that these performances kept the blind students just as separate as they had been previously. Their abilities were still viewed as distinct, they were educated separately, and they were trained in tasks considered appropriate to their sensory condition. But it was because of people like Haüy (and the word spread by his efforts) that the blind could, for the first time, be considered useful members of society. They were marveled at rather than laughed at, and Haüy's continual efforts to keep the blind in front of the public helped, in the long run, to advance their cause.

I'm quite glad that twenty-first-century media would not call those with disabilities "monsters of nature that have loose morals."[38] Despite laws on behalf of the disabled and terminological improvements, though, I would suggest that we could still take a couple of pointers from the Enlightenment attitude toward blindness. In the eighteenth century, many reformers did not see disability as *dis*-ability at all. Instead, they trusted that sensory differences could have positive social effects and that the disabled had unique and important talents. Mérian actually advocated blindness as a form of social improvement (even though, by modern standards, his social stances are quite misguided), and Rousseau thought the ability to navigate without eyesight was an important part of education. Some Enlightenment reforms, philosophies, and initiatives surrounding blindness seem stranger than others, but the projects I've described in this chapter show how difference came to be seen as a good thing. The blind, deaf, physically and mentally disabled—everyone had a social part to play. The Enlightenment goal wasn't just to tolerate the blind or accommodate them. It was to show that the blind had something unique and positive to add to society. Reformers embraced difference and recognized its ability to create a richer, deeper, and fuller world.

⫷ 5 ⫸

Blowing Smoke up the Ass:
Aromatic Medicine and Useful Science

I N THE EIGHTEENTH CENTURY, useful science was every bit
as important as useful citizens. In 1781, the Royal Academy of
Brussels issued a call for scientific papers, and Benjamin Franklin, who was serving as the United States ambassador to France
at the time, wrote an impassioned response—although he never
sent it to the Academy. Instead, he printed his witty essay and distributed it privately to interested parties, including Joseph Priest-
ley, the chemist famous for his work on gases. Like Haüy and the
other reformers from the last chapter, Franklin felt that knowledge should improve human life instead of existing in a theoretical vacuum, and he worried that European academies were
becoming detached from practical considerations.

Thirty-odd years before *Pride and Prejudice*'s "universally
acknowledged" truth "that a single man in possession of a good
fortune must be in want of a wife," Franklin had offered his own
universal truth. He declared, "It is universally well known, That
in digesting our common Food, there is created or produced in
the Bowels of human Creatures, a great Quantity of Wind."[1] He

explained that if the air escapes, it is usually fetid and, as a result, offensive to one's company. Well-bred people will go to great lengths to avoid offending their friends, and instead of giving release to this wind, they opt to forcibly restrain their gas. Yet, Franklin lamented, this discipline often gives rise to pain, and in severe cases, it could contribute to future diseases that could be life-threatening. Therefore, the most useful contribution to science, he reasoned, would be a drug that would make flatulence the sweet-smelling life of the party.

Franklin insisted that this was not just a flight of fancy. People that eat too many onions or who "dine on stale Flesh," often have breath so bad that they can pass gas without it even being noticed. (Perhaps it was for this set of people that Altoids were created in the 1780s?) Furthermore, Franklin noted, we can alter the scent of our urine by eating asparagus, and it was common knowledge that a "Pill of Turpentine no bigger than a Pea, shall bestow on [urine] the pleasing Smell of Violets." Thanks to such examples, Franklin saw no legitimate barrier to altering the scent of flatulence.[2] (It seems that feces were also fair game. According to the historian Alain Corbin, "For nearly a century . . . every eminent chemist tried his hand at deodorizing excrement.")[3]

This pill, to Franklin's mind, symbolized "useful science" much more than any of the abstract discoveries made by the legendary figures of science. Picking on Descartes' theory of planetary motion, Franklin opined, "What Comfort can the Vortices of Descartes give to a Man who has Whirlwinds in his Bowels!" Nor did Newton escape Franklin's wrath, with the founding father's assertion that the seven colors refracted by a Newtonian prism could not hold a candle to the "Ease and Comfort every Man living might feel seven times a Day, by discharging freely the Wind from his Bowels." In this colorful and passionate entreaty, Franklin argued that utility was the most important end of science, and if science wasn't improving man's lot by "bringing Philosophy home to Men's Business and Bosoms," then it was "scarcely worth a FARThing." (Franklin's emphasis, not mine.)

The utility that Franklin praised wasn't just about improving physical comfort; it was also about enhancing people's social interactions. Social reform was key to the Enlightenment, and Franklin suggested that pleasant flatulence could be a boon to human interactions. Considering that "the Pleasures of one Sense [are] little inferior to those of another," he suggested that "instead of pleasing the *Sight,* [the pill-taker] might delight the *Smell* of those about him, and make Numbers happy." The truly generous host could even find out whether his friends prefer "Musk or Lilly, Rose or Bergamot, and provide accordingly." And believe it or not, the benefits did not stop there! The ability to pass gas freely also marked a form of freedom and self-expression. "Surely such a Liberty of *Expressing* one's *Scenti-ments,* and *pleasing one another*," he wrote, "is of infinitely more Importance to human Happiness than that Liberty of the *Press,* or of *abusing one another,* which the English are so ready to fight and die for."[4] Knowing Franklin's dedication to the values of "Life, Liberty, and the pursuit of Happiness," you can see that he had high hopes, indeed, for this pill. Sure, Franklin was somewhat tongue-in-cheek with this essay, but if you only take a moment to imagine the world that he describes, you must agree that it paints a blissful portrait of self-expression.

Franklin's call to action is striking, not least, because of the emphasis it placed on the sense of smell. Historians of odor have argued that smell is undervalued in modern life, and in first-world countries, people have become accustomed to highly anesthetized public environments and subtle body odors. Youngsters are taught to wear deodorant from the time they hit puberty, and products like Febreze, which help eradicate offensive odors, are common.

The modern world's emphasis on objectivity, rationality, and reason, sensory anthropologists argue, has done much to elevate the status of sight and lower that of smell. Furthermore, odors are tricky creatures; they can't be easily contained, which means that some of our most intimate experiences are precisely those that can escape and cross boundaries. We seek to keep our deeply personal odors contained, but try as we might, they sometimes get the best of us. Scholars like David Howes, Constance Classen, and Anthony Synnott have argued that the personal, often transgressive nature of scents, is incompatible with modern society. Today's world emphasizes privacy and discrete boundaries, all of which are subverted by the wafting, free nature of odors.[5]

There are some basic assumptions undergirding these claims. For much of history, many sensory historians and anthropologists argue, people in the West have, often unconsciously, approached the five senses according to these divisions:

SIGHT AND HEARING	TASTE AND SMELL
Operate at a distance	Proximity senses
Objective (Focused on stimuli outside oneself)	Subjective (Focused on personal, internal impressions)
Rational	Emotional
More commonly associated with men or masculine traits	More commonly associated with women or feminine traits

(Touch is ambiguous, moving back and forth between these categories, depending on the circumstances.)

Sight and hearing are "distance senses," meaning that we can look at or hear things from afar without ever interacting directly with them. Because these sensations come from objects at a remove from our bodies, we tend to think of them as objective. We might consider it to be perfectly acceptable for there to be a discrepancy between the ways that you and I taste a particular glass of wine, but we would consider it less acceptable for there to be a discrepancy between the ways we view a particular object. If I were to say that I saw a bird, and you say you saw a cat, a third party would be likely to assume that one of us was, objectively speaking, wrong.

Taste and smell, on the other hand, are "proximity senses," which means that you have to be in contact with a stimulus in order to perceive it. You must be near an odor in order to smell it; you must bring food into contact with your body in order to taste it. Because of this contact, these senses tend to have associations of interiority. We perceive these sensations as being deeply personal, and because of this, we treat them as subjective responses. I might describe a wine as having a leathery taste, where you detect only the flavor of scorched earth. Such discrepancies are normal—even expected—because we think of these senses as emotional and intimate. While sight can tell us about the surface of things, we tend to think that it can't reveal interior knowledge in the way that scent can.

Historically, this led people to treat scents as the bearer of some kind of inner truth. For instance, in the Middle Ages, the corpses of saints were said to smell sweetly of flowers, never succumbing to putrid decay. And, before doctors adopted the idea that diseases are caused by germs, many of them attributed disease to bad smells. Miasmas, or bad air, could invade the pores of the body, spreading illness to the interior body, and miasma theories of disease made it seem like the world was a constant battlefield of odor. Like invisible armor, a cloud of strong odor would prevent other, more sinister, odors from invading the body. For example, to keep the bad air of the bubonic plague out of one's pores, it was preferable to surround yourself with the pungent odor of onions. This is why, during seventeenth-century outbreaks of the Black Death, boatloads of onions were carted down the Thames River, filling London with their penetrating aroma.

Smell's status as a proximity sense meant that it was deeper, striking at the true heart of experience, but because of its interiority, the truths it imparted were harder to verify, universalize, and share. It's precisely because of this conflicted status that I am reluctant to adopt the narrative that smell was marginalized in the eighteenth century. Instead, it's probably best to say that smell occupied a divergent intellectual space in the Enlightenment. On the one hand, smell was viewed as the sense that most directly contributed to self-preservation. Remember, when Condillac's statue came to life, the glorious scent of a rose was his first experience of the world. Condillac's ordering of the senses was far from arbitrary, and he wished to highlight scent's status as the bedrock of human sensation. Although odor may have been fundamental to the first humans, enlightened writers argued that as human communication and commerce developed, olfaction ceased to be quite so important. The physician Albrecht von Haller put it neatly when he said, "The sense of smell was less important to [man than to animals], for he was destined to walk upright . . . social life and language were designed to enlighten him about the properties of the things that appeared to him to be edible."[6] Scent, in this light, was crucial only to uncivilized beings.

On the other hand, enlightened doctors also argued that the nose is the sensory organ closest to the brain, and therefore, olfaction has a deep relationship with intelligence and feeling. Louis de Jaucourt, a prolific contributor to the *Encyclopédie*, argued that olfactory fibers are loose and full of life because of their proximity to the brain, and a number of other authors agreed that fragrances have the power to shake us to our core.[7] A 1761 English essay cautioning "Against the Immoderate Use of Snuff," asserted, "There is no part of the human frame more delicately sensible than the nostrils ... *the brain itself may be said to lie almost naked there.*"[8] According to Rousseau, "smell is the sense of the imagination," and its pleasures were among the most intense, so it was important that "the sense of smell should not be over-active in early childhood."[9] As with the other senses, smell could be refined and aesthetic appreciation could grow, making it a powerful agent of art and culture. And we can't forget our dear friend Franklin, who presented scent as nothing less than the gateway to effective science, human sociability, individuality, and political freedom.

Regardless of whether they saw it as a sense of savagery or civilization, naturalists and physicians all agreed that smell played an important role in scientific and medical practice. We've all heard the trope "the nose knows," but how and what it knew was quite different in the eighteenth century. When you go to the doctor, you probably expect that she will use her eyes to give you the once-over, use her ears to listen to your heartbeat or breathing, or use touch to check your pulse. You likely don't expect her to take a deep whiff as a way of determining whether you're healthy. But during the Enlightenment, the sense of smell was closely involved in the determination of what was salubrious. Odor could give doctors an idea of what was going on deep inside, penetrating to the interior of the body and marking changes in the internal movement of fluids and solids. While the practice was less common than in previous centuries, physicians still inspected patients' urine, blood, and feces, smelling them for signs of internal disorder.[10] Scent functioned as a crucial diagnostic tool, and hygiene and bodily odor played a significant role in ideas about health in the eighteenth century.

The historian Georges Vigarello has written a fascinating account of changing concepts of cleanliness from the Middle

Ages to the nineteenth century, and odor figures centrally.[11] In the Middle Ages, cleanliness meant having no visible dirt on the skin, and the use of water in personal hygiene was rare. Contrary to some commonly perpetuated tall tales, people in the Middle Ages did not think that water was inherently dangerous, but they did think that it posed some potential medical issues if handled improperly. They believed that the body was immensely porous, and water would flush everything out of the pores. This could be good if a person had been exposed to noxious substances, but if one wasn't careful, it could also pose a threat since the pores would be clear and ready to be filled with whatever ambient particles were in the air. Instead of being vulnerable, people wanted to keep their pores filled with healthy or neutral substances, and strong perfumes and slathered-on coatings protected the skin. The vogue in the seventeenth century for perfumes made of the musky excretions of the civet cat or the musk deer did not come from people who arbitrarily wanted to be surrounded by scents capable of singeing the nose hairs; it came from the belief that strong scents had the power to protect the body.

From our perspective, the past may seem like a smelly place: urine in the streets, musk on the body, unrefrigerated meat, and less-than-minty breath. But I have to stress that that's relative to our standards, not eighteenth-century ones, and for a person accustomed to living in early modern Paris, the city would not have registered as a particularly smelly place. Think of it this way: If you worked in a fish market all the time, you probably wouldn't notice the odor after a while. But if you've always bought plastic-wrapped tilapia from the grocery store, the first time that you went to a fish market, your nose would probably be a bit offended. The scents that we perceive as "smelly" are relative to context, culture, and situation, so we can't really chide historical musk-wearers.

Around the mid eighteenth century, new medical theories developed that emphasized the importance of movement within the body, and water was treated as a useful means of stimulating circulation. A new emphasis on "freeing the skin" came to the fore, stressing that external cleanliness was no longer sufficient to maintain health and that the interior of the body needed to be cleaned as well. A smelly body could indicate that the decay attending death had already set in. By the late eighteenth century, microbes were discovered, and physicians began recommending frequent washing to release the body from rotting matter and to protect it from invasion by invisible bacteria, particles, and viruses. These changes in hygiene, as you might imagine, brought along with them a number of social and cultural changes. One such effect is what the historian Alain Corbin has called "collective hyperaesthesia." This term refers to a changing social norm of what constituted pleasant odors and of ones too smelly to bear. Once people started bathing, certain bodily odors were no longer normal, and these smells started standing out more. If you were an eighteenth-century merchant walking around a city square, you may no longer have expected to experience a rich, pungent mixture of body odors. Instead, you might have expected a more benign freshness of deodorized bodies. As these expectations became more and more the cultural norm, Corbin argues, people became hypersensitive to smells, and Western society at large developed a lower threshold for odors, insisting that their public spaces be free and clear of stinky armpits, urine, and feces. (Hence why we think of the past as a smelly place.)

Changes in hygiene also brought about significant shifts in the way that people interacted with one another, and privacy became increasingly important. Before the eighteenth century, separate rooms to bathe, urinate, or defecate were a truly rare feature, and when they did exist, they were usually for show. But as attitudes toward hygiene changed, private bathrooms became more common for the wealthy. However, the bathrooms of this new architecture were not as simple as we may imagine. Architects like Jacques-François Blondel claimed that modern baths required several rooms, including one room for the water heater, one to warm up the linen sheets used to dry off, another one to hold multiple bathtubs with water of varying temperatures, a room for a postbath nap, a room where servants could wait nearby, and a room with a toilet and a sink.[12]

It was this last feature that took off. The flush toilet was one of the great privacy victories of the eighteenth century. Previously, chamber pots had been typical, latrines had been lined up in a row and apparently, few people, regardless of their social status, felt the need to retreat to separate quarters to do their business. Louis XIV, ever the innovator, made the first step toward toilet privacy in 1684, when he asked that a velvet curtain should be placed "in front of his business chair," but he continued to receive visitors and conduct his kingly duty while seated on that other "throne." Stories abound of diplomats who wiped their posteriors while meeting with their peers, nobles who ordered lunch while on the pot, and servants who carried full pots out in front of illustrious guests.[13] But in the eighteenth century, the wealthy increasingly requested that architects design private rooms for these private functions, and plumbing, wash basins, and toilets (first called "comfort chairs") followed soon behind.

As waste became relegated to personal, private spaces, the desire for deodorized public spaces grew. By the 1750s, naturalists started linking the smells of musk, ambergris, civet, and other animalistic odors with the scent of excrement.[14] Instead of using heady, forceful odors as a means of defense, the well-to-do began to favor light, floral scents that would allow them to notice the body's decay, should it arise. These scents were believed to be more "natural," which was just as trendy a word in the mid eighteenth century as the term "organic" is today. (Although, really, is smelling like a civet cat any less natural than smelling like a carnation?) Jean-Jacques Rousseau was at the vanguard of cultural critics who praised everything deemed natural. He argued vehemently against the artifice of high society and claimed that makeup, theater, and complicated social rituals obscured and distorted human interactions. Anything natural, on the contrary, revealed the depths of the self, and helped link souls in sympathetic, meaningful bonds. Delicate, floral scents were among the things that, in the words of Alain Corbin, let the "uniqueness of the 'I' break through."[15]

Marie-Antoinette was at the vanguard of this hygienic shift. She embraced the soft scents of lavender and orange-flowers, which she noted as having a soothing effect. Among her favorite indulgences were a few drops of lemon essence in her bath or a dash of violet, rose, or jonquil perfume.[16] Indeed, bathing was exceedingly important to the queen, and one of the first commissions she gave her royal perfumer, Jean-Louis Fargeon, was for bath sachets. He recommended that the queen sit on a sachet of blanched almonds, pine nuts, linseed, marsh mallow root, and lily bulb, while using two bran-filled sachets for scrubbing.[17] Fargeon was an educated man who read Condillac, Voltaire, Rousseau, Diderot, and Condorcet with enthusiasm, and he saw perfumery as a useful science. "I am a man of science, a follower of progress," he announced proudly. "Paris has become the center of science, of the arts and of taste. In the field of chemistry, a science that has witnessed so many discoveries in recent years, I have explored heretofore untrodden paths."[18] Through the application of scientific principles, Fargeon argued that he could enhance beauty, produce pleasure, and overcome the effects of nature and time.[19] For creators like Fargeon, scent, science, and progress overlapped, and for consumers, wearing these new scents indicated participation in enlightened society.[20]

All these architectural changes, perfume purchases, and bathing sprees required time and money that was not readily available to all members of society. The new technologies that permitted this olfactory shift allowed for clear, bright, floral scents, but they also required an increased quality of raw materials, extra labor hours, and successive distillations, making them quite expensive.[21] *Enfleurage*, a technique that involves setting botanicals in a layer of fat so that the lipids become saturated with scent, allowed perfumers to capture the fleeting and intoxicating essences of flowers like tuberose and jasmine that don't readily yield essential oils. It was an incredibly slow process, requiring a month to obtain a properly scented fat, and the flowers had to be strained and replaced on a daily basis. Delicate scents like those beloved by Marie-Antoinette required a significant amount of skill, attention, time, and money.

As the washed, floral, and clean body became a marker of the beautiful, fresh soul of elite men and women, the unwashed and smelly body of the working class and the poor became ever more noticeable. Prior to the eighteenth century, everyone was in the same musky boat, but as hygiene norms changed, body odor and cleanliness became a clear marker of social status. The very "natural" developments that Rousseau had seen as bringing humans together had the ironic effect of setting them even more visibly (or odorously) apart. In the same way that dialects and noise functioned as class markers in Les Halles, odor increasingly indicated social hierarchies in society at large. An invisible yet potent gauge, scent came to embody differences in class.

Self-expression and social distinction weren't the only functions of scent in the eighteenth century. Enlightenment doctors had long known that certain plants have healing properties, and

they claimed that patients could experience many medical benefits by inhaling the plants' odors. Perfume burners and fumiga-
tors, which were like early versions of Scentsy warmers, were put
to frequent use in the eighteenth century. Aromatics had strong
powers for the human constitution, and by inhaling their fumes,
it was possible to fill your body with their essences. In the words
of Corbin, they "opened the way to the vital principle" and had a
direct relationship to life and energy.[22] Fumigation was an ancient
practice, dating at least as far back as 429 B.C.E., when Socrates
recommended burning odiferous herbs in the streets of Athens in
order to control an epidemic. Enlightenment doctors continued
to trust the wisdom of the ancients, treating scented materials as
valuable curatives, and even as miasmatic theory slowly gave way
to germ theory, scented materials maintained their status as medicines. But it wasn't the Enlightenment style to be content with
the status quo. From the 1740s onward, doctors' use of aromatic
plants moved beyond your average aromatherapy. There were
other, surer, and faster ways for scent to penetrate the body, naturalists argued, and it was their duty to find them.

One such method involved a newly discovered scientific marvel: electricity. At its most basic level, men of science thought of
electricity as an invisible fluid that penetrated the body's pores.
"The body of man," wrote the naturalist Pierre Bertholon,
"which is plunged into the atmosphere just as a fish is in water,
cannot help but to receive electrical fluid from all sides." He continued descriptively, "A dry sponge placed in water gives us only a
weak image of the way in which the body imbibes—if you want
to put it that way—electrical fluid."[23] He carried on, giving an
even more disturbing image of the body by claiming that it was
made up of more than 2,160,000 pores, which functioned like a
bunch of tiny mouths ready to inhale electricity.[24] In other words,
electricity was everywhere, and it flowed freely in and out of the

body.[25] Physicians agreed that electricity had the power to speed up the vibration of fibers and the circulation of fluids (much like the elemental fire described in Chapter Two), and this gave some doctors the idea that they could pair electricity and aromatics to make a potent medical treatment. The quickening actions of electricity would assist the healing properties of the aromatics, and the effects would take hold faster.

Among these innovators was the Italian Gianfrancesco Pivati, and reports of his "medicated tubes" quickly made the rounds through Europe. Pivati got his idea after experimenting with the effects of electricity on different plants. Drawing sparks from a flower, he directed the electric stream toward his nostrils and claimed that he could detect the "very gentle odorous effluvium of the flower."[26] According to Pivati, the sparks would vary based on the chemical composition of the aromatic substance, so different plants would yield different medical effects, and through electrified aromatics, it would be possible to affect "the parts that the medical art cannot reach by means of ingestion."[27] Delighted with Pivati's findings, doctors all over Italy experimented with the method.

In 1747, a seventy-five-year-old arthritic bishop came to Pivati looking for a cure. Pivati filled a glass tube with an aromatic remedy and electrified it so that, upon contact, the tube would draw sparks from the suffering parts of the bishop's body. (Medical electricity at this point was static electricity, so Pivati was not harming his patient.) The bishop, thrilled with the results, "clapped his hands together . . . struck the ground with his feet . . . and cried that he did not know whether he was dreaming or awake. Upon leaving, he got into his boat almost as if he were a vigorous boy."[28]

Not everyone trusted Pivati's methods, though. The pope weighed in, complaining about the craze: "In every correspondence from this or the other side of the Alps, we are electrified, and we feel no other effect but our blood become hot, our head obstructed, and our temperament bilious."[29] The French, at first, were filled with optimism, but they soon changed their tune. The French electrician Jean-Antoine Nollet visited Pivati in 1748 to witness his methods. Shortly after the voyage, Nollet wrote that "most of the electrical healings in Turin were nothing more than passing shadows that too quickly were taken . . . for lasting realities."[30]

While Frenchmen were reluctant to accept these electrical miracles, they maintained that aromatic vapor baths could have salutary effects. The Royal Society of Medicine, created in 1778, was the organization in France that approved the sale of medicines, inventions, foods, and cosmetics. It is perhaps helpful to think of them as a sort of proto-FDA. One of the most notable proposals that they received was Faure de Beaufort's 1782 proposal for "medicinal baths." These baths required a somewhat complicated setup: on one floor, there was a bath; on the floor below it, there was a heater for the aromatic substances, with a tube that brought these vapors up to the bath; on the floor above the bath, there was a second heater and a tube that directed the fumes downward. The body, then, got a double dose of fragrant steam. The Royal Society of Medicine applauded Faure de Beaufort for his invention and insisted that the government should set these baths up throughout the country, but they didn't think that it was unique enough for him to get special rights to the idea.[31]

In cases where baths failed to provide a cure, doctors suggested more invasive methods. One such aromatic treatment was the "urethral anti-venereal candle." These candles were made of all manner of odiferous things, including but not limited to beeswax, walnuts, red wine, olive oil, pigeon, chicken, burned shoe leather, and spermaceti (a waxy substance produced by sperm whales).[32] Given the name, you can figure out where these candles were placed, and they supposedly worked in a manner similar to fumigation, where the medicine's odor would rush into the affected pores. These candles were intended to ease the symptoms of whatever had gone awry in one's private parts, at a fraction of the cost of a trip to a fumigation chamber in a private clinic. Nicolas André, author of *Dissertation on the Afflictions of the Urethra that Require Candles* (1751), did admit that users could expect a "light sensation of pain."[33]

Aromatic fumigations were also used to treat drowning. While the origins of this method are uncertain, the legend is that in 1746 a man's wife was pulled from the water, seeming to be dead. A knowledgeable sailor handed the husband his pipe and instructed the man to insert it into his wife's rectum and "blow hard."[34] The tobacco enema, or more formally, fumigation resuscitation, was born. No matter how it may seem, this sailor wasn't some morbid pervert out to give bad advice to a grieving husband. Indeed, the tobacco enema was a common solution for drowning in the eighteenth century. The first model involved a long tube inserted into the rectum, into which the lifesaver would blow tobacco smoke, but it soon became clear that this method could go badly wrong if the hero accidentally inhaled. Doctors soon developed a device that used bellows to blow the smoke into the drowning victim, and thanks to the efforts of the English doctors William Hawes and Thomas Cogan, these were distributed at key points along the Thames for emergency use.[35] Indeed, Hawes and Cogan were so dedicated to the cause that they put together a *Plan for an Institution for Affording Immediate Relief to Persons Apparently Dead, from Drowning* (1774), which soon became the Humane Society for the Recovery of Persons Apparently Drowned. In 1776, they must have realized the ridiculousness of their name and shortened it to, simply, the Royal Humane Society. (This organization is still in existence in England.)

The society published pamphlets to explain the proper method and gave monetary awards to anyone who could successfully resuscitate a drowning victim. Their efforts inspired a spate of sermons, informational articles, and broadsheets, and newspapers included helpful advice for novice resuscitators. The following instructions appeared in *Jopson's Coventry Mercury* on May 31, 1784: "In the first place, strip [drowning victims] of all their wet cloaths; rub them and lay them in hot blankets before the fire: blow with your breath strongly, or with a pair of bellows into the mouth of the person, holding the nostrils at the same time: afterwards introduce the small end of a lighted tobacco-pipe into the fundament [such a nice word for "arse"], putting a paper pricked full of holes near the bowl of it, through which you must blow into the bowels."[36] Joining in the enthusiastic hullabaloo created by the Humane Society's reported success, similar societies popped up in Venice, Hamburg, Milan, St. Petersburg, Vienna, Paris, and Amsterdam. By 1802, the Dutch Society for the Recovery of Drowned Persons boasted that they had resuscitated 990 people.[37] The Americans even joined the enema party, as demonstrated by a University of Pennsylvania medical dissertation written in 1805, descriptively titled *An Experimental Inquiry into the Effects of Tobacco Fumes, on the System; and Their Use in Cases of Suspended Animation, from Submersion.*[38]

While it seems obvious to us that blowing air into the lungs would be a better option, in the eighteenth century, the rectum seemed just as viable, given that there was not yet a consensus about the cause for drowning. One theory maintained that death was the result of an excess of water in the stomach and intestines. Another claimed that death occurred because water swelled the lungs, throat, and other body parts, such that they cut off the person's air passages.[39] Yet another stated that while the person was submerged, the epiglottis was forced closed so that air couldn't get through. And another, proven by the drowning of dogs, held that water-logged lungs would cause death by suffocation.[40] The tobacco enema relied on the same theories of air, aroma, and healing as other forms of aromatic medicine, and consequently, the question of whether the aroma worked through the skin, rectum, or lungs was not the most important. By injecting the smoke into the rectum, physicians believed that patients would get a quick, stimulating dose of tobacco, which would bring them back to consciousness. It was largely ineffective, as one might guess, hence the modern use of "blowing smoke up one's ass" to signify falseness. But I can certainly see how someone might expect that this method would sufficiently startle an unconscious patient.

Tobacco was a particularly suitable substance for the enema because it was considered to be "dry" matter.[41] It desiccated fibers, depleted mucus, and made "the brain and the nerves drier and steadier."[42] For an unconscious, drowned person, it is evident why you would want to flood her innards with something stimulating and drying. In conscious people, tobacco could lead to "a sound faculty of judgment, a clearer, more circumspect faculty of reason and a greater constancy of soul."[43] And it was particularly good for maniacal men, hysterical women, or women with toothaches.[44] But before you light up, keep in mind that "by virtue of this same desiccating effect, it weakens the erotic passions and steers the lascivious faculty of imagination."[45]

The patient may not have been able to smell the tobacco, but it was still crucial that it was an "aromatic" substance. According to chemists, the aroma of plants came from their essential oils, and these oils were the source of plants' healing essences. According to the *Encyclopédie*, "the aromatic principle is so subtle and so light, so barely material, that . . . it is impossible to identify it by weight or measure."[46] The nose was the only way to access these properties, which made it a crucial tool for the doctor, if not for the patient.

"The odorous part," the physician Jean-André Venel wrote, "has been regarded by pharmacologists as the most valuable element," and the king's physician Henri Rousseau agreed, arguing that "the virtue of medicines, consists almost entirely in the communication of odor or of a certain perfume."[47] Odors carried the very essence of the substance's power, making the lines between medicine and perfumery very thin indeed. The sense of smell was absolutely crucial to effective medical practice in the eighteenth century, and doctors had to pay great attention to odors, not least, because each scent denoted a different medicinal quality. Rosewater and similar floral scents signified purgative substances, while minty odors marked "excellently stomachical" remedies.[48]

The importance of aromas, regardless of whether they were smelled by the patient in question, raises an interesting question. Do we have to be conscious of sensations in order to consider them part of "perception"? Generally, perception is defined as the process of becoming aware of something through the senses, but is awareness truly necessary? In the case of aromatic medicine, a plant's aroma had the power to change the way a person's body worked, even if she didn't consciously perceive the smell. Should we still call the aroma's effects on the body a "sensation"? Many of the eighteenth-century writers you've encountered would probably say yes. In fact, in 1780, the doctor Jean-Claude de La Métherie went so far as to extend the classification of "senses" to all bodily experiences: "The ancients only counted five human senses . . . but there are many other sensations: the back of the throat feels thirst; the stomach, hunger and the sensation of being full; the guts expand and quiver with pleasure, they retract with pain; the genitals give us the liveliest sensation; the urinary passages have their sense; *ultimately there is no part of the body that doesn't have a particular way of feeling.*"[49] Sensation permeated the body, even in ways of which the conscious mind was unaware.

If you still aren't convinced, here's a more contemporary example. We know that the tongue has taste receptors that pick up different flavors as we eat. If you eat dandelion greens, the tongue's receptors activate the parts of the brain that are associated with taste perception, and you register the bitter flavor. This is, of course, a simplified version of the process, but it seems straightforward enough: stimulation → sensation → perception. But in 2007, researchers at the Mount Sinai School of Medicine identified the existence of taste receptors in the intestines. These receptors are the same as those that produce the experience of sweetness on the tongue, but as you're probably aware, you aren't really "tasting" your chocolate muffin when it's in the depths of your gut. Instead, these intestinal receptors regulate the secretion of insulin and the hormones that affect appetite. They may be the "sweet" receptors, but the signals they send your brain are about hunger and hormones, not honey and Häagen-Dazs.

While it's true that we can feel hungry, we can't really "feel" the other things that those taste receptors are doing. So does that mean that the actions of these taste receptors aren't part of perception? Or does it mean that sensation has the power to operate on an unconscious level? Dr. Inge Depoortere, who studies these gut receptors, has described their actions as "chemosensory signaling," which would indicate that *something* sensory is going on, even if it's not conscious.[50] (To be more precise, a chemosensor is a sensory receptor that converts a chemical signal into an "action potential," or a change in the electrical properties of a cell. This, in turn, is transmitted to the central nervous system.) At its heart, this question may come down to basic discrepancies in the definition of perception. Where one person may insist that sensation requires awareness, another might appreciate the murky, unconscious depths of sensation. But no matter which side you fall on, you have to admit that this raises some interesting implications for the ways that we understand sensation. Such considerations raise the basic question of what a sense is, and whether there might be more of them than we imagine.

❧ 6 ❧

What Is a Sense?:
Sex, Self-Preservation, Pleasure,
and Pain

OR THE LAST FIVE CHAPTERS, I've been begging a very important question. I've been assuming that we all understood what was meant when I used the term "sense." But this is not necessarily a fair assumption. So, in trying to figure out what a sense is, here's a seemingly simple question to get us started: how many senses are there? I'll wager that, even if you reasoned yourself out of it, your gut reaction was "five." In the modern West, there is a fairly firm conviction that taste, touch, sight, smell, and hearing comprise our sensory toolkit, and this knowledge is passed on to schoolchildren at an early age. The beloved *The Magic School Bus* book series delves into the question of the senses, and in the opening pages, an essay by the character Carlos, a student, appears, entitled "Without Our Senses, We'd Be Out of It." Carlos writes, "If someone could not see, hear, feel, taste, or smell, that person would not be able to tell <u>anything</u> about the outside world."[1] It seems that Carlos has been reading his Condillac.

But this canonical concept of five senses is actually based more in tradition than in nature. It's not self-evident that our senses are organized this way. Sensory anthropologists have shown that different cultures have radically different concepts of the sensorium—the totality of perception. For example, the Hausa people of Nigeria have one word for sight and another word that stands for "hearing, smelling, tasting and touching, understanding, and emotional feeling."[2] In Java, where there is a five-sense sensorium, the senses are enumerated as seeing, hearing, smelling, feeling, and talking; there is no sense of taste.[3] In contemporary American society, scientists have identified a significant number of other sense candidates, with conservative estimates coming in at ten, and radical estimates going as high as thirty-three. Some of these alternates include balance, blood pressure, sensitivity to temperature, and the feeling of a full stomach.[4] As you've already encountered in this book, the eighteenth-century category of "internal senses" added imagination, memory, reason, and will to the usual five suspects. With all this data, it becomes clear that what started out as a simple question—how many senses are there—is not actually quite so simple.

The five-sense sensorium of taste, touch, smell, sight, and hearing has a long historical basis, stretching back to the Greeks. As far as we can tell, it was first described by Socrates' contemporary Democritus (460–370 B.C.E.), although it's probably a good bet that he didn't invent it. The five-sense schema was fleshed out more fully in Aristotle's On the Soul and "On Sense and the Sensible" (both ca. 350 B.C.E.). Aristotle elaborated on the role that the five senses play in human life, stressing that smell, sight, and hearing, in particular, help humans attain "higher perfection."[5] In Western Europe and the United States, five remains the accepted number, with other candidates having periodically swooped in, only to be ousted again after a few decades. Even though these alternate candidates didn't stick, it's worthwhile to consider how people in the past interpreted the sensorium and why these alternates might have been appealing in the first place.

Before going further, though, it will be helpful to uncover, more specifically, what, in the eighteenth century, made a sense a sense. The *Encyclopédie* (1765) defined it as "a faculty by which the soul perceives ideas or images of objects, whether those come from outside [the body] through the impression of objects themselves or whether they are caused by some action of the soul on itself."[6] In other words, the senses were the means by which a person's internal workings were connected to the outside world. It didn't matter whether the sense was an external one like taste or an internal one like memory. As Carlos from *The Magic School Bus* reminds us, without the senses, humans would be stuck inside themselves, with no capacity to understand or interact with the people and things around them.

The senses had another important characteristic in addition to their ability to bridge mind and matter. All sensations, no matter how small, yielded some experience of pleasure or pain, and these feelings were preservational tools. In the words of Condillac, "Nature gave us organs that, through pleasure, indicate the things that we should seek out, and, through pain, the things that we should flee."[7] Rotten flavors signaled bad fruit; rancid scents marked out the maggoty meat that we should avoid; hot surfaces warned that we should draw back from fire. Because humans are intelligent beings, capable of reason, imagination, and memory, it is possible for us to override these natural instincts. We can ride in cars, jump out of planes, eat poisonous pufferfish, or any number of other dangerous things, but according to sensationalists, in humans' natural state, pleasure was an indicator of things beneficial to our health, while pain forced us away from danger. Because of the drive to acquire pleasure and avoid pain, humans pursue nature's central goals: happiness and self-preservation.

Many other Enlightenment writers agreed that sensation existed to provide experiences of pleasure and pain, which in turn, existed to further the biological impulse of self-preservation. The Anglo-Dutch physician and philosopher Bernard Mandeville wrote in 1723, "There is nothing more sincere in any Creature than his Will, Wishes, and Endeavours to preserve himself. This is the Law of Nature, by which no Creature is endued with any Appetite or Passion but what either directly or indirectly tends to the Preservation either of himself or his Species." He explained that, in order to contribute to this goal, nature has grafted desires into mankind that "either compel him to crave what he thinks will sustain or please him, or command him to avoid what he imagines might displease, hurt, or destroy him."[8]

Similarly, the materialist Claude-Adrien Helvétius argued in 1758 that, because humans are biologically oriented toward self-preservation, everyone is born with a sense of "self-love," which was something like a mixture of self-esteem and self-concern.[9] It's the type of egoism that factors into "do-unto-others-as-you'd-have-them-do-unto-you." Pleasure and pain orient humans toward the things they want for themselves, and this self-interestedness led, in Helvétius's estimation, not only to love, hate, and all the other emotions, but also to all human vice and virtue.[10] What began as an individual means of self-preservation simultaneously worked to preserve the whole human species, because self-love often forces people to be just. Let's say that I saw you on the street on a blistering day, and you were slurping on a large cup of iced tea. Self-love might drive me, with my parched throat, to want to steal it, but self-love would also restrain me, since I wouldn't want to be pummeled or have the cops called on me. In this case, my self-love would make me fear pain more than it made me crave pleasure, and you and I could maintain our just, functional relationship.

In short, nature instilled in humans a biological imperative to stay alive, and a sense was anything that triggered experiences of pleasure and pain, thereby allowing an individual to survive, thrive, and propagate. Taste, touch, smell, sight, hearing, imagination, reason, and memory could all be considered senses because they helped individuals successfully exist in the world, avoiding danger and seeking out benefits. The senses were nature's way of ensuring that living creatures didn't perish as soon as they came into being. What's more, Helvétius and Mandeville would have argued, as humans improved their individual lots, they necessarily improved those of the people around them. Self-preservation and social preservation were two sides of the same coin.

With this definition in mind, let's now consider one of the eighteenth century's contenders for the status of a sense: sex. Driven by a desire for pleasure, humans engage in sexual intercourse, resulting—in many cases—in the continuation of the species. According to a number of eighteenth-century writers, sex had the potential to preserve and extend human life, and as such, it should be considered a sense in its own right. Emanuel Swedenborg (1688–1772), a naturalist-turned-mystic, laid out the steamy details in *The Delights of Wisdom Concerning Conjugial* [sic] *Love* (1768): "Every man hath five senses, seeing, hearing, smelling, taste, and touch; but we have likewise a sixth, which is the sense of all the delights of the conjugial [sic] love . . . and this sense we have in the palms of our hands, whilst we touch the breasts, arms, hands, or cheeks of our husbands, but especially whilst we touch their breasts, and also whilst we are touched by them."[11] Still, Swedenborg believed that he could talk to angels— the spirits of people who had once lived on earth but who had moved to heaven after dying. While engaged in such conversation, a female angel gave this description of sex. (In case you were wondering, angels had sensory apparatuses similar to those of living humans, with one exception: taste.)[12] But you didn't have to be quite as mystical as Swedenborg to believe in sex's status as a sixth sense. Nor did you have to think of it only as part of sweet, angelic, conjugal love.

The naturalist and director of the King's Garden (now the Jardin des Plantes in the center of Paris), Georges-Louis Leclerc, Comte de Buffon, explained sex's relevance by using a more human, if still speculative, example. His epic, thirty-six volume *Natural History* included a passage in which Buffon adopted the voice of a newly created man. Experiencing the world for the first time, this Adam-like figure enjoyed the visual delights of fruit, the sweetness of the garden's perfumes, and the exquisite pleasures of taste. The latter was so intense that it gave the man his first idea of possession, making him believe that the fruit had become part of his own flesh.[13] Finally, having experienced the development of his physical sensations and internal sensations, the man was introduced to a female companion, who promoted the development of the final, most voluptuous sense of all. The man reported, "I would like to give her all my being; this lively desire will complete my existence. I feel born within me a sixth sense."[14] All the delights of the garden combined to sustain and enhance the man's existence, and all the senses, sex included, granted the man experiences of pleasure.

Indeed, from an eighteenth-century medical perspective, sex and other forms of sensation were not all that distinct. Descriptions of the physical response to sensory pleasure sounded very much like sexual arousal. Dr. Victor de Sèze, with whom you became acquainted in the first chapter, explained that all pleasurable sensations—everything from tasting a scrumptious strawberry to listening to a catchy song—would "cause an erection in the organ that enjoys it, a type of intumescence of all fibers." Pain, on the other hand, would cause fiber shrinkage, "as if in offering less surface, it could try to escape the sensation."[15] Sexual stimulation and other sensory stimulation varied only in that they affected different organs.

One of the most forthcoming advocates of sex as a sense was Jean-Anthelme Brillat-Savarin. Born into an old, respected family of provincial lawyers, Brillat-Savarin took up the family trade, and in the early phases of the French Revolution, he served as a moderate representative in the National Assembly of 1789. Five years later, during the Terror—the notorious part of the Revolution, when the guillotine was in full force—he was accused of befriending royalists and escaped to New York. There he gave French lessons and played the violin in an orchestra. In 1796, Brillat-Savarin was allowed to return to France. He spent the latter part of his life in Paris, pursuing his hobbies. A man of diverse interests, he authored a *Historic Treatise on the Duel* (1819), but his true love was food. For years, Brillat-Savarin collected notes for a book on gastronomy, and in 1825, he published *The Physiology of Taste* under the pseudonym "The Professor," before dying of acute pneumonia the following year.

Physiology used food as a gateway to philosophizing about all aspects of life, and it ranged widely in subject matter and style, including chapters like "On the End of the World," "On the Influence of Diet on Rest, Sleep, and Dreams," and "Theory of Frying." Brillat-Savarin was the master of witty aphorisms, and he came up with the phrase "Tell me what you eat: I will tell you what you are," which was updated to the more familiar "You are what you eat."[16] Apropos, Brillat-Savarin now has a cheese named after him that is (appropriately) extra smooth, somewhat salty, and faintly sour.

The first chapter of *The Physiology of Taste* focused on the senses, and I will let Brillat-Savarin make his own case about their number: "The number of senses is not fewer than six, namely [sight, hearing, smell, taste, touch] . . . and lastly, the sense of *physical desire*, which brings the two sexes together, and procures the reproduction of the species. It is astonishing to observe that this important sense was scarcely recognized before the time of *Buffon*, having been confounded until then with the preceding one of touch, or rather included as a part of it. The truth is, however, that the two have nothing in common: the organism of the sixth sense is as complete as are the mouth or eyes."[17]

According to the gastronome, humans are fundamentally driven by a love of pleasure: "The stream of time, flowing onward over the human race, has brought new perfections without end, the cause of which, almost imperceptible but continually at work, will be found in the insatiable claims of our senses to be agreeably occupied."[18] If he sounded a lot like the Enlightenment writers of an earlier generation, Brillat-Savarin also sounded remarkably like Sigmund Freud, who nearly one hundred years later declared that most human behavior could be linked to a sexual instinct. But, Brillat-Savarin claimed, sex wasn't content to stop there. Sex (and its attendant desire) was at the core of all scientific achievement.[19] So, you can thank lust for your computer, toaster, and smartphone. This makes sense on several levels. Reproduction is at the heart of human achievement because, otherwise, why would we strive to improve the future? We, as a society, trust that there will be people to whom we can pass our successes. But what Brillat-Savarin was saying was more than this. He followed Condillac's assertion that pleasure and pain "give birth to [humans'] ideas, desires, habits, and talents of all kind," and argued that human achievement—in all areas—was linked to a fundamental, natural desire for pleasure.[20]

If Buffon and Brillat-Savarin were content to elevate sex to the sensory pantheon, others were not quite so certain. In his *Lectures on Ethics* (delivered in the 1770s and '80s), the philosopher Immanuel Kant called the "sexual impulse . . . whereby one human being is pleasing to the appetite of another" the "sixth sense." But it's unclear whether he was truly convinced of this fact, since he questioned it in *Anthropology from a Pragmatic Point of View.*[21]

Kant's uncertainty raises the valid question of why, if sex so neatly adhered to the definition of a sense, some philosophers may not have seen it as such. Unfortunately, writers didn't tend to refute the theory outright. Instead, they ignored the question, and when they rehearsed the standard roster of senses, they left sex off the list. There are a few indications, though, of what their objections might have been. Take, for instance, Voltaire's description of love. Voltaire maintained that humans were more capable than animals of appreciating the sensations of sex. Most animals, he asserted, take basic physical pleasure in sex, and once their lust is satiated, they no longer desire their mates. In contrast, when humans make love, they encounter pleasures unknown to animals (and, Voltaire added, pains unknown to animals as well, thanks to venereal disease).[22] Where animals only feel lust, humans are able to bring emotions, memories, and other sensations to bear, heightening the act beyond physical sensation. Voltaire suggested some physical means of improving love, like staying clean and paying attention to one's physical health, which could improve the sensation of touch. But these physical improvements were not the only means by which humans could heighten their sexual pleasure; the internal senses were equally important. For example, the imagination is able to foster feelings like friendship and respect, which give love a more ornate character. Pride adds even more fuel to the fire, since we applaud our own choice of mates.[23] An appreciation for the sharp wit or keen intellect of your partner can only enhance the pleasure.

In this description of love, Voltaire did not directly reject the notion of sex as a sixth sense, but he did suggest that sexual experience was a composite of sensations rather than a sense in its own right. Humans are complex beings, with similarly complex sensations, desires, and sexual appetites. To form an exquisite experience of sexual pleasure, humans' external and internal senses collaborated, bringing them delights unknown to the rest of the animal kingdom. But ultimately, when it came to sexuality, the actions of the senses were cumulative and could not be reduced to a separate, sixth mode of perception.

The conservative English writer Edmund Burke raised another potential objection. In his treatise *A Philosophical Enquiry into the Origin of Our Ideas of the Sublime and Beautiful* (1757), Burke separated human experience into two categories. The first was oriented toward the preservation of the individual, and these experiences "turn mostly on *pain* or *danger*."[24] For example, if I notice someone pointing a gun at me, my fear of pain will kick in, and I will run in order to save myself at all costs. But pleasure, he argued, belonged to an entirely different category: that relating to the preservation of society. Because of the importance of preserving the species, nature had created sexual pleasure as a "great incentive," which was "therefore attended with a very high pleasure." Indeed, Burke, who wasn't particularly known for his saucy tendencies, even went so far as to confess that it was "the highest pleasure of sense."[25] Where pain worked to deter individuals from their destruction, pleasure worked to inspire social and sexual relationships.

According to Burke, both impulses—to preserve oneself and to preserve society—were natural, but they were distinct, as were the sentiments of pleasure and pain to which they connected. He dismissed the idea that pain was the lessening of pleasure and pleasure the lessening of pain.[26] However, Burke believed that a sense, in order to effectively fulfill nature's mandates, had to be capable of inspiring both pleasure and pain. Under those conditions, sex didn't make the cut. It yielded intense sensory pleasure and served to preserve society, but it had no connection with pain or the preservation of the individual.[27]

While these debates show that sex's status as a sixth sense was, by no means, agreed upon, they also reveal that, by and large, philosophers shared a unified concept of what constituted a sense in the first place. Enlightenment writers concurred that sensations were nature's way of protecting, encouraging, and supporting humans and their communities. Pleasure and pain regulated human interactions and guided individuals through a world filled with danger and joy. As one of life's key sources of pleasure, sex was an important test case for understanding the limits, purposes, and biological implications of sensory pleasure, even for philosophers who rejected its status as a sense in its own right.

All this talk of pleasure may conjure images of sun-dappled sexual bacchanals, but on the whole, sensationalists didn't argue for a hedonistic pursuit of desire. In Chapter One, you read how Tissot, Le Camus, and others argued that sensory experiences had to be carefully managed such that a perfect balance of stimulation was struck. Like other forms of sensation, sexual pleasure wasn't to be overindulged. According to Helvétius's materialist colleague d'Holbach, "The more lively [pleasure] is, the more fugitive, because man's senses are only susceptible of a certain amount of motion. When pleasure exceeds this given quantity, it is changed into *anguish*."[28] In other words, the experience of pleasure had diminishing marginal returns. Overstimulated fibers would vibrate too much, and the experience would overwhelm the mind and body. Having too much sex will make you sore. Rubbing velvet for too long will make your fingers ache. Eating too much chocolate cake will make you ill. Pleasures, like every other type of sensory stimulation, had to be carefully regulated. D'Holbach affirmed, "The same elements, which under certain circumstances serve to nourish, strengthen, maintain the animal, become, under others, the principles of his weakness, the instruments of his dissolution—of his death."[29]

Libertines didn't seem to understand this need for moderation. In the eighteenth century, legendary libertine Giacomo Casanova cavorted with courtesans, gambled, and collected forbidden books. If anyone could be said to live life's pleasures to the fullest, without paying attention to moderation, it would be that Italian adventurer. Casanova's memoirs are full of intrigue and scandal, but even if a reader wasn't privy to their full contents, Casanova's devotion to one small object would have perfectly revealed to eighteenth-century audiences just how much of a libertine he truly was. Casanova was an adopter of the unpopular "English raincoat," which you may know by its more common name of "condom." During the eighteenth century, condoms tended to be made from cloth or, more commonly, animal intestines, bladders, or skins. Known for a "smell of Fish and feel of Slime," the condom was tied to the man's appendage by means of a ribbon.[30] Some libertines were reluctant to give into the allure of the condom, because they were so thick that they often numbed sexual sensations or, thanks to a misplaced seam, could lead to chafing and discomfort. In 1717, the English doctor Daniel Turner noted, "by reason of its blunting the Sensation, I have heard some [libertines] acknowledge, that they had often chose to risque a Clap rather than engage *cum Hastis sic clypeatis* [with spears sheathed]."[31] Of course, the eighteenth century was no chaster a time period than any other, and extramarital sex, prostitution, and promiscuity abounded. But the condom still had a reputation for being a shameful, licentious piece of equipment, used only by the most debauched people. By thwarting reproduction and engaging in wanton pleasure, libertines were sowing the seeds of pleasure with no intent of reaping their fruits.

Casanova, blowing up his "English raincoat" as a titillating party trick.

You might wonder why so many people would care that other people were engaging in nonprocreative sex. (Indeed, in certain quarters, the same might be asked about our own era.) One significant reason comes from the fact that people in the early modern era used population to judge the power and success of their kings. A prosperous, growing society was the indicator of the glory of a nation, and beginning in the seventeenth century, French royal ministers began to express fear that the population of their fair nation was on the decline. These warnings turned into a full-blown depopulation anxiety in the eighteenth century, and during the reigns of Louis XV (reigned 1715–1774) and Louis XVI (reigned 1774–1792), it was a commonly accepted narrative that the French population was in a downward spiral. Never mind that social statistics were in their infancy in the eighteenth century and that there was little empirical basis for this belief. (In fact, the French population rose over the eighteenth century, growing from somewhere around 22 million in 1700 to 28.1 million in 1801.)[32] In an era in which outright criticism of the monarchy was forbidden, criticisms about the decline in the population were a roundabout way to needle the king and his legitimizer, the Catholic Church.[33]

Sex, then, was a political matter, and the fact that libertines so openly flaunted the laws of nature carried a great deal of symbolic importance. Sensory pleasure, as a mechanism for biological preservation, held the key to social cohesion and a flourishing state. But used in the wrong way, it also had immense negative potential. Sexual and political critiques centered on the fear that pleasure, taken out of its natural context, might have the power to tear society apart. Libertines' sexual practices dissociated physical pleasure and reproduction, and consequently, their behavior suggested to fearful moralists that shifting cultural norms and technology—like the condom—could alter the healthy, generative instincts furnished by nature.

One of the most notorious philosophers of the eighteenth century, the Marquis de Sade, latched onto these fears and showed just how easily pleasure and pain could undermine even the most universally accepted standards of morality. The Marquis de Sade is best known for his salacious fiction, and to read it is to enter a world where there is no sense of "wrong." People are murdered, children are deflowered, bodily orifices are sewn shut, and God is nowhere to be found. If ever an author deserved a "trigger warning," it's the Marquis de Sade. (That said, his texts are also peppered with darkly funny moments. For example, one of the main characters of *The 120 Days of Sodom* is named "Bum-Cleaver.")[34] His personal history was nearly as colorful. After a lengthy series of prison stints for various sexual offenses and violent episodes, the Marquis was declared insane in 1803. He was then transferred to the mental asylum Charenton, where he lived until his death in 1814. It's understandable why these juicy particulars would cement his reputation as a debauched human being. But what people don't remember as readily is just how significant his philosophical interventions were.

Sade never clearly addressed the question of whether sex was a separate sense, but he did treat sex as the form of sensory experience that could demonstrate the truths of human existence, more than any other. The Marquis de Sade was a sensationalist, and as such, he granted all forms of sensory experience power. Odors, tastes, touches, sounds, and sights fill his books, and his mantra was that nature had created humans with strong desires, "for the sole purpose of yielding to them and satisfying them," so that they might fulfill "Nature's fundamental designs."[35] In his writings, the Marquis explored the same questions of self-preservation, pleasure, and pain that had occupied so many of his peers. All sensation mattered, even though sex occupied the majority of his attention. Where Sade differed from most other sensationalists was in the way that he investigated these ideas' implications for morality.[36] He pushed sensationalist philosophy to its extremes by creating dark, fictional worlds in which responses to pleasure and pain formed the core of all human action.

One didn't have to go to Sadean extremes to agree that sex

brings about a great deal of pleasure. Helvétius and Buffon weren't making waves when they claimed that between platonic love and sexual love, sex was "more pleasing."[37] But even though sex might have won the prize for "most fun," that didn't mean that it was necessarily the most intense sensation. Writing on sublime experiences—experiences that are equal parts terror and wonder, like staring at a vast, never-ending ocean, or staring over the edge of an immensely high cliff—Edmund Burke argued, "where the chances for equal degrees of suffering or enjoyment are in any sort equal, the idea of the suffering must always be prevalent."[38] According to Burke, pleasure is something that humans often choose to experience, but because we don't usually submit to pain willingly, it always seems more powerful. Unlike pleasure, pain carries the emotional baggage of violence and terror, which elevates its intensity.

This question of pain's intensity was one that intrigued Sade greatly. Intense experiences would shock the system, causing the blood to flow, the body to tremble, and the imagination to run wild, but where writers like Tissot and Le Camus had warned against the dangers of such intense stimulation, the dear Marquis didn't seem to be concerned. Sade's *The Story of Juliette, or the Prosperity of Vice* (published 1797–1801) featured a nymphomaniac murderer who was, appropriately enough, raised in a convent. One of the many libertine characters that Juliette met over the course of her depraved doings, a wealthy government minister named Saint-Fond, explained, "I believe in the senses alone, I believe in the carnal habits and appetites . . . in self-seeking, in self-aggrandizement, in self-interest."[39] In doing so, Saint-Fond turned the sensationalist principle of self-love into something bleak and limitless, rejecting Helvétius's conviction that self-love would lead to virtue and justice.

Later in the novel, Saint-Fond elaborated on this statement, explaining how the senses provide pleasure and pain: "Only by undergoing the greatest possible upheaval in the nervous system may [a person] procure himself the drunken transport he must have if he is properly to enjoy himself. For what is pleasure? Simply this: that which occurs when voluptuous atoms . . . clash hard with and fire the electrical particles circulating in the hollows of our nerve fibers. Therefore, that the pleasure be complete, the clash must be as violent as possible."[40] True pleasure then, for Sade, meant shock to the nerves, the imagination, and his readers, who would be getting pleasure from the shocks given to and by the characters. Pain gave the greatest shocks, and it mattered little whether one experienced the pain or watched it, although the Sadean hero was usually the person in the drivers' seat. Hence the term "sadist" for someone who likes to inflict pain.[41] In Sade's writing, sex's purpose was to generate sensation, but it mattered little whether the sensation was pleasurable or painful, as long as it was powerful. This is a long way from the perspective that the senses were created by nature to preserve the individual and the species. By this reasoning, the senses (and sex as their agent) might just as easily destroy. Indeed, Sadean ethics, such as they were, even encouraged murder. *Philosophy in the Bedroom* ended with Eugénie, a once-innocent girl, drawing her sexual and philosophical education to a close by murdering her mother in a horribly grotesque way.

It might seem that Sade's love of shock went against the sensationalist idea that pleasure and pain were mechanisms that furthered nature's intent. But mother-murder and blood-fondness aside, the Marquis wasn't totally removed from his sensationalist brethren. According to Sade, the senses were still, fundamentally, preservational tools. Bear with me as I explain his viewpoint here, because at first blush, it may seem like odd logic. The literary scholar Caroline Warman has written the best, most succinct summary of Sade's philosophical system.[42] She breaks it down to five main points, which I will paraphrase, adding some of Sade's own words. First, Sade was a materialist who argued that life is nothing more than matter. Secondly, he believed that there is a finite amount of matter. When it's formed into people, plants, and objects, then it is removed from nature's stockpile of resources, limiting nature's power to create. Third, he claimed that destruction is just as much a part of nature as creation. By destroying things, we are releasing matter back into nature. If I eat a plant, it becomes something new. Some of the matter becomes part of my body, some of it goes back to the earth in the form of waste, and from there, it becomes something new again. "Destruction being one of the chief laws of Nature," Sade argued, "nothing that destroys can be criminal."[43] In fact, he claimed, destruction is just an illusion, since matter is simply transformed, and anyone who "commits [murder] does but alter forms; he gives back to Nature the elements whereof the hand of this skilled artisan instantly re-creates other beings."[44] Fourth, nature's true purpose is to keep moving, creating, and transmuting matter. It's only humans' pride that leads them to think that they are special in the natural order, but in truth, "the whole extirpation of the breed would, by returning to Nature the creative faculty she has entrusted to us, invigorate her; she would have again that energy we deprive her of by propagating our own selves."[45] In other words, nature doesn't need humans. Whether humans are in the world or whether they're extinct, nature will keep on creating new forms. For Sade, pleasure and pain weren't about encouraging reproduction. Fifthly and finally, the more matter there is in circulation, the better. Turnover is the most crucial element of this natural cycle. This is where pleasure and pain had the most significant role in continuing nature's work. According to Sade, nature has just as much need of vice as of virtue, and murderous libertines, in the eloquent words of Warman, helped "feed the dead matter into nature's recycling system."[46] For Sade, the senses were less related to humans' self-preservational mechanisms than to nature's. And sexual satisfaction, regardless of whether it inclined toward pleasure or pain, helped nature achieve its goals.

There's a reason why Sade's books were banned and he was locked up in a mental asylum. Most people in the eighteenth century did not agree with his controversial ideas about morality. That said, he's still an important figure for the Enlightenment because his works show how the optimism that drove so much Enlightenment reform could have latent potential for social destruction. Nineteenth-century writers looking back at the bloodshed of the French Revolution often blamed the Enlightenment for the ideas that inspired such turmoil. Many revolutionary supporters cited Jean-Jacques Rousseau's political ideas on general will and transparency, and they self-consciously positioned themselves against the superstitious corruption of the *ancien régime* (the "Old Regime," a term that revolutionaries applied to the aristocratic society that existed before the Revolution purportedly set the nation aright). Enlightenment battles against superstition and artificiality found articulation in the bloody, fraught political processes that took place at the end of the eighteenth century. Theories of physical perfectibility, so important to writers like Antoine Le Camus, had a dark legacy in nineteenth- and twentieth-century racial theory and eugenics. (Indeed, one could already see the stirrings of trouble in the Comte de Buffon's ideas about "marriage broking" among peasants. Buffon argued that people who lived on higher terrain would be "agile, well-disposed, well-made, spiritual," while on the flat ground or in the valleys, where the soil is heavier and the air is thicker, "the peasants are thick, weighty, badly formed, stupid, and the *paysannes* [peasant women] are almost all ugly." By mixing these two groups, a happy medium could be reached, whereby nature could be perfected, and ugly women would be no more.)[47] Also, writing in the aftermath of World War II, the German-Jewish philosophers Max Horkheimer and Theodor Adorno claimed that the Enlightenment's obsession with reason created a mindset that was compatible with political regimes like fascism and totalitarianism.

Generally speaking, there's very little that the Enlightenment hasn't been credited or blamed for. Even though there were plenty of religious philosophers in the Enlightenment, it's been described as the modern moment that gave rise to anti-Christian secularism. Even though there were plenty of people stressing sentiment and feeling, it's been described as an era that advanced cold, scientistic views. And even though there were plenty of conflicting economic theories being tossed around, it's been viewed as the era that gave birth to capitalism, which will mean something different to you depending on whether you feel more love for Karl Marx or for Milton Friedman. Suffice it to say, the Enlightenment, perhaps more than any other historical period, has had the power to be all things to all people. According to Enlightenment writers, it stood as the bearer of all that is light and good, but for many others, it has been conceived as the bearer of all that is twisted and bad. From my perspective, the Enlightenment is no different from any other historical moment in that it was neither "good" nor "bad." It was an era of intellectual flourishing and social reform, which meant that new ideas circulated everywhere. Some of these ideas were abysmal, while others were genius, and as with all reform, some changes were more effective than others.

A number of eighteenth-century writers argued that the senses contributed to individual and social good. Sex, either as a sixth sense or as an agent of pleasure, incentivized humans to improve, reproduce, and flourish. Sade, using sex as a synecdoche for sensory experience, turned many of these claims on their head. Through his macabre fantasies, he demonstrated that sex did not always lead to social growth; pain did not always lead to the impulse to flee danger; and personal pleasure did not always lead to social gain. Ultimately, he destabilized the notion of an anthropocentric world, showing that the things that benefitted nature did not necessarily benefit humans. Whether you find his account convincing, Sade raised crucial questions about human agency, the purposes of pleasure, and the forces of nature that exist beyond the scope of human life.

Debates about whether sex counted as a sixth sense, and more generally, about the implications of sexual pleasure, opened up huge topics for Enlightenment philosophers. Talking about sex meant talking about the purposes of sensation, how instinct informs human action, and how humans understand their place within nature. *Philosophes* may have agreed that the senses were preservational mechanisms, but the question as to whom, or what, they preserved was still wide open. And they may have concurred that sensation furnishes experience, but the question remained, "What does a person do with that experience?" This was not an insignificant question, and it may go some way to explaining why the Enlightenment has earned such a Janus-faced legacy. The dictates of joy and anguish, love and hate, and good and evil are never as cut-and-dried as they initially may seem. Perhaps what Sade understood better than most was the necessity of these internal tensions. Pleasure and pain may be common to all, but that doesn't mean that humans respond to them in the same way. Or at least, that's my understanding of his thought. But in the next chapter, you'll meet Louis-Bertrand Castel, an inventor who would disagree with me entirely.

⫷ 7 ⫸

Harmonious Nature:
The Cat Piano, the Ocular Harpsichord,
and Scales of Scent and Taste

A<small>T THEIR CORE</small>, the senses might be about self-preserva-tion, but they are also the means by which we are wooed and wowed. There's a reason that pop concerts incorporate bright lights, flashy videos, and elaborate costumes and that celebrities give it their all on the red carpet. You should never underestimate the power of a grand entrance. This is a lesson that Philip II, the king of Spain, took to heart when he went to visit his father, the Holy Roman Emperor Charles V, in Brussels in 1549. Philip's procession was led by a bull with flaming horns that carried a small devil; next came a horse whose tail and ears had been cut off, being ridden by a young man in a bear skin; and ended with a person costumed as the archangel Michael. The most impressive part of the whole affair, however, was an organ that played "the most singular music that you can imagine."[1] Instead of pipes, "there were twenty rather narrow boxes, each of which contained a cat; their tails were sticking out and were connected to the keys by a string, such that, when someone pressed one of the keys, the corresponding tail was strongly pulled, producing a lamentable

Tred all hee bij sehs wee der schönst sij
aber zelt mich auch sij ich bin der bas in der cantrij

76

AVRICVLIS MIDAE NON MVSICA GRATIOR VLLA EST·

A varied troupe indulges in the many delights of the a cat piano.

meowing each time."[2] Welcome to the cat piano. And lest I forget to mention, the organ was played by a bear and followed by dancing monkeys, wolves, and deer.

This is the most fanfare-filled account of the cat piano, but it was far from the last. Its next appearance was in Johann Theodor de Bry's *Emblemata saecularia* (1596), a deeply fascinating book that begins with a discourse on love and ends with fifty engravings. The cat piano appears in the forty-eighth image, titled, "There is no music sweeter to Midas's ears," and in it, a merry band of men and animals gathers around the instrument to create auditory gold.

The cat piano remained a lasting trope throughout the next few centuries, popping up in a number of unexpected contexts and inspiring a number of other fanciful instruments.

I should probably reveal that there is no evidence that a cat piano ever existed, and some historians suspect that it was a hypothetical instrument. Given the less-than-generous attitude toward cats in early modern Europe (you'll discover more on this in a bit), the piano was not too far-fetched an idea, but thanks to a lack of documentation, its existence also can't be verified. In my estimation, the world may never know whether cat choruses had flesh-and-blood audiences or merely fictional ones. But even if the cat piano was simply a long-lasting trope or conceit, it had real effects on musical theory and the development of novel instruments, and the very fact that it had such staying power is telling. Where did this fascination come from? And aside from the fact that it involved hearing, what did it have to do with the senses?

The ancient concept of the Harmony of the Spheres maintained that the universe was governed by harmonic, mathematical relationships, structured by patterns of proportionality. This harmony was not always audible, but for centuries, philosophers, theologians, and naturalists had argued that certain sounds could elevate humans, bringing them nearer to this celestial, divine order. Hearing, as a sense that had a strong, long-standing connection to spirituality, was considered capable of opening up the mysteries of the universe. This chapter will carry you through a series of musical innovations that were, at least in part, inspired by the cat piano: the pig piano, the donkey chorus, the ocular harpsichord, the perfume organ, and the liquor organ. The creators of these instruments all attempted to tap into the underlying rules of nature, linking music to the very harmonies of the universe. Through the melodious yowls of tortured cats, the amorous brays of donkeys, the sonorous appeal of colors, the brassy tenors of tastes, and the sweet music of scent, musicians, artists, and philosophers dug deeper into the long-standing belief that the senses are deeply connected. If cats could harmonize, then so could colors, sounds, taste, smells, textures—just about anything a person could imagine. The senses not only granted access to pleasure, but they also lifted Nature's veil, allowing humans to understand the deeper patterns of the world. These instruments were tools not only for entertainment, but for truth, knowledge, and power.

It's not coincidental that the cat piano made its first appearance in a royal procession. Royal spectacles were about testing the limits of possibility. They involved showing everyone around the king that he could accomplish the unthinkable and that his power was not subject to the usual restraints of money, imagination, or nature. By parading his bear-powered cat piano through Brussels, Philip II was showing the world that he was undaunted by convention and that people should marvel at all the wonders that his reign could produce. Pierre Bayle, a source of inspiration for many Enlightenment thinkers, recounted a story in his *Historical and Critical Dictionary* (1690s) that highlighted similar links between power and display. According to Bayle, King Louis XI (1423–1483) used musical means to demonstrate the extent of his power, although it seems that he didn't get the memo that cats produced the finest tones. Louis XI commissioned the Abbé de Baigne to "get him a consort of swines' voices, thinking it impossible." Not long thereafter, the cleric showed up at court with a velvet tent that contained an organ-like instrument and a "great number of hogs, of several ages." As he played the keyboard, little spikes pricked the pigs, making them "cry in such order and consonance as highly delighted the king and all his company."[3] Louis' concept of the impossible was quickly revised, as was that of all of the noble onlookers who witnessed the spectacle. Remember, even the King Midas of myth popped up in the de Bry engraving, showing the deep connections between fantasy and royal power.

While the story of the cat piano may begin with a display of royal power, it quickly became clear that it had a cultural power all its own, and the fascination with cat music made its way from the courts of kings to the fairs of common people. What began as a means of accessing the mysteries of the divine glided easily into the realm of farcical entertainment. In the eighteenth century, the dictionary writer Valmont de Bomare noted that popular crowds had been charmed by a cat-based spectacle at the Saint-Germain Fair in Paris. It was called the "Concert Miaulique," and while the author makes no mention of torture, it does seem that the cats came together to form ludicrous melodies. "These animals were placed in stalls, with a sheet of music in front of them," he reported. "And in the middle was a monkey who kept time; at his ordered signal, the cats made cries or meows that, in their diversity, formed sounds that were more high-pitched than deep, and altogether laughable."[4] Entertainments featuring cats seemed to be quite fashionable in the seventeenth and eighteenth centuries. In London in 1758, the animal trainer Samuel Bisset staged a "Cats' Opera" that also included performances by a horse, a dog, and some monkeys. The house was packed, and reportedly, Bisset raked in a thousand pounds in just a few days. And according to Harrison Weir, who was the president of the National Cat Club in 1889, cat stage companies were still all the rage in London in the late nineteenth century.[5]

Laughter seemed to be a common theme when it came to the cat piano. In 1650, the German Jesuit scholar Athanasius Kircher reported that a cat piano was created for an Italian prince who was melancholic because of the demands of his royal position. The musician picked cats whose natural voices were of different pitches, and when a key was pressed, a sharp spike was driven

My favorite image of the cat piano, from an 1883 science journal. The cat on the left seems resigned, while the one on the right looks utterly mystified.

into the appropriate cat's tail. According to Kircher, the cats' cries became more frenzied as they became more desperate to escape, and the prince could not help but to laugh at the music. Bracketing the poor cats' misery for a moment, it's important to notice that Kircher wasn't just advocating the cat piano as a form of entertainment. It actually had the power to pull the prince from his melancholic state, meaning that it also served a medical function.

Kircher wrote in an era that predated the development of psychiatry, but his observations on the cat piano's psychological power were noted by others. One of the early-nineteenth-century founders of psychiatry, Christian Reil (1759–1813), argued that the cat piano, or *Katzenclavier* in German, was the key to treating patients who were lost in constant reverie. Daydreamers, he argued, had trouble paying attention to objects in the real world, but the bizarre, jarring nature of the cat piano would have the power to jolt them back to reality. In his book *Rhapsodies on the Application of Psychological Methods of Cure to the Mentally Dis-*

turbed, he wrote, "A fugue played on this instrument—when the ill person is so placed that he cannot miss the expressions on their faces and the play of these animals—must bring Lot's wife herself from her fixed state into conscious awareness."[6] According to Reil, mental illness was an affliction of the nervous system, and all psychological problems could be traced back to the malfunctioning of the brain and nerves. Sensory jolts, like the cats' yowls and their pained expressions, had the power to bring the mind back to itself. Music, in particular, could have beneficial effects on patients, since it "quiets the storm of the soul, chases away the cloud of gloom, and for a while dampens the uncontrolled tumult of frenzy."[7]

These examples show why the cat piano might have been appealing to early modern audiences, but they still don't explain why people were obsessed with cats in particular. Nor does it explain why they generally didn't seem bothered by the instrument's cruelty. For most modern readers, the abstract idea of the cat piano may be chuckle-inducing, but if they think more deeply about how those meows were produced, most people would find it less amusing. Since it's not the best historical practice or even the best common sense to think that everyone in the past didn't mind torturing animals, we have to ask, what *was* going on?

For one, the cat piano can be viewed as an extension of a folk tradition dating from the Middle Ages, called "charivari" (pronounced "sharivary" or "shivery"). The word comes from either the Latin word for "headache" or the Greek term for "heavy head," which should give you an idea as to just how pleasant and melodious this custom could be. When a community was displeased with the actions of one of its members, charivari was their method of shaming, punishing, and enforcing right conduct. Community members would gather beneath the culprit's windows, bringing the noisiest pots, pans, horns, and whistles that they could muster. Then the caterwauling would commence. In some cases, the culprit would be forced to ride a donkey backward, holding its tail, and the ceremony would end with a mock trial. Charivaris often resulted in violence. Sometimes the person being shamed would fight back, the punishment of the culprit would get out of hand, or the guilty person would commit remorseful suicide. These riotous processions were common around Carnival, right before Lent, when boundary-testing, hilarity, and ribaldry ran high, and cats were often a part of the celebrations. For example, in Burgundy, it was common for youths to pass around a cat while mocking their charivari victims. They called this ritual "doing the cat," and they would pull the cats' fur, eliciting screeching yowls. In Germany, charivaris were even called *Katzenmusik*, indicating that tortured felines probably played a key role in those rituals as well.[8]

In the 1980s, the historian Robert Darnton uncovered a curious story about cat-killing in Paris in the 1730s. Some mistreated print shop workers banded together to exact revenge on their unfair boss, and they did so in a way that they found riotously funny. Their methods included smashing the spine of the boss's wife's cat, clambering over rooftops and bludgeoning every cat they could find, dumping sacksful of cat corpses into the courtyard, and holding a mock trial in which the animals were found guilty and sentenced to hang. They reported the episode as bringing much "joy," "laughter," and "disorder," and they pantomimed the massacre at least twenty times in the weeks to come.[9]

Darnton asked what made cat murder so funny to the workers. While his answers centered on this particular cat massacre, they also help explain why the yelps of boxed-up piano cats would have been so hilarious to early-modern spectators. Darnton notes that cats had long been a part of European cultural rituals. In addition to charivaris, which date back at least to the twelfth century, cats were roasted at public festivals in central France; they were tossed and smashed as part of a game in southern France; and they were shaved, dressed as priests, and hanged in Reformation London.[10] Cats had a longstanding association with witchcraft, and popular folklore maintained that the best way to protect yourself from sorcery was to maim a cat. Cats had a number of other taboo associations. However, if you used them properly, their occult powers could be channeled for good. Unfortunately, "using them properly" often meant harming or killing them. Finally, symbolically speaking, cats smacked of sex and cuckoldry. Cats frequently represented female sexuality, as is made clear by the vulgar English term "pussy" and its French equivalent, *chatte*.[11] Since charivaris often centered around sexual impropriety, these associations make it clearer why "doing the cat" would have been popular at these events.

Aside from the cat piano's power and ability to amuse, there was one other aspect that intrigued the instrument's advocates. Some writers claimed that the cat piano highlighted the boundless possibilities of nature, and they took its musical and sensory potential to heart. Kircher, the seventeenth-century Jesuit writer who originally suggested the cat piano as a cure for melancholy, was a font of knowledge about the musical capacities of animals. In addition to his observations on cats, Kircher revealed that the sloth "perfectly intones the first elements of music" and sings a beautiful diatonic scale spanning a sixth, and he put a number of bird songs into musical notation. According to Kircher, animals' singing was evidence that music was natural, not man-made, and these songs enshrined the "sound of nature."[12] His student Gaspar Schott also indicated that animal music formed a "rare delight," and that it could "refresh the mind" and "rival Angelic Music." He cited his teacher's writings on the power of the cat piano but added his own reflections on a donkey chorus organized by a seventeenth-century Sicilian that he felt elegantly revealed God's power. The Sicilian selected four vigorous male donkeys whose voices fit together naturally in a scale, and he dabbed a large piece of silk with female donkey urine. Excited by the odor, the donkeys brayed their calls of love, and the conductor managed to create a magnificent polyphony by strategically placing the silk in front of the amorous asses.[13]

In 1725, fellow Jesuit Louis-Bertrand Castel entered the conversation, and while he credited Kircher with giving him the "seed for his discovery," he ultimately proposed another musical instrument that he believed would more accurately reveal nature's universal music. The first mention of the instrument was in a letter to M. Decourt published in the November 1725 edition of the *Mercure de France* newspaper. In it, Castel suggested that "colors follow the proportion of musical tones, and that each tone corresponds with each color."[14] These correspondences were not just representational, like a pale pink going with a sweet melody. According to Castel, certain colors and sounds were linked in nature, and they directly mapped onto each other. This instrument, which he called the ocular harpsichord, would simultaneously emit sounds and colors, producing two different kinds of music at once.

This letter proved suggestive enough to kindle imaginations, but it was not until 1735 that Castel developed the idea at any length. In a series of six extended letters to Montesquieu, Castel outlined what he called his "physico-moral system of taste," a system of connections he saw between the senses, mental faculties, and aesthetic taste.[15] He further elaborated the color system in his 1740 *Optics of Colors*, and the idea took on a vibrant life of its own, infusing French philosophy for over a century. Using acoustical theory as his guideline, Castel assigned colors to the seven pitches of the diatonic scale (described by the syllables that we now refer to as *do, re, mi, fa, sol, la, and ti*), as well as to their chromatic alternations (by which *do, re, fa, sol,* and *la* are raised by a half-step). Together, these seven diatonic pitches and their five chromatic alterations comprise the twelve-note chromatic scale. Based on contemporary musical practice, Castel claimed that of these twelve, three were essential: *do, mi,* and *sol,* which comprised the "tonic triad." Using this musical-theoretical system as his basis, Castel created an analogous system of colors. As with sounds, there is an infinite continuum of color, but Castel asserted that our senses could discern only a limited number of distinct shades. He identified the twelve colors of the chromatic scale (a doubly appropriate term here) as blue, celadon, green, olive, yellow, rosy gold or tawny, nacarat (a red-orange color), red, crimson, violet, agate, and blue-violet. These colors analogically corresponded to the musical chromatic scale, and blue, red, and yellow furnished the three essential "sounds" of the tonic triad.[16]

The parallelism continued further. In the same way that there are twelve degrees of pitch, Castel argued that there are twelve degrees of chiaroscuro [lightness and darkness]. These degrees, confusingly named, are as follows: black, black/black/gray-black, black/gray-black/gray-black, gray-black, gray-black/gray-black/gray, gray/gray/gray-black, gray, gray/gray/gray-white, gray-white/gray-white/gray, gray-white, gray-white/gray-white/black, gray-black/white/white, and white. As colors got darker or lighter (or as notes got higher and lower) they followed this second scale of twelve units. For example, a pale blue and a dark blue were both analogous to *do,* but they differed on the chiaroscuro scale, indicating that they varied in "pitch." On the other hand, a "gray-white" red, and a "gray-white" crimson, would vary in "sound," but not in "pitch." When all the twelve possible colors/ notes were combined with the twelve possible degrees of shading/

pitch, it became evident that "in all, there are 144 degrees of colors nuanced with harmony, as there are 144 degrees of tones or of harmonious sounds." Thus, an ocular harpsichord, designed to represent all discernible notes and colors, would have 144 keys.[17]

According to Castel, musical harmonies corresponded with color harmonies, and where musical melodies produced pleasure and emotion, so would the melodies of the corresponding colors. For example, playing a piece from Bach's *Das Wohltemperierte Klavier* (*The Well-Tempered Clavier*) would result in a series of color projections that were equally enjoyable and that matched the music in subtlety, tone, and mood. The colors would not simply accompany the Bach piece; they would *be* the Bach piece in a different form. With the ocular harpsichord, Castel argued, a deaf person would be able to judge music and a blind person would be able to judge colors.[18] In other words, Castel was describing synesthetic experience before synesthesia was a topic for scientific investigation.

Synesthesia, which means "union of the senses," is a neurological phenomenon in which one sensory pathway is linked to another, leading to mixed forms of sensory perception. A synesthete might be able to taste music, for instance, or she may experience tactile sensations when she hears certain sounds. Neurologists and psychologists have identified a number of different forms of synesthesia, including a type called "chromesthesia," where sounds are associated with certain colors. Castel would not have had this frame of reference, given that the first medical description of synesthesia was not published in Europe until 1812, and the term "synesthesia" didn't enter the scientific vernacular until 1892, when Jules Millet suggested the term in his thesis on color-hearing.[19] Nonetheless, Castel's ideas were harbingers of medical knowledge and cultural fascinations to come.

There is a major distinction to be made between Castel's protosynesthesia and our twenty-first-century notions, though. We understand synesthesia as a neurological phenomenon experienced by few people. Castel thought that anyone had the power to experience color music. He believed that all sensory experience derived from the action of objects on nerves. Stimuli struck fibers, causing them to tremble, and these sensations were transmitted through the nerves to the soul, where pleasure was felt.

This depiction of nerve fibers may have been fairly orthodox, but the conclusions that Castel drew from it were not. Unlike many of the doctors encountered in previous chapters, Castel argued that the fiber vibrations caused by sensory stimuli had very little to do with the state of the fibers themselves. Weak or strong, tense or elastic—it barely mattered. The vibrations that mattered were those of the stimulus itself, e.g., the vibrations that music causes in the air or the vibrations of light particles as they hit the eye. From Castel's perspective, regardless of whether one was the most amazingly trained classical musician or someone who had previously never heard music, a song would cause the same vibrations in her aural fibers. Jean-Philippe Rameau's song "L'amante préoccupée" ("The Worried Lover") would be "L'amante préoccupée," no matter who was listening.

Drawing on his work in mathematics and music, Castel insisted, "Everything that is in numerical proportion is in harmonic proportion."[20] In other words, if you could figure out the rates of color vibration, then you could figure out their harmonic relationships, just like people had done with musical vibrations. In a perfect octave, the vibrational frequency of sound occurs at a ratio of 2:1, so it stood to reason that in a perfect "octave" of colors, the hues would strike the ocular fibers with a 2:1 vibrational ratio as well. An example of a color octave would be the pairing of a dark blue with a lighter blue of the same intensity. These vibrational frequencies were crucial to Castel's theory of pleasure, because in his system, when different tones of color or light combined, a person experienced pleasure if the ratios of these rates were simple rational numbers.[21] This is why octaves and perfect fifths are so enjoyable, and in just the same way, this is why blue and crimson can be considered harmonic colors. Stated more directly, "The pleasure and displeasure of all our senses consist in the same type of vibrations, that is to say, in vibrations and harmonic proportion."[22]

This might seem somewhat reasonable at first blush, but there is an odd assumption at the base of this theory: that pleasure has nothing to do with the perceiver at all. Instead, pleasure comes from the mathematical relationships between objects, and if you could figure out the relationships, it would be possible to systematize pleasure. If you follow this line of thought, human emotions result from the effect of objects outside the body, and it would be possible to calculate which sensory stimuli would give a person joy. Castel described shifts in colors as the "vital force of the soul," going so far as to argue that colors could inspire the passions. Green, which corresponded to *re,* could give one a natural, laughing, pastoral feeling, while red, which corresponded to *sol,* led to "bloody, choleric, terrible" tones.[23] Think of it. In this system, all of your happiness, pleasure, and treasured moments have nothing to do with your individual likes, feelings, or proclivities. They have everything to do with the material objects that are in the world and the natural vibrations that they produce when they interact with the human body.

I'd guess that few people today have sat down to develop a fully formed theory of pleasure, but I would say that most of us, intuitively, tend to fall somewhere between the subjective and objective interpretations. In a somewhat Castelian move, Western interior design color psychologists maintain that blue is an appetite suppressant, so it's not suitable to dining rooms, and red is an energetic color, probably not suited to restful sleep in a bedroom. Such principles are fairly dogmatic, assuming that the same colors will affect different people in the same way. If you've been steeped in the cultural assumptions around certain colors, these theories probably seem "correct" to you, giving them the appearance of objectivity. When you think of red, you think of blood. Or courage. Or war. Or love. It carries potency, passion, and energy. Blue? Calming and restful. Green? Nature, life, envy, and money. Yellow? Sunlight and happiness. But modern culture also strongly stresses the power of personal preference and subjective opinion. If you want a red bedroom, then by all means, have a red bedroom. I may like blue kitchens, but you might hate them. Fine. So be it. To each her own. This attitude certainly would not align with Castel's notion of mathematical pleasure. Furthermore, most of us also recognize that color preferences are culturally specific. For instance, in Chinese culture, red signifies happiness, but in American culture, it represents anger.[24] To his credit, Castel did mention the fact that different cultures have different preferences, but he wound himself into philosophical knots trying to explain why this happens even though pleasure is objective, universal, and mathematical.

For the moment, though, let's appreciate Castel's idea and follow him down the philosophical rabbit hole. If pleasure operated at fixed ratios, then it made sense that once humans understood the math, it would be possible to tap into nature's bounty to make more pleasurable creations. Painters could produce more beautiful paintings, textile makers could make more sumptuous goods, and audiences could have an even deeper experience with music. By going a step further and uniting the music of the eyes and the ears, Castel wanted to enhance the links between the internal and external senses, stimulating the mind and eyes in one fell swoop.[25] Delighted at the prospect of uncovering the mathematics behind all sensation, Castel anticipated that the theories behind the ocular harpsichord were "of the greatest consequence for pleasure and for the whole of public utility, perhaps even for the entire state of humanity," and that it would revolutionize life as we know it, "making us more enlightened and better."[26] He ever-so-modestly continued, "The harpsichord is going to be like the renaissance of humanity."[27]

Many of his readers seemed to agree. The poet Descazeaux wrote a piece that attributed Castel with "lift[ing] the obstacle that kept our mind in chains," and he described the harpsichord in rapturous terms.[28] As you might expect, people desperately wanted to witness these raptures for themselves, and Castel had a ready audience for his instrument. Unfortunately, theory and practice don't always align, and Castel had a devil of a time producing the ocular harpsichord. At the end of his life, after thirty years of work on it, Castel wrote a series of letters to his benefactor and former student the Comte de Maillebois. In these letters, Castel claimed that he had originally intended the harpsichord as a theoretical instrument, and he fully expected that someone else would have built it since he didn't have the necessary technical skills. But no one had attempted it, and Castel had tried to appease the public by building the machine himself. By 1730, Castel had produced a model that operated by means of "colored flips of paper" and a spring mechanism attached to the harpsichord keys.[29] Dissatisfied with these results, Castel reported to his friend Montesquieu in 1734 that he was working on another model, and in 1739, he described his forays with different lighting techniques like rockets, oils, and lanterns.[30] Then there was the question of other materials. Colored ribbons, colored crystals, painted panels, and painted lanterns were among the variations Castel tried over the years, but none of them seemed to satisfy the inventor or his public. "If I had not persisted with too great

The caption reads: "If only they had all occupied their time on the same machine. Father Castel links sounds and colors."

an idea of Perfection, my harpsichord would have been made 12, 15, or even 20 or 25 years ago," Castel opined.[31] Before his death, Castel was able to put on a semisuccessful demonstration of the machine. On December 21, 1753, fifty people had witnessed its glory and demanded four encores. On January 1, 1754, the harpsichord had an even larger audience, and Castel reported to his correspondent Rondet that an audience of two hundred had met his instrument with applause.[32]

By and large, though, over the course of his pursuit, Castel felt that the public had "abandoned him," leaving him attacked by an audience pitted against his harpsichord.[33] Castel did endure some harsh criticism. This stinging caricature by Charles-Germain de Saint-Aubin, created sometime between 1740 and 1757, shows just how ludicrous some of Castel's audience found his creation: Castel sits at the instrument, ready to play, but instead of being greeted by the blissful harmonies of Paradise, he is greeted by an arc of water coming from an enema syringe. What Castel intended as an impressive pursuit, Saint-Aubin depicted as a ridiculous mess.

The ocular harpsichord had been only the first piece of Castel's musical puzzle. Originally, he had intended to devise an "entire music," or "sensible" music—which included musics of sound, sight, taste, smell, and touch—and other instruments of sensible music that would have been equivalent to violins, flutes, cymbals, and trumpets.[34] But because of the difficulties he had with the harpsichord, Castel never got underway with the others.

Castel's theories may have been a failure on a practical front, but they continued to fascinate scientists, writers, and artists for years to come. In 1753, Antoine Le Camus—the same man that developed the "mental medicine" of Chapter One—argued that taste could be reduced to a science similar to Castel's music-color system. He speculated that, like the seven tones, there might be seven base flavors. Thus, "It would be possible to have in flavors a harmony even more real than that which could be formed by the ocular harpsichord."[35] Following suit, the marvelously named Polycarpe Poncelet published a book called *Chemistry of Taste and Odor* (1755), in which he argued that liquor could be used to "transmit agreeable sensations to the brain."[36] To better orchestrate these agreeable sensations, Poncelet proposed a music of taste that was comprised of seven flavors (acidic, bland, sweet, bitter, bittersweet, sour, and spicy). Such an analogy was possible, he argued, because flavor comes from particle vibrations that affect the sense of taste, just like vibrations in the air affect the sense of hearing. In the second edition of the book (1774), Ponce-

The components of Polycarpe Poncelet's savory symphonies.

let described a prototype of a liqueur organ that he had produced according to Castel's theories. He constructed a small buffet with two bellows and a series of acoustical tubes, alongside which were a series of vials filled with liqueurs that represented the primitive flavors. Pressing on a key would uncork the bottle and trigger a mechanism that would let the liqueurs flow into a reservoir. Poncelet admitted that he had not been scrupulous enough in choosing the liqueurs since he picked things that he knew would taste good together instead of truly testing the music's ability to create delightful concoctions.[37]

About one hundred years later, the liqueur organ resurfaced in the novel *Against the Grain* (1884) by Joris-Karl Huysmans. The book follows the decadent exploits of a disaffected, eccentric man named Jean des Esseintes. Tired of the typical bourgeois life, and bored with the usual pursuits, he retreated to a house that he tried to make into an ideal aesthetic world, filled with the most exquisite sensory experiences. Huysmans dedicated entire chapters to the colors that des Esseintes selects, the décor he chooses, and even the pets that he keeps (a jewel-encrusted turtle that became so heavy-laden that he could no longer move). But one of the most intriguing scenes involves des Esseintes' "mouth organ," which was composed of a number of tiny casks controlled by a set of spigots and buttons. Each liqueur corresponded, not with a particular note, but with a particular instrument, and Des Esseintes, who "sipped here and there, enjoying the inner symphonies, succeeded in procuring sensations in his throat analogous to those which music gives to the ear." Des Esseintes ultimately became so skilled at "hearing in his mouth" that he was able to "transfer to his palate real pieces of music."[38] Castel, who had argued that it was possible to taste cymbals and flutes, and who believed that natural harmonies existed between the senses, would have been delighted with Huysmans' organ. That said, he probably would have been far from delighted with the rest of the novel, which was described during the proceedings of the Oscar Wilde trial as a "sodomitical" book. *Against the Grain* is categorized as part of a nineteenth-century aesthetic movement called "decadence," and much as its name implies, the style was marked by its emphasis on indulgence and moral decline. Decadent literature tended to emphasize characters who had lost sight of reality and who focused on sensory details to the detriment of the bigger social picture.

Against the Grain appeared at the same time that synesthesia was moving from a specialized medical concept to a culturally pervasive one. Psychologists and physicians had studiously taken up the issue of color-hearing in the 1870s, and the concept did not escape the attention of a group of young artists, with whom Huysmans became friends. This group, which included Charles Baudelaire, Arthur Rimbaud, Paul Verlaine, and Stéphane Mallarmé, became known as the Symbolists, and they believed that great truths could only be described indirectly. They wrote in a highly metaphorical manner and focused on the fluidity of experience, with sensory experience figuring front and center. Synesthesia was one of their prized concepts, and the Symbolists believed that "all refined nervous systems" should be able to experience the unity of the senses.[39] Baudelaire, a longtime laudanum user, must have had the most refined nervous system of them all, because he produced a poem called "Correspondences" that became the epitome of the Symbolist movement:

> *There are perfumes fresh like children's flesh,*
> *Sweet like oboes, green like meadows,*
> *—And others, corrupt, rich, and triumphant,*

> *Having the expansiveness of infinite things,*
> *Like amber, musk, benzoin, and incense,*
> *Which sing of the transports of the soul and the senses.*[40]

Like Castel, Baudelaire understood the world to be full of unrecognized correspondences, but unlike his Enlightenment predecessor, he trusted intuition, experience, and opium—not mathematics—to give him access to these connections.

Artsy, eccentric, and drug-addled though they may have been, the Symbolists weren't alone in their hopes. The fascination with sensory correspondences also appeared in less artistic realms like chemistry, medicine, psychology, and botany.[41] The English chemist George Field composed a treatise on color that explored "aesthetical chromatics," in which the "harmonic analogy of colors" played a significant part. He criticized Castel's method but maintained that color music was possible and that there was an "entire conformity of the systems of colours and sounds," as long as one considered them, not as arithmetical ratios but as geometrical ones.[42] In 1905, the perfumer S. Piesse adopted Field's method to create a similar music of odors, based on their intensity and their propensity to linger. "Definitively, the best way, I believe, to understand the theory of odors," Piesse maintained, "is to consider them as particular vibrations that affect the nervous system, like colors affect the eye, like sounds affect the ear."[43] In short, Castel's dream for a universal music had not gone unnoticed, and throughout the nineteenth and eartly twentieth centuries, others took that dream and made it their own.

Advocates of universal music tended to see sensory unity as a way to access the hidden truths of nature, but their concepts of nature were not all the same. Where the cat pianists saw nature as a playground for wonder, Castel saw it as regular, discernible, and regimented, and the Symbolists viewed it as a metaphysical swirl of emotion and ineffable beauty. For some, nature was comprised of a complex series of mathematical equations, with numbers acting as the invisible supports for everything from planetary motion to human emotion. For others, nature offered a glimpse of God, who in all his infinite power, had created things of such beauty and charm that even their shadows could enchant the imagination. And for others still, nature was made up of the chaotic, unknown beyond. It marked the highest planes of spirit, so far removed from the body, that one could access it only through the most transcendent and syncretic of experiences.

Varying visions of nature aside, these creators shared the idea that the senses formed a tightly interwoven system. They argued that what we often divide into separate categories—like sight, taste, and hearing—are actually interconnected and do not operate in isolation. Indeed, they claimed, the lines that we draw between our senses are much more arbitrary than we realize. Antoine Louis Claude Destutt, Comte de Tracy, a French philosopher who wrote on the senses in the early nineteenth century, argued in his multivolume *Elements of Ideology* that humans rely on imprecise and flawed language to describe experience. "All the classifications that men make to put their ideas in order are very imperfect," he asserted, "and while we use them because they are convenient, we should never forget that [these categories] always confound things that are quite distinct or separate things that are quite similar."[44] Distinctions may be helpful, de Tracy argued, but it could be equally helpful to consider the connections between different domains of experience. It was precisely these connections that so captivated the proponents of universal music, and rather than fixating on the senses as separate faculties, they focused on the ways in which the senses were similar and bound together. These creators stressed the fact that experience is often fluid and pertains to multiple senses at once.

They also shared the conviction that sensory correspondences could have marked social effects. George Field, writing in 1824, stressed that universal analogies existed, not only between the "physical and sensible" sciences, like color and music, but also between the moral sciences of ethics, politics, and theology. Nature existed as "one uniform design, pervading, actuating, and regulating, harmoniously, all nature, science, and art," and the same relationships that guided aesthetic questions (like color music) also guided questions of human interaction.[45] Field argued, "Man has the same triple nature in which our universe is founded; he begins in *matter,* proceeds to *sense,* and thence to *intellect.*" He explained that the individual will is forged out of these three parts, and when that individual desire harmonizes with God's will, or "universal will," the result is individual happiness and moral harmony among all humans.[46] In other words, the interconnectedness of the senses was simply one small expression of the interconnectedness of human society. Sensation, individuality, ethics, and God existed like a series of *matryoshka* dolls, resembling each other in larger and larger scale. These resemblances meant that the tiniest aspects of human existence were able to provide insight into the largest questions of human sociability. Small though they may have seemed, sensory correspondences carried a great deal of power.

Castel, ever the optimist, also emphasized the large-scale conclusions that could be drawn from color music. He argued,

"There are many harmonious bodies; there is only one harmony." This single harmony led him to the parallel conclusion, "There are many men; there is only one humanity."[47] In other words, understanding sensory correspondences could help clarify the correspondences between human beings. Like colors and sounds, humans seemed infinite in their dispositions, talents, and proclivities, but by identifying patterns and creating a system, society could be harmonized and made better. Such a sentiment resonated with a much larger Enlightenment fixation: how to incorporate everyone into society and how to reconcile the many differences between individuals in order to fashion an efficient society that worked well for all. According to Castel and his nineteenth-century successors, the unity of the senses opened up the possibility for the unity of society and human experience.

8

Calling It Macaroni:
The Politics of Popular Pigments

I F COLOR MUSIC promised the possibility of unity, other forms
of color promised social distinction. Modern depictions of the
eighteenth century portray it as a colorful time, at least when it
comes to the decadent lives of the aristocracy. From the frothy
frocks of Marie-Antoinette to the vibrant rooms of the finest
homes, we have a Technicolor image of the eighteenth century.
And certainly, there's good reason for this. As mentioned in
Chapter Two, foreign and colonial trade flooded Europe with
new foods, drinks, and spices, stimulating the tongue in new,
exciting ways. The eyes also had their treats, as places like Mex-
ico and India offered up brilliant shades of carmine, peacock, and
egg-yolk yellow. New animals, vegetables, and minerals meant
fresh visual delights, and lively hues were more diverse and more
readily available than ever before. These intense colors were often
quite difficult and expensive to produce, but they were in high
demand by those who could afford them.

While the wholesale market of Les Halles operated in the
dark, other types of commerce centered wholly on seeing and

This dapper macaroni wears spotted trousers, striped stockings, and the finest floral corsage. It is not a color print, but thanks to the many patterns, it's easy to imagine what a vibrant figure he must have been.

being seen. Amazed by the unfamiliar, wealthy consumers indulged in vivid fashions and interiors, surrounding themselves with bright, jewel-box colors. In the 1770s in England, outlandish figures emerged who bathed themselves in extravagant colors and patterns: the "macaroni." These were young men who had traveled to Italy and developed a taste for the finery and food that they discovered there. Bringing these passions back to England, they dressed in bright, bold clothes, often involving animal prints, and styled their hair in poufs that seemed to reach to the heavens.[1] The term "macaroni" came to signify something that was very *à la mode*, and so when Yankee Doodle went to town and stuck a feather in his cap, he naively thought that the feather was sufficient adornment to be called macaroni.

The macaronis were a short-lived phenomenon—although their cousins, the fops and the dandies also had their day—but one didn't need to be so outlandish to participate in the color craze. Greater textile production, the introduction of cheaper, colorfast cotton fabrics, and changing attitudes toward consumption meant that plenty of people, even if they couldn't afford the most expensive hues, still had access to new, vivid tones. For example, the historian Joan DeJean has shown how crimson, originally a royal hue, became a more common, casual accent color from the 1680s onward, thanks to the import of dyed cottons from India.[2] Grinding pigments had been an extremely labor-intensive process, but several eighteenth-century innovations helped make paint and dyes less expensive and more accessible. One such innovation was the packaging of pigment pastes in animal bladders. The bladder was pierced with a tack, which then allowed the painter to squeeze out the desired quantity of color into basic white lead paint. By 1734, English writers took note that "several Noblemen and Gentlemen have by themselves and Servants painted whole Houses without the Assistance or Direction of a Painter."[3]

Choices in fabrics, colors, and styles quickly multiplied in the eighteenth century, creating what the historian Daniel Roche has called a "revolution of appearances."[4] Visually, the world became a new place. Intense colors were novel, and they could be an excellent way to show off your status. For instance, one way that the artist William Hogarth portrayed the immense wealth of a countess in his *Marriage-à-la-mode* series was to depict her sitting room as having deep green walls. "Fine Deep Green," as this color was called, was an incredibly expensive paint color, costing about six or seven times as much as an ordinary paint color. Eighteenth-century viewers immediately would have recognized this visual signal of wealth.[5] George Washington had brilliant verdigris walls in his dining room at Mount Vernon, and notoriously, the dining room of Thomas Jefferson's Monticello was a cutting-edge, eye-popping yellow that the former president selected in 1815, shortly after the color was developed in France. The paint cost more than thirty-three times the price of a basic white paint, and Jefferson was thrilled with its palpable mark of scientific advancement.[6]

By and large, though, the changing experience of color didn't manifest in deep, saturated colors, the proliferation of jewel-tones, or a dazzling array of bright shades. As you might expect from an era called the "Enlightenment," a new emphasis was placed on light, luminous, and soft colors. It was a more muted color revolution, and subtle tones proliferated, partially because of their cost. "Common colors" was the term for those that were affordable and frequently applied, and the most common of them all was a color called "stone."[7] "Stone" actually covered a range of hues. Paints inspired by the honey-colored limestone of Bath differed greatly from those modeled on the cream-colored stones so characteristic of later, nineteenth-century Parisian architecture. Despite the particular shade of "stone" people chose, though, the most popular colors were relatively light in tone.[8]

Similarly, in clothing, a taste for heavy, dark silks shifted to a passion for lighter, pastel ones and delicate floral motifs.[9] By the 1750s, men's suits, in the words of the fashion historian Stella Blum, "had taken on a distinctly feminine tone" (although, I should point out that the eighteenth-century standards for "masculine" and "feminine" fashion were rather different from today's). With slimmer and more form-fitting cuts, these suits were made of light-colored satin or taffeta, and they were trimmed with floral embroidery and lace.[10] The new colors were those that brightened, lightened, and lifted the spirits, and while intense colors could indicate wealth, there was nothing like a dose of soft pink, light blue, or creamy white to express a lighthearted outlook.

If you compare early-seventeenth-century interiors with their eighteenth-century counterparts, the first thing you will notice is the dramatic tonal difference. To stroll through the Musée Carnavalet, the museum of the history of Paris, is to forge through a series of dark-and-light ups-and-downs, with the eighteenth-century rooms registering like the pale frosting on a rather ornate wedding cake. They are a stark visual contrast from the dark-paneled, brocade-lined rooms that were more characteristic of the sixteenth and early seventeenth century. The historian Joan DeJean argues that in the late seventeenth century, "white had become for the first time a color, the dominant color in modern homes."[11] Mirrors, glass, gilding, and high-gloss finishes added reflectivity, making interiors seem highly luminous, even in candlelight. If the light of reason could sweep away the darkness of the mind, then the light of the home could sweep away the shadows of the soul. Eighteenth-century churches also adopted this interior Enlightenment. Whitewashed walls and the removal of heavy, colored stained glass windows signified the visibility of Christ, who shone as the Light of the World.[12]

Where intense colors often connoted wealth and status, soft colors indicated delicacy, beauty, and refinement. In his 1757 *Philosophical Enquiry into the Origins of Our Idea of the Sublime and Beautiful,* Edmund Burke declared that soft tints truly were the only way to go. "As to the colours usually found in beautiful bodies," he declared, "first, [they] must not be dusky or muddy, but clean and fair. Secondly, they must not be of the strongest kind. Those which seem most appropriated to beauty are the milder of every sort; light greens; soft blues; weak whites; pink reds, and violets."[13] Sofia Coppola's film *Marie Antoinette* made use of soft pastel colors, and it did so with good reason. In the Petit Trianon, Marie-Antoinette's retreat from the world of the court, the queen selected a palette of grays, beiges, and pastels, and she favored light, delicate patterns to the bold, large-scale patterns that had been characteristic of aristocratic dress earlier in the century.[14] In the English colonies of North America, gentlemen adopted a new style in the early eighteenth century that moved away from flamboyant colors, fabrics, and jewelry, favoring white linen shirts and jackets in subdued colors. Indeed, the love of stone colors was so pronounced that by the 1760s Horace Walpole, the English politician and author of the sorrowful Gothic novel *The Castle of Otranto*, seemed utterly fed up: "I have seen but one idea in all the houses here; the rooms are white and gold, or white. . . . I could not perceive any difference, but in the more or less gold."[15]

The pure, delicate powers of soft colors dominated not just interiors and fashion, but the world of food as well. According to Jean-Jacques Rousseau, children preferred pale, sweet foods— milk, cheese, butter, pastry, fruit, creams, fresh eggs, and rice puddings. These foods preserved their innocence and wholesomeness, whereas a diet dominated by red meat would destroy their character. Rousseau beseeched his maternal readers not to give their children the "unnatural" taste for meat: "For how can one explain away the fact that great meat-eaters are usually fiercer and more cruel than other men?"[16] Likewise, he advised that sensitive, refined adults looking for a therapeutic diet should also subsist on light-colored foods. The historian Rebecca Spang has charted the history of the restaurant, and she has shown that at its beginning, a "restaurant" was not a location where one could buy food. Instead, it was a light broth that was designed to restore (*restaurer*) its eaters to health. The light broth counteracted the effects of heavy, rich, decadent foods and warded off the languor and torpid morals that were thought to accompany them. As Spang has beautifully shown, "Mild, white foods such as these stood in opposition to the regularly brown (or black) bread of the common people, as they did to the sanguine meat and red wine associated with Homeric heroes and the sturdy early Gauls."[17]

There has been a long-standing medicopsychological claim that certain colors have the power to affect our bodies and mental states in intense ways. The Persian physician Avicenna (980–1037 C.E.) warned that one should avoid looking at red objects while having a nosebleed, since red was a color that stirred the blood. Similarly, physicians from ancient India, China, and Greece argued that visual stimuli could have deep and lasting effects on the body, particularly when it came to the bodies of pregnant women. Supposedly, the things that women saw could alter their organs, manifesting in their children. For example, a woman who looked too often at a portrait of a dark-skinned Moor might have a "maternal impression" that would give her baby culturally undesirable dark skin.[18] Vision had power, and the presumed emotional effects of light colors were potent in the eighteenth century. To eat white, dress white, live white was to be pure, clean, sensitive, and healthy.

As you might imagine, these theories entailed a great many assumptions about class and race. While Rousseau valorized the pastoral life, harping on country air and rustic life, a true shepherd never could have afforded the "simple" foods he lauded, which often involved refined (and therefore expensive) sugar and flour.[19] Candles, lantern oil, mirrors, glass, and other light-related goods were often priced beyond the reach of the average family as well. It was no accident that Marie-Antoinette was known for her pale hair and fair complexion, which made her sheltered status immediately evident. Similarly, it was no accident that the wigs that were so fashionable among the upper and middle classes were coated in powder and flour in an array of white and pastel hues. (In fact, French revolutionaries scorned wig-wearing, not only because of its association with aristocracy, but because it signified a waste of important food resources for the poor. Flour, as the main component of bread, was a mainstay of the lower-class diet, and instead of going into hungry mouths, it was going to waste on ostentatious heads.)

In the American colonies during the eighteenth century, white linen bore the mark of "decency," and to reveal one's cosmopolitan identity, refined character, and gentility, one had to wear linen of the purest white, connoting religious piety and civil purity. Per capita ownership of linen grew rapidly, and men of sufficient means changed their shirts as often as possible. Daniel Defoe, the author of *Robinson Crusoe*, maintained a standard for linens that his desert-island solitary could never have achieved. He argued that "nicer" English gentlemen should change their shirts twice a day.[20] This zest for white linens marked out those who could not afford frequent clothing changes or whose occupations made them filthy. Today we use the terms "white collar" and "blue collar" to distinguish those who work at desk jobs from those who perform manual labor, showing the continued power of historical color associations.

The love of white linens also imposed Anglo-American concepts of purity and hygiene onto other cultures. The historian Kathleen M. Brown has shown that "white linen also symbolized the social 'whiteness' of the wearer, no matter what his complexion, a sleight of hand made possible by the conflation of the shirt with the skin."[21] Native Americans who adopted the subtle colors of Anglo-American fashion were seen as having taken a step toward civilization, while slaves, who were issued "broun Linnen" clothing of coarser textures and darker colors, were considered to be lower on the ladder of civilization.[22] Race was visually signified not only by the color of skin but also by the color of clothing slaves were allowed to wear.

The twenty-first-century art theorist David Batchelor has argued that in Western cultures, "colour has been systematically marginalized, reviled, diminished, and degraded."[23] This chromophobia, or fear of color, manifests as the valorization of white as the color of rational, clean, controlled spaces, while color is seen as dangerous, superficial, and potentially contaminating. Obviously, white is a color, so the opposition of these terms might, at first, seem a bit simplistic. But what Batchelor is interested in is the idea of "generalized white," or the "negative hallucination" of white—the fact that even when color is present, as in the minimalist art of Piet Mondrian or Donald Judd, we still tend to be blind to that color, thinking only of the white space and tending to privilege form over color.

Your initial objection might be that it's quite simple to look around us and see plenty of color: green trees, blue sky, vibrant flowers. But consider this: in the things that we make or buy, color tends to be reined in. Generally speaking, we think that bright colors are acceptable only in limited doses, and too much vivid color can seem tacky or like an assault on the senses. For instance, it would be considered fashionable to wear a bright pink tie, as long as the suit is gray, but in general, we would find it eccentric or odd to wear a bright pink suit with a gray tie. (Obviously, the "we" I refer to here is a generalization about American culture; there are plenty of individuals, communities, and cultures that don't view color in this way. But just watch HGTV or talk to a realtor about resale values if you think that there's not an overwhelming propensity toward muted, neutral palettes.) Chromophobia is marked not just by the desire to eradicate color, but also a desire to control it and master its forces. When we do use color, there's some sense that there are definite rules to its use.

There is a pervasive idea that color gets us in the gut; it's seductive, emotional, compelling. It carries intense cultural assumptions and associations—so much so, in fact, that the anthropologist Michael Taussig has even argued that color should be considered a manifestation of the sacred.

According to some art critics, sensory anthropologists, and historians, this mutual attraction and repulsion to color has centuries-old roots, bound up in a colonial past. Taussig has shown that in the seventeenth century, the British East India Company centered much of its trade on brightly colored, cheap, and dye-fast cotton textiles imported from India. Because of the Calico Acts of 1700 and 1720, which supported the interests of the wool and silk weaving guilds, these textiles could only be imported into England with the proviso that they were destined for export again, generally to the English colonies in the Caribbean or Africa. These vibrant textiles played a key part in the African trade, and especially in the African slave trade, where British traders would use the textiles to purchase slaves. According to Michael Taussig, these trades are significant not only because they linked chromophilic areas like India and Africa, but also because "color achieved greater conquests than European-instigated violence during the preceding four centuries of the slave trade. The first European slavers, the Portuguese in the fifteenth century, quickly learned that to get slaves they had to trade for slaves with African chiefs and kings, not kidnap them, and they conducted this trade with colored fabrics in lieu of violence."[24] Ironically, many of these slaves were then put to work in the colonies cultivating plants like indigo, which yielded dyes whose monetary values sometimes surpassed that of sugar.

In England, contemporaries often called the Indian textiles "rags" or "trash" and scorned their bright colors, and in Europe more generally, bright colors were taken as a sign of degeneracy and inferiority. The German writer Goethe famously stated that "men in a state of nature, uncivilized nations and children, have a great fondness for colors in their utmost brightness," whereas "people of refinement" avoid vivid colors (or what he called "pathological colors").[25] In short, a love of bright color marked one as uncivilized, lacking in taste, and "foreign" or other. Color, for people like Goethe, represented the "mythical savage state out of which civilization, the nobility of the human spirit, slowly, heroically, has lifted itself—but back into which it could always slide."[26] This danger of falling into degeneracy, disorientation, and excess resulted in a valorization of the "generalized white" mentioned above. According to Batchelor, prejudice against color "masks a fear: a fear of contamination and corruption by something that is unknown or appears unknowable," and the highly minimal, white spaces of contemporary architecture mark an attempt to rationalize and strictly limit an interior, to stop its merging with the world outside. The "hollow, whited chamber, scraped clean, cleared of any evidence of the grotesque embarrassments of an actual life. No smells, no noises, no colour; no changing from one state to another and the uncertainty that comes with it."[27]

I would not be too quick to argue that the history of the West's relationship with color (even inasmuch as one can say that there is such a thing as a "Western" relationship to color) is so neatly linear or stable. Victorians were infamous for their love of pattern and color, and a glimpse at the painted ladies in San Francisco or the love of neon in the 1980s will show that certain eras have a relationship to color that doesn't fit neatly into the narrative above. But it does appear that many of the fears described by Taussig and Batchelor seem to have been present in the eighteenth century. According to some of the period's naturalists, different climates, foods, and other nonnatural influences had caused certain portions of humanity to degenerate, and darkened skin was one sign of this decline. In a section of his *Natural History*, Buffon discussed "the degeneration of animals," focusing first and foremost on how these elements had created different races of people. He maintained that from the outset of creation, there had been only one kind of human, and any racial differences were the product of environmental factors. (This is called a "monogenist" account of humanity. It stands in opposition to a "polygenist" account, which maintains that different races come from different origins.) According to Buffon's monogenism, if one race were implanted in the climate of another, it would only be a matter of time before they resembled each other. "To conduct an experiment on the human species' change in color," he argued, "it would be necessary to transport some members of the black race of Senegal to Denmark, where men all have white skin, blond hair, blue eyes, [since] the difference in their blood and their color is the greatest. It would be necessary to cloister these Blacks with their women, and scrupulously keep them from interbreeding. This is the only means that one could employ to know how much time it takes to reintegrate man's nature in this manner; and, for the same reason, how much time it takes to change from white to black."[28]

Given that social status, racial stereotypes, and cultural fears and anxieties readily manifested in the colors that people selected, it is probably unsurprising, then, that politics also found a powerful platform in the visual language of fashion. The cultural historian Caroline Weber has extensively researched the ways in which Marie-Antoinette's clothing choices symbolically and consciously marked her political stances. Ostentation functioned much in the same way for the Austrian-born queen that it did for Louis XIV in the seventeenth century. Fine fabrics, impeccable gowns, over-the-top hairstyles, and decadent jewelry indicated Marie-Antoinette's power, and in a rush to please a powerful queen, her subjects faithfully emulated her every action. For example, many people are familiar with the showy *poufs* for which Marie-Antoinette was famous. Because of the queen, three-foot-tall piles of hair, replete with battleships to signify military success, or sky-high hairstyles celebrating the fact that the king had been inoculated for smallpox graced the finest heads in the nation. (Vaccines were just as much a hot-button issue in the 1770s as they are in certain circles today.)

Although the revolutionary image has colored our understanding, all told, Marie-Antoinette's spending was not particularly anomalous for a royal. What was anomalous, though, was the fact that she relied, not on the court fashion of Versailles, but on cutting-edge fashion, created by Paris's most fashionable *marchandes des modes* (the guild of fashion merchants, which rose to prominence in the second half of the eighteenth century). By patronizing these fashionable merchants, the queen violated centuries of court etiquette, which stipulated that those who dressed the queen could dress no one other than the queen.[29] For the first time, people with sufficient connections, money, and power could obtain the unconventional fashions of an unconventional queen.

Historians have talked about the development of a "consumer revolution" in northwestern Europe and the American colonies in the eighteenth century, stressing the creation of new commercial relationships and the immense expansion of consumer choice. But it may not be evident to most people just how quickly things revolved in this new commercial world. As the art historian Kimberly Chrisman-Campbell has pointed out, "When a fashion becomes accessible to the masses, it can no longer be considered fashionable, and must be replaced by a new fashion," and in the late eighteenth century, this cycle of replacement was very quick indeed. The fashion magazine *Cabinet des modes* was published every fifteen days in its first year, and demand was sufficient enough to move the production to every ten days in subsequent years.[30]

Stop for a minute and let that sink in. Imagine if *Vogue* came out every ten days, full of new things that people had to wear, buy, and try if they wanted to seem like part of the social elite. Together with the *marchandes des modes*, the elite created these new fashions, and people from lower social classes copied these trends, whenever and however they could. Thanks to innovations like fashion dolls and fashion magazines, information about the latest and the greatest sartorial trends was at the fingertips of more and more people. There was a robust secondhand clothing market, and after a particular garment went out of style, ladies and gentlemen would generally pass the garment down to their servants or sell it at the market, allowing someone of a lower social status to enjoy it. Ironically, the fact that Parisians of all classes donned elegant clothing drew even more attention to the dire living conditions that the majority endured. The aspirational poor, who could not even afford basic clothing items, struggled to obtain status symbols like wigs and swords.[31]

In the spring of 1775, a series of riots called the Flour War erupted, following an increase in grain prices. Fueled by rumors of monopolization and new government policies favoring more laissez-faire economic policies, the poor rose up, claiming that the monarchy had broken its centuries-old pledge to protect the well-being of its subjects. Order was restored by May, thanks to military intervention and food assistance, but unrest and distrust remained, and the structural weakness of the French economy, strapped from centuries of warfare, had become clear to a much larger public. In the wake of this turmoil, Marie-Antoinette's profligate spending no longer had the same political valence out-side court circles. What once counted as a display of spectacular royal power now smacked of thoughtlessness and a lack of empathy. The tide of public opinion began to turn against her flashy ways, earning the queen the nickname of "Madame Deficit." The king, in an attempt to temper Marie-Antoinette's spending habits, made a joke about a new pinkish-tan gown that she had just purchased. Trying to dispel her passion for the faddish hue, he remarked, "It is the color of a flea [*puce*, in French]." But instead of quelling the queen's fashion bug, *puce* took off. Soon, according to the Baroness d'Oberkirch, "every lady at court wore a puce-colored gown, old puce, young puce, flea's belly, flea's back, etc.," and its influence didn't stop there. "As the new color did not soil easily," the baroness continued, "the fashion of puce gowns was adopted by the [Parisian] bourgeoisie."[32] The queen may have been criticized for her spending, but it didn't stop her ready public from buying the latest fashions. The allure of "fast fashion" had begun, and consumer society was on the move.

When Marie-Antoinette switched to less decadent fabrics like muslin and linen in the late 1770s and early 1780s, as part of a shift to Rousseauean "stylized simplicity," she was criticized for favoring imported, British fabrics rather than French-produced silks. But the silk-makers got a boost again in 1780 when Marie-Antoinette's mother, the empress Maria Theresa, passed away, inspiring the French queen to spend liberally on silk mourning dresses. Marie-Antoinette requested gowns in an array of violets, blues, grays, and whites. All of these were typical mourning colors, but the queen insisted on changing gowns at a dizzying rate. After her mourning period, she continued these quick changes, shifting from scarlet "Opera-fire," a color that commemorated the burning of the Paris Opera in 1781, to "prince poo," a greenish-brown hue that was inspired, so to speak, by the newborn prince's diapers.[33] Wealthy nobles and up-and-comers spent the equivalent of thousands of dollars to wear clothing the color of baby poop as a way to show their support for the monarchy and to demonstrate how fashionable they could be.

Although the changing patterns of consumption coincided with technological shifts that made production more efficient, silk-makers were still unable to keep up with the queen's ever-changing desires. As soon as she popularized one color, sending its sales through the roof, she would switch to another hue. Suppliers were often left with bolts of cloth in highly specific, often quite costly, colors whose values declined rapidly, diminishing the possibility of profit. The escalating popularity of monarchical colors and the mounting cost of keeping up with the trends encouraged, on the positive side, a burgeoning consumer society, but on the negative side, a view of the aristocracy as profligate and capricious. As the French Revolution drew nearer, the economic considerations at stake in these types of practices became more acute. In 1788, the French government fell into bankruptcy, and in 1789, they called a meeting of the Estates-General, a political assembly comprised of representatives from the three French "estates": the clergy, the aristocracy, and everybody else (the estimated 95 percent of the population known as the Third Estate). By that point, steep rises in the price of grain meant that bread absorbed between two-thirds and nine-tenths of an urban worker's wages.[34]

The French Revolution was a complex series of political events that transpired over the course of ten years, and no simple explanation will suffice to explain its many twists and turns. To advocate any particular interpretation of the Revolution is to invite contention, confusion, and a lot of detailed theorizing. The most common narrative that people seem to know, which still seems to be the high-school history version, is of class warfare, where the poor rose up to overthrow the aristocracy and the monarchy. This simplified version of events overlooks some of the Revolution's deepest causes and implications, and historians have spilled countless amounts of ink in an attempt to do justice to the complexity of the period.[35]

That said, it is undeniable that revolutionary rhetoric often centered on the distinctions between the "haves" and the "have-nots," and the lines between these two groups were often drawn through symbols that could be expressed through colors and clothing. One macabre trend emerged in 1789, shortly after the infamous storming of the Bastille prison. On July 17, the controller-general of finances, Joseph Foulon de Doué, fled Paris to the country estate of his friend the former lieutenant-general of police, Antoine de Sartine. Thanks to the catastrophic state of the French coffers, Foulon was unpopular. The tax collectors who served under him thought that he was too restrictive and gave him the nickname *âme damnée* (demon, or damned soul), and the poor resented his wealth. Foulon was rumored to have responded to famines with the pithy response, "If the people cannot get bread, let them eat hay," a statement that resembles Marie-Antoinette's similarly apocryphal statement, "Let them eat cake."[36] Foulon, eager to escape the wrath of the Paris mobs, tried to spread rumors of his own death, but he was captured and carried back to Paris, where he was brought to the Place de Grève and was hung from a lamp-post. Unfortunately, the rope from which he was hung kept breaking, and he was ultimately beheaded. Foulon's head was placed on a pike, and his mouth was stuffed with hay. In the wake of this event, revolutionaries signaled devotion to their cause by wearing ribbons dyed with a red color called *sang de Foulon*, or Foulon's blood.

As revolutionary tensions intensified, almost all colors took on a deep political implication. It became possible, at a glance, to identify a person's political loyalties. In the early portion of the revolution, black cockades (ribbons affixed to clothing or hats) signaled sympathies with the aristocracy. The royal family had worn black for much of 1789 in order to mourn the loss of the crown prince, Louis-Joseph, who died that year at the age of seven. Black also signaled those who mourned the loss of the old way of life and its familiar landscape of traditional feudal rights, estate categorizations, and hierarchical privileges. Additionally, black and yellow were the colors of the Austrian Habsburgs, and black was often seen as signifying foreign loyalties, like those presumably felt by Marie-Antoinette and the mercenary soldiers that filled Parisian streets. The revolutionary journalist Camille Desmoulins suggested green as a possible color for the radical cause, but he soon remembered that it was the livery color of the Comte d'Artois, the grandson of Louis XV, who fled the French Revolution (the ultimate sign of treachery in the eyes of the revolutionaries) and later went on to become King Charles X of France during the Bourbon restoration (1824–1830). Purple, which had long been a symbol of royalty, was another color that set the aristocracy and their sympathizers apart from the revolutionaries. Wearing these colors—yellow, black, purple, or green— immediately signified one's loyalty to the monarchy. When Marie-Antoinette returned after the "flight to Varennes," her first clothing order was for garments in Artois green and royal purple.[37] That same year, the *Journal of Fashion and Taste* featured a "counter-Revolutionary suit" for men that consisted of a black jacket, yellow waistcoat, and green cashmere stockings.[38]

Desmoulins' pitch for liberty green may have failed, but the revolutionaries found better options. The most widely recognized French colors are the *tricolore*: red, white, and blue. The precise origin of this family of colors is lost in the mists of time, but according to centuries of lore, St. Martin of Tours was one of the first apostles of Gaul, and Gallic warriors adopted the saint's blue banner as a sign of protection. When Paris became a more important French city, the *oriflamme* (a red banner that was the emblem of Saint Denis, the Parisian patron), joined the blue. During the fourteenth century, when English kings began claiming their sovereignty of France, the red rose of the English house of Lancaster was easily confused with the French *oriflamme*, and in the early fifteenth century, Charles VII, adopted the white color, signifying the protection of the Holy Virgin.[39] Red, white, and blue were the colors of France, but white was the color most readily associated with the king. The royal standard of the King of France had a white background, and white was frequently associated with the Bourbon family. When the French Revolution began, the wearing of red, white, and blue signaled a love of France, but as the king became distinct from the nation, so, too, did the king's colors. Along with green, purple, black, and yellow, pure white came to signify the Bourbon family, the aristocracy, and their interests.

The tricolor cockade, a pleated circle of ribbon in red, white, and blue worn by revolutionaries, came to be the most enduring symbol of the revolutionary cause. In 1789, as tensions initially mounted, the king summoned the renowned Flanders Regiment to the palace as a form of protection. Once they arrived, Louis found the courage to voice his reservations about the Declaration of Rights and other revolutionary decrees. Obviously, this displeased the revolutionaries, and rumors began to circulate in Paris about a reception given by the king's bodyguard to welcome the Flanders Regiment. Apparently, after a number of drunken toasts, the national cockade was said to have been trampled underfoot, and according to the historian William Doyle, "by 4 October all Paris believed that counter-revolutionary orgies at Versailles were the prelude to a new attempt to starve the capital."[40] The following day, a mob of 60,000 stormed the palace at Versailles and led the king and queen on a nine-hour march back to Paris. After the march on Versailles, a popular image of the raucous Flanders Regiment dinner circulated, in which the trampled red, white, and blue cockade of the nation functioned as the antithesis of the foreign, aristocratic black of its opponents. According to the engraver, a single symbolic act against these colors was enough to spark the political action of thousands of people.

In July 1792, it became compulsory for men to wear the tricolor cockade, and selling these ribbons became a booming business. Cockades could be found in virtually every market stall and shop, and female ribbon-sellers stood on the street, selling them by the basketload. In a drive to attract customers, cockade manufacturers often varied their materials. Leather cockades endured, silk ones shone, and wool ones held their color well. Augustin Liébert, a merchant who had declared bankruptcy in 1788, experienced a comeback thanks to the cockade, and he offered a subscription service that guaranteed the delivery of a clean cockade each month.[41] Lucrative though this business may have been, the grip on cockade manufactures tightened as the Revolution progressed. Wearing a silk cockade could prove to be dangerous, not only because of silk's connotation as a luxury good, but also because it was not a colorfast fabric. Getting caught in the rain with a silk cockade meant that one might suddenly, and inadvertently, lose the blue and red coloring of the ribbons and be left standing with only the dreaded royal white. During the Terror, when people were being guillotined *en masse*, the last thing one would want to do would be to wear a monarchical ribbon. Consequently, when the revolutionary representative Jeanbon Saint-André was sent to the rainy coast of western France, he banned all silk cockades, and stressed that only wool ones would be allowed.[42]

In the 1790s, red, white, and blue articles filled the streets, striking the eyes at every turn. As aristocratic hues like flea and prince-poo disappeared, primary colors came to take their place. Even the most mundane of objects became a space for advertising one's political sentiments, and invisible opinions, increasingly, were rendered visible through the symbolic language of color. The nation was written into the very fabric of the population, and donning red, white, and blue became a common means of outwardly expressing one's interior self. In this era, sight was key to identifying whether an individual was friend or foe, and the color one wore could easily mean the difference between life and death.

In 1832, shortly after another French revolution (the July Revolution of 1830), the *Encyclopaedia Americana* was published in Philadelphia, and it included a lengthy entry on the French *tricolore*. Thinking deeply about why small visual symbols like the cockade can have such significant political effects, the author wrote, "Whenever a great principle or interest, good or bad, brings large bodies of men into direct opposition, it is the common and natural course of things for some distinguishing cry or badge to be adopted by all those who espouse the same side; and the more active and absorbing the opposition is, the more significant becomes the sign. There is not time to give or receive long explanations: the questions will be, Are you whig or tory? patriot or royalist? a friend of the government or of revolution? Do you fight for the red or white rose? Do you wear the white riband on your sleeve? &c."[43] In other words, when the stakes are high and when passionate emotions take control, we rely on gut reactions to identify like-minded members of our "tribe." We expect that the interior can, with the aid of a simple color, be inscribed onto our bodies. Complex emotions and beliefs find their shorthand in small emblems, and in intense times, we tend to trust that people are being honest and honorable in the emblems they adopt.

This astute American encyclopedist continued, "The *tricolore* was adopted, originally, by accident, but has become a historical sign; and even if the elder line of the Bourbons could regain any permanent power in France, it could only be by adopting the *tricolore*; i.e. by yielding to the spirit of modern France, by becoming *national*."[44] Small markers, like the *tricolore,* come to bear the weight of our deepest hopes and fears, developing a life of their own. They are like a language, laden with connotations, tones, and hidden meanings, subject to interpretation and redefinition. Colors draw from the shadows of our psyches, giving them the power to bring deep-seated feelings to the fore. Through the simple act of wearing a color, painting a room a certain hue, or selecting objects in a certain shade, we, often unconsciously, reveal the deep essence of who we are. Through the language of color, others receive a vivid portrait of a person's social status, cultural identities, political beliefs, and emotional charges. And through our own choices and the assumptions that we make about the choices of others, it is possible to find deeply buried stereotypes, sympathies, and sentiments.

9

The Gourmand's Gaze:
Visual Eating in the
Postrevolutionary Period

LIKE MANY CHILDREN raised in less-than-ideal conditions, Alexandre-Balthazar-Laurent Grimod de La Reynière harbored a great deal of bitterness toward his mother and father. His mother came from an ancient family with a great name but little money, and she seemed consistently disappointed with her life with her husband, an immensely wealthy tax collector who feared thunder and adored copying the paintings of the great masters. Grimod's birth in November 1758 did not improve their marriage, and the child was born with deformed hands. Ashamed of their son, Grimod's parents spread the rumor that he had fallen into a pigpen, where his hands had fallen victim to hungry hogs. When he grew older, Grimod had fake hands built out of iron and springs, and as an adult, he took joy in heating his metal hands over the fire and telling unsuspecting folks that it was safe to follow suit.[1] He wore a bizarre *toupée* that made him look like a hedgehog, and he went for daily walks through the Les Halles market, wearing a mechanical hat that he could tip at ladies without lifting a hand. In addition to these antics, he was a respected lawyer, theater critic, and man-about-town, known for his art patronage and connoisseurship of food. Overall, Grimod was fiercely intelligent and darkly funny with a bit of a mean streak.

On February 1, 1783, Grimod threw a dinner party that would live in infamy, whose dual purpose was to honor his new mistress and to dishonor his stodgy family. Having ensured that his parents would be out of the house for the evening, Grimod sent out 300 black-edged invitations that resembled funeral notices. On the evening in question, a select number of guests (between sixteen and twenty-two, depending on different accounts) passed a checkpoint where they were required to answer whether they were going to be received by M. de La Reynière, the "oppressor of the people," or M. de La Reynière, the "defender of the people." (Obviously, Grimod considered his father to be the former and himself to be the latter.) If they passed the first test, guests were brought before a man dressed as a judge who collected invitation cards and passed final judgment on the guests' worth. Guests deemed worthy were then allowed to enter a dark room that gave way to a banquet hall lit by 365 lamps. The room was decorated in black, and the centerpiece of the table was a catafalque, the stand that holds the coffin of a person lying in state. Coffins were situated behind the guests' chairs. This funereal theme was designed to poke fun at Grimod's mother, who had failed to mourn the recent death of a woman who was, supposedly, one of her best friends.[2] Unfortunately, little is known about the menu, with the exception of the first course, which consisted of pork, and the second, which consisted of items cooked in oil. These dishes allowed Grimod to make jokes at his father's expense; supposedly, his family was descended from a line of butchers and his father often covered the house in oil as a way of warding off lightning. Afterward, guests were treated to coffee and liqueurs in an adjoining room while they watched electrical demonstrations and a magic-lantern show.[3]

Meanwhile, the overwhelming majority of the guests—which, mind you, numbered in the hundreds—were led to a balustrade overlooking the banquet, where they could watch the macabre festivities below. The dinner lasted until seven the next morning, and spectators were offered biscuits and other light refreshments, but they were not given a full dinner, nor were they allowed to leave. Grimod locked the doors, which (understandably) angered his guests, and one of his colleagues was so upset that he supposedly yelled, "They will send you to the madhouse and strike you from the list of members of the Bar."[4] Grimod was not sent to a mental institution, nor were his legal credentials revoked, but his parents, infuriated by his insolence, had him exiled from Paris. He only returned ten years later, in February 1794, at the height of the Terror.

Notorious as it was, this wasn't Grimod's only funeral feast. On July 7, 1812, well after the Revolution, Grimod staged another macabre feast. In the wake of Napoleonic defeat, Grimod defied his mother's wishes and married his mistress of twenty-four years, Adélaïde Feuchère. The couple and their adopted daughter packed up and moved to a country house, where they began a new life, away from their usual Parisian social circles. Ever the jokester, Grimod designed a second funeral feast, this time in honor of his own death, as a way to commemorate the passing of his old life. A month prior to the feast, he locked himself up in his family home and spread rumors that he was ill. At the end of Grimod's confinement, his friends were devastated to hear that their comrade had departed this world. His grieving widow invited them to the funeral, and mourners arrived to find the coffin laid out in state. As guests stood about discussing their friend's life, doors swung open to reveal a table draped in black with a coffin for a centerpiece. At the head of the table sat Grimod himself, who called the shocked mourners to dinner, explaining, "This way I am certain to have dined with my friends." His true death came twenty-five years later.[5]

Grimod de La Reynière seems to have jumped the gun with his 1783 black feast.[6] If lighter colors marked the court of Louis XVI and Marie-Antoinette, in the wake of the French Revolution, "black triumphed," and "a colourless male society" dressed in a way that declared decency, austerity, and gravity. The historian Daniel Roche noted, "The soberly dressed bourgeoisie manifested the virtues appropriate to capital and to work."[7] Many people had lost friends, family, and acquaintances to the Revolution, while others had been disappointed politically. War-weary and emotionally drained from ten years of turmoil, many people found the restrained civility characteristic of nineteenth-century bourgeois culture an attractive alternative to vitriol and violence. Having survived an era when speaking out too brashly could cost you your life, people had learned the value of silence, restraint, and caution.

On the other hand, as the specter of war dissipated (albeit briefly, since France would be rocked by a revolution virtually every fifteen years throughout the nineteenth century), nobles returned to France, to live alongside their wealthy bourgeois neighbors. One of the lasting effects of the French Revolution was a shift in social values, such that one's status was no longer determined exclusively by birth. Wealth increasingly came to determine one's place in the world, and new opportunities were open to merchants, bankers, and other individuals of their ilk. People with adequate money and leisure were eager to enjoy what their money could buy, and, in the words of the historian Jean-Paul Aron, after the Revolution, "a passion for pleasure and self-indulgence affect[ed] the exhausted society like a madness, reconciling Royalists and Republicans."[8]

One of the areas in which this self-indulgence took hold was in eating. During the French Revolution, shortages had been the norm, and one often had to *diner par coeur* ("dine by heart," meaning "to do without"). Even if a person had the means to dine out, it hadn't always been a pleasant experience. Grimod bitterly remembered having to dine in silence during the Terror, for fear that he would say the wrong thing and be denounced to the Revolutionary tribunal.[9] Once the clouds lifted, his first aim was to "save French cookery from the shipwreck of the Revolution."[10] He wasn't alone in this mission, and the new science of "gastronomy" took hold of the nineteenth century, first in France, and soon, all over Europe. Today, if we use the term "gastronomy" at all, it generally refers to fine dining, or a somewhat upscale eating experience (think of the trend for gastropubs). But in the nineteenth century, gastronomy was considered a science with a wide-ranging scope. In Chapter Six, you encountered one of gastronomy's pioneers, Jean-Anthelme Brillat-Savarin. Here's how he defined its breadth: "Gastronomy is the reasoned comprehension of all that relates to the nourishment of man," and as such, it pertains "to natural history . . . to physics . . . to chemistry . . . to cookery . . . to commerce . . . to political economy, through its value as a source of revenue and a means of exchange between nations."[11] In other words, the science of gastronomy extended its reach to anything even remotely having to do with food. While the indulgence in culinary pleasures carried significant class distinctions, all human life was touched by the science.

Gastronomical literature is a thing of beauty. If you want entertainment, then you can certainly find it in the pages of Grimod de La Reynière, Brillat-Savarin, William Kitchiner, Launcelot Sturgeon (a pseudonym), Dick Humelbergius Secundus (also a pseudonym), and their culinary companions. Gastronomy texts ranged widely in genre, and a single work often

mixed dialogues, medical language, recipes, informal anecdotes, scientific asides, gossip, rambling accounts of dreams, and
poetry. Pure miscellanies, these works often featured sharp wit,
incisive social commentary, and amusing turns of phrase. Just to
give you a few examples (and truly, these are just a few), here are
some of my favorites:

- GRIMOD DE LA REYNIÈRE: "One must take possession
  of wines as they leave the vat, just as, in days past, one
  would take possession of a young girl as she left the
  convent."[12]

- LAUNCELOT STURGEON: "If either want of appetite, or
  want of sense, should lead you into a warm discussion
  during dinner—don't gesticulate with your knife in
  hand, as if you were preparing to cut your antagonist's
  throat."[13]

- WILLIAM KITCHINER: "There is not a more absurd
  Vulgar Error, than the often quoted proverb, that
  Cheese is a surly Elf, Digesting all things, but itself."[14]

- THE ALDERMAN: "I cannot refrain from offering a few
  remarks on the engrossing subject of Toothpicks. So
  poetical a theme calls for higher powers, perhaps, than I
  may modestly lay claim to."[15]

- W. BLANCHARD JERROLD: "Sir, the man who would
  mangle a capon would kill a child."[16]

Aside from serving up a healthy dose of humor, gastronomical writings illustrate the two postrevolutionary tendencies I
mentioned above: 1) the valorization of civility and certain forms
of restraint; and 2) the desire to indulge in material pleasures.

These food manifestos are exceedingly detailed, both about the joys of food and the manner in which it should be eaten. Gastronomers adhered to strict rules about everything from meat carving to conversation, leaving no stone unturned. Even chewing was subject to scrutiny: "It has been calculated by a learned physician, who devoted the greatest part of a long life to experiments upon his own stomach, that a mouthful of solid meat requires thirty-two bites, of a perfect set of teeth, to prepare it for deglutition."[17] It may be tempting to think of gastronomers as gluttonous hedonists, but they weren't just the foodie equivalent of libertines. They demanded restraint, discernment, and etiquette, and their requirements were quite strict. Grimod acknowledged the rigors of gourmandism, explaining, "The Gourmand's Code contains an abundance of rules that one must follow so as not to seem like a savage, but which would lead a reserved gentleman who observed these laws faithfully to die of starvation at a four-course dinner."[18]

It would be quite natural to wonder why the gourmands thought it was necessary to have all these rules if even the most devout eater couldn't possibly observe them. Rules were supposed to enhance the experience of the dining experience. With proper chewing technique, one could savor all the juices of the finest pheasant; with the right carving technique, the best cuts of meat made it to the table in prime condition; and with the right types of conversation, one could socialize without being distracted from the food. Another significant aspect of gastronomical rules, though, was to quickly delineate different groups of people. Those who knew the proper way to enjoy the finest delicacies were set apart by their elite knowledge and elite tastes. The rules made it easy to identify those who didn't live up to the title of a true gourmand. A man whose cook boiled his pig instead of roasting it? Shame! A man who canceled a dinner invitation at the last minute? Shame! A woman who drank to excess or indulged in hearty cuts of meat? Even more shame!

As I mentioned in the last chapter, the visual signifiers of status changed radically over the course of the eighteenth century. This declining trust in the visual meant that "the eighteenth century had to invent new, more subjective (and ultimately arbitrary) standards of differentiation."[19] Consequently, "taste," as an intimate proximity sense, became a powerful metaphor for a person's internal capacities for aesthetic appreciation.[20] In "Of the Standard of Taste" (1757), the philosopher David Hume argued that beauty is not inherent in objects; it's a subjective trait. But, he continued, "it must be allowed, that there are certain qualities in objects, which are fitted by nature to produce those particular feelings."[21] In other words, Hume expounded that individual experiences may be subjective, but there is still a durable, universal Standard of Taste that determines what is beautiful. This argument may sound somewhat like Castel, who argued that pleasure had an objective basis, but Hume didn't think that everyone should or would experience everything the same way. Instead, the universal standard was more like a consensus that could only be figured out over time. Things that were truly beautiful would last, and things that were faddish or coarse would disappear from the record. For example, van Gogh may not have been appreciated in his own era, but over time, we have come to see the value of his works. While only time would tell what good taste was, Hume did think that people with more refined and practiced senses would appreciate beauty in their own time. Those best equipped to recognize lasting value had achieved "the perfection of every sense or faculty."[22] Good taste often accompanied wealth in the social world of the eighteenth and early nineteenth centuries, but ultimately, it ran deeper than money.

"Taste" may have been the operative metaphor, but epicures'

notions of taste were actually quite expansive, extending to all of the senses. Launcelot Sturgeon wrote: ". . . all the senses should be in unison with that of taste: his eye should be penetrating, to direct him in the first choice or rejection of what is before him; his ear quick, to catch, from the farthest end of the table, the softest whisper in praise of any particular dish; his extended nostrils, uncontaminated with snuff, should faithfully convey the savoury intelligence of what surrounds him; and his ample tongue should dilate each copious mouthful, both to protract the enjoyment of mastication and to aid the powers of deglutition."[23] Similarly, Grimod proclaimed that "all his senses must work in constant concert with that of taste, for he must contemplate his food before it even nears his lips."[24]

Notably, there was a huge visual component to the new regimes of "taste" in the eighteenth and nineteenth centuries. Being "seen" in society and "keeping up appearances" were both important. Exterior markers like etiquette, refinement, and comportment hinted at something much more fundamental and intrinsic to one's being. Appearances may have been deceiving, but they were still the expression of the deeper proclivities of the soul. A dinner's visual appearance transitively revealed a great deal about the taste of the host. Grimod argued that, just as all women's complexions could be divided into dark and light, dinners could be divided into "brown" and "blond." A brown dinner would be composed of ragouts, stews, hashes, stewed turnips, and other items more properly belonging to "popular cooking than to *haute cuisine*." A gourmand would immediately recognize the inferiority of such a dinner, because brown foods were easier to make, and the dark colors made it easier to cover up mistakes.[25] A blond dinner, on the other hand, was comprised of "those dainty and subtle dishes whose color comes closer to white than to any other—like Béchamels, quenelles, chicken fricassees, cucumber émincés, chicken *à la reine*, sautés *au suprême*, braised veal garnished with cockscombs, and a multitude of other such complex and difficult dishes."[26] (In case you were wondering about Grimod's taste in ladies, a racial component extended through his treatment of both food and people.)[27] Color revealed the deeper qualities of the chef and the host, and taste and appearance were inseparable parts of the same process. Taste, for Grimod, relied as much on the eyes as on the tongue.

True gourmands appreciated spectacle, and there's a reason that Grimod was both a gourmand and a theater critic. As his funerary feasts attest, dining was an opportunity to put on a show. Even the more mundane gastronomes, who didn't indulge in Grimod's outrageous theatrics, still valorized the spectacle of the table. In theory, every element of the meal, down to the smallest gesture, was choreographed. In *Essays, Moral, Philosophical, and Stomachical,* Launcelot Sturgeon walked readers through each step of a dinner in detail: "To commence with your entrance into the dining room—don't stand bowing at the door, as if you had a petition to present; but stride confidently up to the lady of the house, and so close before you make your obeisance, that you nearly thrust your head into her face."[28] He then continued to explain what to do when dinner was announced, when to be seated, when to get seconds, when to get wine, when to drink the wine, when to speak, when to carve the meat—a task that, if tackled improperly, could result in having a mangled turkey deposited in a neighbor's lap (should this happen, Sturgeon advised, do not apologize)—when to ask for dishes to be passed, when to bid the ladies goodnight, and when to stretch the legs after dinner. Luckily for his readers, Sturgeon left off when the food should be digested and passed. The gastronomic experience depended integrally on the presence of all these rules, rites, and rituals, and because of them, it was possible to exhibit one's good taste.

Guests' behavior may have been a large part of the spectacle, but the foods served by gastronomes were no less impressive. The legendary chef Marie-Antoine Carême (1783–1833) produced some of the most exquisite postrevolutionary marvels. During the French Revolution, cooks had moved from the kitchens of the aristocracy to the public fora of restaurants and taverns. Under Napoleon, when aristocrats returned, the situation was more complex, with some chefs choosing to remain in the public world, others opting to work for private households, and others still deciding to work on a freelance basis, catering *extras*, or special banquets. This period of political shifts fostered instability in certain contexts, but it also encouraged social mobility. Thanks to the many opportunities available to talented cooks like Carême, this was the era of the first "celebrity chefs." Carême began his career around the age of ten as a kitchen boy, and in 1798 he became an apprentice at a pastry shop. He quickly moved through the ranks, first serving as a private chef to the diplomat Charles Maurice de Talleyrand-Périgord (whom Napoleon once called "shit in a silk stocking"), then becoming a bakery owner, and eventually working as a freelance chef for the finest households in France, England, Austria, and Russia.

Among Carême's most noted talents were his *pièces montées*. These *pièces* were large, sculptural centerpieces made out of edible substances like sugar and marzipan that weren't actually intended for consumption. *Pièces montées* had previously had a place in French cooking, but Carême's *pièces* went well beyond their predecessors in terms of scale, number, and detail. In 1815, he published *Picturesque Pastry*, a book that contained over one hundred designs for *pièces montées*, which took their inspiration from "pavilions, rotundas, temples, ruins, towers, belvederes, forts, waterfalls, fountains, pleasure palaces, cottages, windmills, and hermitages."[29] Carême maintained that architecture was one

A "Grand Chinese Pavilion" designed by Carême.

Grand Pavillon chinois

of the five fine arts—alongside painting, sculpture, music, and poetry—and that it could be effectively explored through pastry. In fact, he went so far as to argue, "The principal branch of architecture is confectionery," a claim that many architects would probably be flabbergasted to learn.[30] For Carême, the two disciplines were so intertwined that he presumed to publish not only on culinary matters but also on architecture. In the 1820s, he followed up his best-selling cookbooks with *Projects for the Architectural Embellishment of St. Petersburg* (1821) and *Projects for the Architectural Embellishment of Paris* (1826). These were fairly expensive and did not sell as well as his cookery manuals, but for the public, the link between Carême's two lifelong passions was quite clear. While flavors, odors, and textures mattered to

Carême, the eye had its own delights, many of which had little to do with the act of tasting. The dinner table was the place to display some of the finest arts of humankind and where architecture from all over the world could be assembled for all to see.

Carême is perhaps best known for his show-stopping centerpieces, but I should point out that he was responsible for major olfactory and gustatory shifts as well. Paul Metzner has argued that Carême dispensed with overpowering aromas, which had traditionally hidden the foul odors of improperly stored foods. Instead, he favored simple and subtle scents like orange, rose, and lemon, a gustatory preference that resembled the concurrent olfactory shift to lighter perfumes. Similarly, in flavor, he stressed the harmonious blending of a few key flavors, such that a good dish came to be signified by restraint rather than of an assortment of costly, motley mixtures of rare ingredients.[31]

It was only the finest families that could afford spectacles quite as grand as those of Carême, but the dissemination of information about cooking was greater than ever before. Middle-class households could buy Carême's cookbooks at 10 francs (which was not cheap, but was within the realm of possibility). Gastronomical newspapers and manuals were available at affordable prices, and eating out was a much more common practice than it was fifty years earlier. Even when they couldn't host the finest dinners, bourgeois families emulated elements of high dining. Culinary manuals taught hosts to make the most of the ingredients that they could afford and to use flowers and plants as centerpieces to make the table look full. In *A New System of Domestic Cookery* (1806), the author Mrs. Rundell advised using the eyes to shape the gustatory experience. "The brighter the things the better they appear," she wrote. "Jellies, different coloured things, and flowers add to the beauty of the table."[32] The productions may have been on a smaller scale, but when guests came to dinner, even middle-class families put on a show.

The historian Andrea Broomfield has argued that industrialization made nineteenth-century society even more fluid, and middle-class men's work carried them outside the home, increasingly making women the rulers of the private sphere. In America, a whole genre of literature had developed by the 1830s to teach women how to perform their duties at home, and culinary experts successfully convinced genteel and bourgeois women to take up cooking.[33] The many cookbooks that appeared in this period aimed to help the new middle-class wife "feel more confident and secure with her status by making visible to her the seemingly invisible codes of conduct and protocols to which she was now expected to subscribe."[34] By the 1860s, families were increasingly aware of what their food choices said about their socioeconomic status, and "what one ate was not necessarily what one most craved."[35] For example, eating onions, leeks, or garlic marked one as a lower-class individual. Blue cheese was considered to be in poor taste as well, since its mold *surely* indicated that it was in a state of decay. And indeed, cheese in general was looked down upon in most polite society because, like salad, it was thought to be rough on the stomach.[36] On the other hand, one wanted game on the table, because in England until 1831, it was only available to those with shooting rights (hence, the landed classes). The cultural capital of a good pheasant or grouse wore on for a long time. As with clothing, food made otherwise intangible social boundaries quite visible.

But perhaps the most prominent element of nineteenth-century visual eating was the tendency to dominate nature by garnishing one's food or metamorphosing it so that it no longer resembled the original source. Cookbooks like Russell Thacher Trall's *New*

Hydropathic Cook-book (1873) pointed out how "brutalizing, sensualizing, and degrading" traditional depictions of animals were, and instead sought to include "engravings which lead the mind away from scenes or thoughts of blood and slaughter."[37] Many books advocated new recipes for foods like beef balls, meat croquettes, and oyster patties, teaching cooks to transform meat into regular, nonnaturalistic shapes.[38] The daily meals of middle-class families were much simpler than those they hosted for guests, and often, the abundance of food left over after a party would be served for days thereafter. Garnishes allowed recycled versions of half-eaten foods to look dainty and palatable, and families strove for a style of cooking that food historian Dena Attar has called "economical display."[39] It looked elegant and artful, serving as a treat for the eyes, but it still made use of basic ingredients like potatoes, peas, and cheap cuts of meat. By effacing the "natural" look of the food and jazzing up appearances, middle-class dishes were elevated above the food consumed by the lower classes, which were described as "savory messes." Inventiveness and imagination were the elements that elevated the middle-class table above its simpler, more rustic, and less spectacular counterparts.

Victorians are generally stereotyped for having an aversion to things that referred too openly to the body. In most cases, this stereotype extends to debates about their sexuality—or supposed lack thereof—but it can also be read in light of their food practices. The unnatural look of nineteenth-century food, "which put so much distance between the genteel diner and the coarse productions of nature," could signify, Attar suggests, "a contemporary inability to deal honestly with bodily appetites."[40] This book is not the place for me to sort out the facts and fictions about Victorian sexuality, but Attar's claims do point toward a tendency that remains quite strong in modern America. As foods became more "unnatural," it seems that many people became more accustomed to seeing them this way, and many Americans today have become, either willingly or in many cases unconsciously, unable to handle the corporeal realities of their food. Meat in grocery stores is plastic-wrapped and cut into shapes that no longer resemble the animal. Supermarkets rarely sell meat with the animals' heads still attached, and many people couldn't tell you from which part of the body a porterhouse steak comes or what goes into hot dogs. Actually, we may willingly try to ignore this latter bit of information. Furthermore, we have a number of false understandings of our food. For example, people often say that they want their meat cooked well done so that it won't be "bloody." In fact, there is no blood in raw meat; the animal's blood is drained when it's killed. The red juices are water mixed with a substance called myoglobin, which is a protein that stores oxygen in muscle tissues. And even the most ardent meat eaters often have an aversion to seeing animals butchered.[41]

I can make similar arguments about food transmutations when it comes to vegetarian food. Mashed potatoes, tofu blocks, seitan, and tempeh in no way resemble their origins. But this overwhelming desire to avoid the "backstory" of our food does highlight some important social characteristics. In 1939 the sociologist Norbert Elias argued that over time Europeans (and by proxy, Americans) have undergone a "civilizing process" whereby their codes of conduct have become more and more strict. Social boundaries are enforced by strong codes of conduct that separate the "civilized" elite from the "uncivilized" masses. As part of this process, people have "sought to suppress in themselves everything that they feel to be of an animalic character," and "they have likewise suppressed such characteristics in their food."[42] While someone in the Middle Ages would have found it a great pleasure to carve a whole boar with all of his dinner guests watching, now many people would be aghast if an animal were served with eyes, ears, and snout still intact. Elias argued that over time people have developed increased "thresholds of repugnance" that make them more inclined to experience disgust when something is too close to an animal or is something they consider "uncivilized" or "barbaric." (Obviously, these are culturally loaded terms, which is precisely what Elias wanted to suggest.)

The transformation of nineteenth-century foodstuffs fits into this narrative, because as upper-class food became more visual and as middle-class food followed, it became more "civilized" and "normal" for food to bear no resemblance to its source. When dishes contravened these new norms, they were considered "low" or "base," a sentiment that, with time, transformed into "disgusting" or "repugnant." The people who were "civilized" grew further and further from the processes of production and the coarse realities of blood, guts, and the body. Accordingly, the metamorphosis of foods into chicken nuggets, plastic-wrapped breasts on Styrofoam platters, and tubes of sausage offers consumers distance from the circumstances by which it appears on our plates. These thresholds of repugnance provide psychological protection from the types of "animalistic" behavior that the polite elements of the modern world have increasingly seemed to reject.

When it came to the poor in the nineteenth century, though, the sight of meat—bloody or no—would have been of little concern since their diets were almost entirely comprised of starch. As the price of sugar dropped and as the amount of time that working families had for cooking decreased, many workers began "convenience eating," which included meals of cheap store-purchased bread, jam, hot tea with sugar, and other calorie-heavy but nutritionally barren foods. Porridge and potatoes were common fare. The folks of the upper and middle classes may have increasingly focused on visual presentation, but in the lower economic brackets, diet tended to hinge more on the invisible aspects of food. The next chapter will focus much more on food adulteration practices, but suffice it to say that the poor had to be wary that their bread did not include plaster, chalk, or other harmful substances, and they had to be vigilant that the candies their children consumed did not contain poisonous additives. (Between thirty and forty children fell victim to the wares of the same candy seller in the mid nineteenth century. It was later discovered that his confections contained arsenic, copper, lead, iron, and zinc.)[43]

In this period, people also became much more aware of the invisible agents of illness that could contaminate their bodies. The germ theory of disease was finally gaining traction in the nineteenth century, and people began to understand that what they couldn't see in their food might have been just as important as what they could. Cholera was a fairly common affliction during the century, and it was primarily caused by drinking water that had been contaminated by the feces of an infected person. After a severe outbreak in London in 1854, the physician John Snow identified the public water pump as the source of the infection, and he used microscopic observations to prove his claims. A poem from the popular comic paper *Punch* shows that common folk in London were well aware of the hidden dangers in their river water:

> *All beside thy sludgy waters,*
> *All beside thy reeking ooze. . .*
> *All her foul abominations*
> *Into thee the City throws;*
> *These pollutions, ever churning,*
> *To and fro thy current flows.*
> *And from thee is brew'd our porter —*
> *Thee, thou guilty, puddle, sink!*
> *Thou, vile cesspool, art the liquor*
> *Whence is made the beer we drink!*[44]

An 1850 cartoon depicted a single drop of Thames water containing bugs, death, pestilence, and more than enough cause for alarm, and the figure of "Father Thames" was often portrayed as a muddy, water-dripping old man with a dead cat on his head.

By the 1870s, the middle classes had adopted new styles of dining and the lower classes were keeping their eyes peeled (so to speak) for invisible dangers, but the science of gastronomy had begun to lose its steam. At the beginning of the century, gourmands depicted a world of delight. Discernment and enjoyment combined to create ideal experiences, and nothing was beyond the bounds of taste. This philosophy depended on the new, flourishing consumer world, but there was a paradox at the heart of gourmandism that became increasingly evident as the nineteenth century progressed. Gastronomy popularized the love of food, but at its heart, it also advocated a form of elitism that was incompatible with popularization. According to men of taste, they alone had the palates to appreciate the aesthetic delights of the world. Still, every bourgeois family sought to reproduce those delights on their own tables. Gastronomy, in many ways, resisted the very commercial ideology that had made it possible in the first place.[45] People continued to want to eat well and spectacularly, but the philosophical core of gourmandism began to fade away.

By the end of the nineteenth century, those who continued to dedicate themselves to the strict aesthetic philosophy of gourmandism started to come under scrutiny, and in certain circles, gourmandism gained subversive associations. In Chapter Seven, I introduced Joris-Karl Huysmans' 1884 decadent novel *Against the Grain*. This book centered on the life of the fictional Jean des Esseintes, a wealthy eccentric who loathed nineteenth-century bourgeois life. To escape his misery, des Esseintes retreated to a remote country home, where he tried to regulate every detail of his sensory world. Taking inspiration from Grimod's funerary dinners, the book includes a mourning feast as part of des Esseintes' program of sensory indulgence. This feast featured rye bread, olives, caviar, black pudding, chocolate creams, plum puddings, and various other black foods. The table was covered with a black cloth and decorated with baskets of black violets. Guests drank red wine from tinted glasses. To spice things up, "the guests were waited on by naked negresses wearing only slippers and stockings in cloth of silver embroidered with tears," and a hidden orchestra played funeral marches. Fittingly, the invitations had described this somber event as "the farewell dinner to a temporarily dead virility."[46]

While Grimod took refuge in the delights of the senses, praising spectacle and food as one of the main ways to improve culture, science, and society, Huysmans depicted it as one of the last resorts for a man who had lost the ability to relate to society and appreciate the pleasures of the real world. Grimod had gathered crowds for an elaborate social joke, but for the jaded des Esseintes, the funerary feast was no joke. It marked the death of his interest in anything other than personal pleasure. The self-indulgent des Esseintes lacked all the qualities that Grimod had insisted were crucial in a good host. As he dug deeper into his pleasure-seeking tendencies, des Esseintes' "contempt for humanity deepened.... Already, he was dreaming of a refined solitude, a comfortable desert, a motionless ark in which to seek refuge from the unending deluge of human stupidity."[47] Huysmans did not use the sensory pleasures of the feast to illuminate good taste, strong character, or adept sociability. Indeed, Des Esseintes' sensory indulgences were the antithesis of sociability.

Having read *Against the Grain,* the critic Jules Barbey d'Aurevilly remarked, "After such a book, there is nothing left for the author but to choose between the barrel of a pistol or the foot of the cross."[48] This is a fairly harsh take on the situation, but it does highlight the fact that not everyone appreciated the new world of sensory delights made possible by postrevolutionary consumer society. The nineteenth century might have made new experiences available to everyone who could afford them, but as commentators like Barbey d'Aurevilly pointed out, the true cost of these experiences may not have been readily apparent.

⋘ 10 ⋙

Digesting Nature:
Exotic Animal Dining Clubs in
Nineteenth-Century England

IT WAS NOT UNCOMMON for William Buckland (1784–1856) to become excessively animated during his lectures at the University of Oxford. Passionate about nature to the point of always having natural history oddities on his person, Buckland delivered his show-and-tell lectures with undeniable vigor. His colleague Nevil Storey-Maskelyne reported that "Dr. Buckland's wonderful conversational powers were as incommunicable as the bouquet of a bottle of champagne," and students described him as effervescent.[1] Humorous, passionate, charismatic, and folksy, Buckland ran contrary to the stereotypical image of the stodgy, tweed-clad Oxfordian and instead seems to have been more like a nineteenth-century version of Bill Nye the Science Guy. Many years after the fact, Sir Henry Acland, one of Buckland's former students, remembered Buckland in the lecture room: "He had in his hand a huge hyena's skull. He suddenly dashed down the steps—rushed, skull in hand, at the first undergraduate on the front bench—and shouted, 'What rules the world?' The youth, terrified, threw himself against the next back seat, and answered not a word. He rushed then on me, pointing the hyena full in my face—'What rules the world?' 'Haven't an idea,' I said. 'The stomach, sir,' he cried (again mounting his rostrum), 'rules the world. The great ones eat the less, and the less the lesser still.'"[2]

Buckland was a man of his word, and when he declared his devotion to the stomach, he was not exaggerating or using metaphorical language. In fact, he was quite well known for his food choices. Toasted mice, crocodile, and battered hedgehog were only a few of the delights that he reported sampling, and these were some of the more common items that crossed his table. Arguably, the weirdest thing that Buckland ever ate was part of the embalmed heart of Louis XIV. The heart belonged to Lord Harcourt of Nuneham, who had purchased it while he was in Paris during the French Revolution. Nuneham, who normally kept the sliver stored in a silver casket, showed the item to Buckland, who promptly mused, "I have eaten many strange things but have never eaten the heart of a king." Before Nuneham or any of the other guests could stop him, Buckland had indulged his whim, and the Sun King's heart had disappeared down the professor's gullet.[3]

Buckland may have been something of an eccentric, but he was respected in the scientific community, and guests relished their visits to the Buckland home and frequently wrote about their enlightening experiences at Buckland's table. John Ruskin, the preeminent art critic, lamented the occasion that he had to miss "a delicate toast of mice," and remembered with delight one summer morning when Buckland invited two Carolina lizards to join the party so that his guests would not be bothered by flies.[4]

Buckland was certainly not alone in his tendency to indulge in unusual eating practices. His son Frank, who became a prominent Victorian naturalist, carried on the family interest in edible oddities. Through an arrangement with the Regent's Park Zoo, Frank had regular access to supplies of exotic meats, and guests to his home could expect such delicacies as elephant trunk soup, roast giraffe, or partially rotted panther.[5] Charles Darwin was a member of the "Glutton Club" at Cambridge, a group that met weekly to seek out and eat "strange flesh," and he eagerly described how he ate the same foods as native inhabitants during his travels in South America. Among other sumptuous morsels, he was treated to armadillo (which apparently tastes like duck) and a twenty-pound rodent, which he claimed was "the best meat I ever tasted."[6] Sir Richard Owen, the Hunterian Professor of the Royal College of Surgeons, and his wife Caroline enjoyed delicacies like sea snake and ostrich, and Charles Waterton, an independently wealthy naturalist, enjoyed ant-bear, toucan, and howler monkey.

In 1826, Sir Arthur de Capell Brooke formed a dining club composed of world travelers called the Raleigh Travellers' Club, which later merged with the Royal Geographical Society (because if you can't eat 'em, join 'em). The group's aim was "to collect, digest, and print . . . new interesting facts and discoveries."[7] Digestion was taken quite literally, and each member was expected "to present any scarce foreign game, fish, fruits, wines, etc., as a means of adding greatly to the interest of the dinners." Their inaugural dinner consisted of a haunch of reindeer, Swedish brandy, North Cape *Flad Bröd* (rye cake), Gammel Ost (a Norwegian cheese), and preserved cloudberries.[8] Numerous scientific societies like the Zoological Society and the Acclimatization Society of Great Britain followed suit, regularly holding extravagant exotic animal dinners, and private menagerie owners bred exotic livestock with eating in mind.

Certainly, the average Briton was not eating kangaroo steamer or sea slugs, but these exotic dining practices were fairly common among the educated elite. By 1866, the Acclimatization Society boasted 270 members, all of whom were eager to try these out-of-the-ordinary animals at their regular meetings. Add to this number the hundreds of men who participated in similar dinners at other clubs and multiply it by the number of meetings—the Royal Geographical Society alone held over 200 meetings between the 1850s and 1870s—and you have a large population, or at least a high frequency, of upper-class people eating exotic foods.

On one level, it might be easy to chalk this up to eccentricity, extravagance, or a desire for (quite literal) conspicuous consumption. But on another, these dinners became trendy at precisely the moment when the Regent's Park Zoo opened (1828), when science was increasingly concerned with classification and taxonomy, and when people were deeply worried about the ability to feed the booming populations of growing cities like London. A more generous historical perspective is to consider these dinners as one of the ways that curious men and women handled the unique mixture of excitement and anxiety that came along with modernity. As learned individuals across Britain grappled with vast amounts of new information about animals, naturalists sought inventive means by which they could experience and understand them. Eating became an important way for people to engage with new ideas about the animal kingdom and humanity's relationship to it.

Exotic eaters like Buckland considered taste to have the power to convey objective truths about nature. While eating could have personal, intimate, and emotional effects, it also was an effective way to discern the truths of nature and to interact with the world outside oneself. For many naturalists, a moral interaction with an animal was one that maximized its utility to man. Instead of focusing on preservation, conservation, or habitat research, the early zoo served as storehouse for animals who would eventually be dissected.[9] Natural history at that time primarily focused on the use of taxidermied specimens and on osteology, the study of bones, meaning that meat would have been the least useful part of the animal, scientifically speaking. With the amount of large animals in the zoo, this meant that tons of flesh were literally being discarded yearly. Some of this meat was sold to cat food vendors, but for the most part, its disposal was at the discretion of the naturalists overseeing the dissection.[10] Many naturalists saw the potential of this meat, and in the search to make science moral, they decided to make use of the whole animal in order to discover new food sources for the hungry.

Several decades before the rise of the zoo, the English cleric Thomas Malthus wrote his notorious *Essay on the Principle of Population* (written and published in 1798 but revised continuously until 1830), which argued, contrary to the optimistic attitudes of earlier Enlightenment thinkers, that the limits of human progress and human population were not boundless. Instead, he prophesied that any prosperity leads to a rise in population, which necessarily leads to food shortages, an increased labor force, and a decrease in wages. Poverty and starvation were the necessary outcome of this "natural" principle of population, and one of the only ways that humans could combat it was to show moral restraint and keep themselves from indulging in sexual congress. According to Malthus, the poor should not be given aid, since this was a natural cycle, and welfare was simply a stopgap. In other words, starvation was God's way of teaching humans to practice abstinence.

For more than half a century, Malthus was the name on reformers' tongues, and a great deal of political, social, and religious attention was turned toward the question of food supplies for the poor. Such debates were not idle speculation; food in this period was scarce for a great many people. The Irish Potato Famine of 1845–1852 killed 1 million people and forced another million to emigrate, causing the total population of Ireland to drop by nearly 25 percent. Rapid urbanization and industrialization meant a significant rise in individuals who were, for the first time, separated from agricultural production and traditional modes of food distribution. Even though wages rose steadily throughout the century, so did prices, and malnutrition was common among working populations who had an imbalanced, carbohydrate-heavy diet and little time to eat during excessively long factory shifts. For many workers in British cities, the questions of where the next meal was coming from and what it would consist of were not negligible.

There was also a considerable question not only about food supplies in general but more particularly about the availability of Britons' favorite part of a meal: meat. Throughout the nineteenth century, numerous British cookbook writers, naturalists, gourmets, and dieticians lauded both the quality and quantity of British livestock. An 1866 cookbook reported that each resident of London ate 107 pounds of butcher's meat per year while Parisians consumed only 87 pounds, and, drawing from the "good authority" of a French correspondent, English food writer Peter Lund Simmonds cited British meat consumption to be a half-pound per diem while the French languished under the "astonishingly small" one-sixth of a pound daily.[11] Given the long-standing rivalry between the British and the French, these comparisons should not be taken as accurate portrayals of the French situation, but they do demonstrate the way in which Britons rhetorically used meat to define themselves. To be British was to love meat and to consume it in great quantities.

This principle can be even more clearly seen in the proliferation of eating clubs like the Sublime Society of Beef-Steaks, which was founded in 1735 by Henry Rich (often known as John), a "celebrated harlequin and machinist."[12] Members of the SSBS wore blue coats that bore an insignia of a gridiron (a metal frame used for grilling over an open fire) and the motto "Beef and liberty." The membership was capped at twenty-four, and all members had insignia rings that also bore the words "Beef and liberty," reinforcing the group's dedication to the oddly inter-twined English values of freedom and bovine flesh. The club experienced great success—so much so, in fact, that the Prince of Wales joined in 1785 to celebrate the great English protein. The "Rump-Steak or Liberty Club," which also called itself the Patriots Club, was a similar society that was well known for its opposition to Sir Robert Walpole, the first British prime minister. Comprised primarily of disgruntled aristocrats who saw Walpole as a *parvenu*, the Rump-Steak Club took British beef as a symbol of blue blood and British heritage. Clearly, from the eighteenth-century perspective, it was possible to judge the wealth and wel-fare of a nation by the availability of its meat. But for all the tales of tastiness and praise of overflowing pastures that circulated in cookbooks and domestic manuals, the reality could not match. One writer bemoaned the problems associated with the popular-ity of meat, remarking, "Beef and mutton, and mutton and beef, no matter what their price, John Bull will not dispense with; and although they are 40 or 50 percent dearer now than they were ten years ago, and although we import animals largely from abroad, and our cattle-breeders do their best to meet the demand, cattle and sheep will not increase and multiply fast enough to bring down the price for the consumer."[13]

And if quantity and price weren't sufficiently complicating fac-tors, there was also the question of quality. The nineteenth century was rife with accusations of food adulteration. Watered-down milk was made to look like cream with the addition of pulped calves' brains, or it was also possible to thicken it by tossing in a handful of snails, whose mucus would cause a delightful froth to form. Tea was laced with iron filings, and bread was filled with ground bones, white lead, chalk, plaster of Paris, sawdust, and lime. Supposedly, sausages often contained horsemeat, which, being of a dense con-sistency, helped keep the links firm, and cat meat was popularly suspected to be a key ingredient of street vendors' pies.[14] In 1846, the character of Sweeney Todd, the most notorious and sinister food adulterer, made his first appearance in the penny dreadful *The String of Pearls*. Todd, the demon barber who murdered his clients and disposed of their flesh by way of Mrs. Lovett's meat pies, was fictional, but the fright inspired by this wicked figure was heightened by the fact of real food tampering. As early as 1820, the prevalence of these practices had inspired the chemist Frederick Accum to publish his descriptively named *A Treatise on Adulterations of Food, and Culinary Poisons, Exhibiting the Fraudulent Sophistications of Bread, Beer, Wine, Spiritous Liquors, Tea, Coffees, Cream, Confectionery, Vinegar, Mustard, Pepper, Cheese, Olive Oil, Pickles, and Other Articles Employed in Domestic Economy, and Methods of Detecting Them*. The title page, bearing a skull and crossbones, declared, "There is death in the pot."

But with a slab of meat, adulteration was harder. The introduction of more meat to the market might lower its cost, and with the rise of the railroad, buying food from afar became more plausible as refrigeration methods and rapid transport increased the freshness of the goods. As new horizons were opened by trade, colonization, and travel, many men of science saw no reason that there shouldn't be a similarly increased range of fare. Britons' passion for meat could remain, but the methods of procurement needed to change. Thus began the drive for acclimatization, or the attempt to breed new animals on English soil for the purpose of "utilizing them in places where they were unknown before."[15] The writer George Bompas reminded his readers: "We are apt to forget how large a portion of the animal and vegetable food of this country has been introduced from abroad. . . . In England it is said that but four additions have been made to our domesticated animals since the Christian era; viz. in 1524 the turkey, in 1650 the musk-duck, in 1725 the gold-pheasant, and in 1740 the silver-pheasant."[16]

Thanks to colonization and the expansion of the British Empire, this paltry number of domesticated species could and should have been increased upon, to naturalists' minds, and the types of protein expanded. The entomologists Vincent M. Holt, William Spence, and William Kirby tried to convince popular audiences that insects were a clean, "vegetarian," and nutritious food source.[17] In *The Curiosities of Food* (1859), Peter Lund Simmonds emphasized man's taxonomical position as the "universal eater," qualified by his anatomical structure to consume food of all kinds. Such a privileged position should not be wasted on the ever-increasingly pricey mutton and beef, Simmonds claimed, and he entreated his readers to take the advice of a "recent writer": "Make use of every material possible for food." The only meat that he did not recommend was that of the rat.[18]

Edward Smith-Stanley, the thirteenth Earl of Derby and a founding member of the Zoological Society of London, converted his park at Knowsley Hall into a sprawling 100-acre menagerie with more than 345 mammals, one-third of which had been bred in the park. Most of the animals were of the ruminant variety, intended not "for the gratification of whim, for the sake of mere collecting, or for ostentatious display," but for the sake of acclimatizing the breeds for English consumption. At his death, Derby willed his "useful" breeds to the Zoological Society, and it was this endowment that led to the creation of the Acclimatization Society of Great Britain.[19] The inaugural dinner of the Acclimatization Society was held on July 12, 1862, and over one hundred attendees dined on birds' nest soup, Chinese sea slugs, Axis deer sinew soup, a hybrid duck breed (courtesy of the Hon. G. Berkeley), "Leporines" (a rabbit/hare crossbreed), and kangaroo steamer, among numerous other exotic courses. Most of these animals were incredibly expensive to import, and the transportation of the kangaroo even proved so difficult that by the time it was served it "was a little 'gone off,'" an indication that if these foods were, in fact, intended as eventual food sources for the poor, such a goal would have been a long time coming.[20] Indeed, most of the acclimatization projects were failures, with the notable exception of the Society's focus on fish hatcheries.

In the 1850s, Lord Powerscourt introduced Japanese deer to his Irish estate, and Japanese deer, American turkeys, Indian black buck antelopes, mouflons (a type of wild European sheep), hog deer, and gazelles populated the grounds of Sir E. G. Loder's Sussex park. The Duke and Duchess of Bedford introduced over 73 new species of ruminants to Woburn Abbey, and Lionel Walter Rothschild raised ostriches and kangaroos. Frank Buckland urged the domestication of beavers and kangaroos, and a contributor to *All the Year Round* wrote in 1861 that the capybara, "the largest rodent in the world, strongly tempts the domesticator."[21] All over England, new species were vying for the attention and tongues of the British people, and exotic animal eaters took charge in the effort to determine which species were most suitable for the English palate and pocketbook.[22]

The prejudices of the English people were considered to be the largest obstacle to acclimatization efforts. An anonymous writer for the popular magazine *All the Year Round* expressed concern that popular prejudice would "wall in and imprison many of [the Acclimatization Society's] efforts."[23] But men of science had the perfect antidote for these deep-seated prejudices. Thanks to a highly particular nineteenth-century concept of the sense of taste, naturalists could serve as experts who had the power to claim "good" and "bad" flavors as matters of scientific fact. Following in the steps of their seventeenth- and eighteenth-century predecessors, nineteenth-century naturalists trusted in an empirical approach to nature. They believed that all knowledge comes from our senses, and as a consequence, scientific knowledge is directly reliant on experimentation, observation, and experience. Such a perspective may not seem radically different from our own, but the Georgians and Victorians took the idea of "sensory experience" much further than scientists and cultural critics today. Nowadays, a visit to a museum only involves the use of one's eyes. Paintings are viewed at a distance, ancient artifacts are protected under glass cases, and a visitor would never dream of smelling or licking mummified remains. But in the early nineteenth century, it was not unusual for museumgoers to lift and handle artifacts, sniff specimens, and taste exotic items.[24] According to Britons in the long eighteenth century, one's eyes had the power to deceive. An artifact that looked light could, in fact, be quite heavy, or a seemingly smooth surface could in reality be rough to the touch. Smell gave insight into the deepest intrinsic virtues of an object, and it was only through taste that one could fully experience the rare and wondrous medicinal effects of some artifacts. For example, mummy flesh, plant and animal specimens, and ground-up fossils were all considered to have medical applications. And for the impotent, powdered mammoth tusks were considered to be an especially powerful aphrodisiac. Thus, a true understanding of the nature of an object could only come from the cooperation of all the senses.

Seen from this angle, William Buckland's goal to eat "his way straight through the whole of animal creation," was consistent in its scientific logic.[25] For nineteenth-century naturalists, taste was just as valid a way to learn about nature as sight or touch. Buckland was a collector of experiences, and he mentally catalogued the sensations of every object he encountered, gathering details until they came together to reveal natural truth. For instance, while on a vacation with his son Frank, William used his gustatory prowess to disprove an instance of what he felt to be Catholic superstition. One of the cathedrals on their tour boasted fresh, dark splotches of martyr's blood. Upon hearing of the miracle, Buckland immediately took matters into his own hands, dropping to touch the flagstones with his tongue. "I can tell you what it is," he proclaimed. "It is bat's urine!"[26]

For better or for worse, in order to identify the mysterious substance, Buckland must have known what bat urine tasted like. Rather than accepting prepackaged laws or explanations, Buckland hoped to experience everything for himself, and the tongue was a perfectly valid instrument with which he could gather knowledge and draw conclusions about nature. Indeed, one has to admire the devotion these empirical eaters displayed in their investigations. Buckland and his fellow naturalists were willing to eat any and all things for the sake of knowledge, regardless of whether the experience would leave a good taste in their mouths. Archibald Young, a colleague of William's son Frank, explained that Frank "never stat[ed] anything as fact, of which he had not satisfied himself by actual experiment." Young reported, "I once found him cooking a piece of dead kelt." (A kelt is a salmon that has returned to fresh water to spawn and whose physical condition has deteriorated.) "'Good gracious!' I said, 'how can you eat anything so abominably nasty?' 'No doubt,' he said, 'it is nasty enough, but how can I say so unless I have tried it?'"[27]

This devotion to firsthand experience—even when it led to unsavory and highly specific conclusions like the fact that boiled porpoise tasted like broiled lamp wick—was a characteristic that can be traced back to Frank's early childhood. As you might imagine, living with a father like William meant that he was exposed to plenty of natural history and interesting foods. Frank's schoolmates at Winchester College remembered him largely for his mouse-eating and taxidermy projects, which he carried out in the lavatory. Buckland also took up the care of a pet hedgehog around the same time that he started keeping a diary. One of his schoolmates remembered prying into the diary's contents only to find entries of "'lost hedgehog,' 'found hedgehog,' and the like on alternate days, till at last there came the final and fatal entry of 'ate hedgehog!'" [28] By the time Frank attended Oxford, he had gathered his own private menagerie, the most popular members of which were Tiglath Pileser, a bear, and Jacky, a jackal who had eaten his own tail. After graduating, Frank became a surgeon for a while, but his real calling was zoology, and in addition to founding and editing the periodical *Land and Water*, he wrote numerous articles on animal life, which he later compiled into his bestseller *Curiosities of Natural History*.

For Frank, his father, and a number of other exotic eaters, firsthand experience was the most valuable tool in understanding nature. That said, even Frank's stomach had its limits. On one occasion he discovered a large oyster of an indeterminate species that was, apparently, "almost as big as a cheese-plate." Young reported that Frank "looked at it once or twice with an evident wish to experiment upon its flavor, but although blessed with a very strong stomach, his resolution failed him, and he resolved to make the experiment vicariously." Frank recruited a garbage collector, promising him a shilling if he would eat the gargantuan oyster. Evidently, the man's spirit was willing, but his stomach was weak, so Frank upped the ante by promising him a pot of porter beer to go along with it. The garbage collector made it through half of the bivalve before running away, and Young and Buckland were left to lament that "the precise flavor of that oyster [was] still locked unrecorded in the dustman's breast."[29]

In addition to inspiring serious sympathy for that poor garbage collector, this episode reveals a great deal about the way that exotic eaters viewed the value of their endeavors. For one thing, Frank saw his culinary exploits as "experiments," and he considered them a function of science, duty, and necessity, instead of leisure, aimless curiosity, or pleasure. (From the dustman's reaction, I think that one can safely say that this exploit was less than pleasurable.) For another, this episode indicates that Buckland and Young believed that foods had a "precise flavor" that was inherent in the oyster and that didn't depend on the subjective experience of the taster. Regardless of how much porter the taster washed the oyster down with, his sense of taste was capable of revealing natural laws that were just as definite, durable, and objective as the principles of anatomy, light, or physics.

This position was widely shared by other nature enthusiasts of the Victorian era. In 1867, Jane Loudon, the author of many popular gardening manuals and the much-acclaimed science fiction novel *The Mummy!: Or a Tale of the Twenty-Second Century*, published another well-respected book, *Mrs. Loudon's Entertaining Naturalist, Being Popular Descriptions, Tales, and Anecdotes of More than Five Hundred Animals*.[30] This informative and comprehensive tome was intended to give readers information on the functions, habits, and utility of various animals. Mrs. Loudon combined the scientific offerings of well-known zoologists with popular anecdotes, such as the tale of a pet panther who became kitten-like the moment he smelled lavender-water. Through her anecdotes, Mrs. Loudon hoped to present a clear, organized, and systematic vision of the world, and taste figured prominently among the characteristics she used to formulate her classifications. The flesh of arctic fox cubs "is said to be very good," skunk meat is "considered excellent food" despite the animal's odor, and "in autumn, when [American black bears] are become exceedingly fat by feeding on acorns and other similar food, their flesh is extremely delicate, the hams in particular are highly esteemed, and the fat is remarkably white and sweet."[31] Nearly all of Loudon's entries included at least one mention of the animal's flavor, except for those on insects and the radiated animals like starfish and coral.[32]

Mrs. Loudon's enterprise fit in with a larger Victorian fascination with classification. New animals like the kangaroo (first
brought to England in 1790 and originally called the "Cun-
quroo") piqued the public interest, and the flood of new specimens did not slow. By the late nineteenth century, an average of
1,000 new genera of animals were described each year. Men of
science spent decades fighting over how these new animals should
be classified, and taxonomy, the branch of science concerned with
the classification of organisms, was a hot topic in popular culture.
A cartoon from *Punch* showed how perplexing these new categories could be. Confronted with the question of whether she
would have to buy a "dog" ticket for traveling on a train with her
pets, a lady received the answer ". . . cats is 'dogs,' and rabbits is
'dogs,' and so's parrots; but this 'ere 'tortis' is a insect, so there ain't
no charge for it!" The porter's dedication to precision, despite his
unusual categorization, reveals just how thoroughly the impulse
for collecting and sorting had penetrated British society.

Animals from new lands were not the only ones of note.
Those of the distant British past also captured the popular attention, given that the first dinosaur bones were collected during
this period. In 1842, Sir Richard Owen coined the term "dino-
sauria," which means "terrible lizard." This classification is one
that current paleontologists would deem incorrect, but to Owen's
credit, it is just as accurate as the classification of a tortoise as an
insect. These great lizards caused such a stir that between 1852
and 1854, Benjamin Waterhouse Hawkins and Owen collaborated on a series of sculptures for the Crystal Palace Park that
represented the most cutting-edge knowledge of the creatures.
Staying true to Frank Buckland's claim that Englishmen always
connect their natural history research with food, Hawkins invited
some prestigious guests to join him for dinner inside the belly of
the iguanodon model. *The Illustrated London News*'s 100,000 sub-

The Iguanodon Dinner, featuring Richard Owen as the "brains" of the operation. Note the honorific plaque dedicated to William Buckland in the upper left-hand corner.

scribers eagerly read about this "socially-loaded stomach," filled with twenty-one prestigious Victorian businessmen, naturalists, and investors.[33] *Punch* made sure to "congratulate the company on the era in which they live; for if it had been an early geological period, they might perhaps have occupied the Iguanodon's inside without having dinner there."[34] They feasted on an extravagant seven-course meal that included mock turtle soup, hare, turbot hollandaise, pigeon pie, hashed partridges, woodcocks, and salps (a gelatinous sea creature).[35] Since flavors were considered to be a key characteristic by which one could classify the world, exotic animal dinners became a way to rally the best scientific minds and tongues so that they could accurately identify the "precise flavors" of the world's foodstuffs.

Today, we tend to think of taste as a very personal sense. I might prefer a dish with more salt, while you already find it to be sufficiently salty. I might like liver, while you detest it. Or I might think that ketchup on eggs is "good," where you think no such thing. We also are very conscious of the way that different seasonings alter the flavor of a dish, and we also trust that the method of cooking has some bearing on the final product. Very rarely would we state dogmatically that a food has a flavor that *everyone* should agree upon. The closest we might come would be the pronouncement that something "tastes like chicken," or that a certain meat "tastes gamy." But for Buckland and his compatriots, a food's flavor was "precise," such that you could discern it, document it, and categorize it in a way that would be universally accepted, regardless of one's subjective taste. Assuming that Hume was right that there was a "universal standard of taste," these men wanted to get it pegged down without waiting centuries for a consensus to form.

For Georgians and Victorians, "good" and "bad" taste, to a large extent, existed as verifiable scientific fact. Naturalists' descriptions of the "well-tastingness" of hedgehog or the "horribly bitter" taste of blue-bottle flies usually made no reference to the eater's subjective experience or even to its preparation. For Mrs. Loudon, the hare was a "favorite food, notwithstanding the dark color of its flesh," and the meat of the hedgehog "is said to be well-tasted, and to have an abundance of yellow fat."[36] In such statements, the meat itself is the source from which the taste derives, and each protein had a distinct, identifiable quality. The taste was located in the animal itself, not in the tongue of the eater. Zoological Society member C. J. Cornish claimed that, in fact, a good food source needed no special treatment; its inherent flavor and consistency should be what determined its worth. And according to one writer for *Bentley's Miscellany*, preparation only entered the culinary picture when it was necessary to cover up the bad quality of meat. Because Britons "posess[ed] the finest, meat, fish, and vegetables," he opined, they did "not think it necessary to heighten their savor by any extraneous aid."[37] Flavors in their natural states, apart from any culinary crutches, took the center stage in British gastronomical thought, or at least that advanced by naturalists. And this perspective might explain partially why British cuisine had, for quite some time, been accused of being tasteless or for consisting entirely of boiled foods.

In order to determine the "well-tastingness" of a particular food, it was necessary to have an expert consensus, and exotic animal dinners were perfectly suited to bring naturalists together into a "committee of taste." On February 29, 1868, the Society for the Propagation of Horseflesh as an Article of Food brought together 168 illustrious guests to test out nine courses featuring horse-derived products or horse-themed foods: horse soup, filet of sole in horse oil, filet of roast Pegasus, turkey with horse chestnuts (the single "horseless" dish), sirloin of horse stuffed with Centaur, braised rump of horse, tongue of Trojan horse, and jellied horses' hooves in maraschino. I don't know what's more shocking—that they managed to create dishes out of mythological creatures or that they got 168 people to join a club called the Society for the Propagation of Horseflesh as an Article of Food.

Frank Buckland, one of the attendees, reported that he went to the dinner "without fear or prejudice, and came back from it a wiser and sadder man." In every preparation, he reported that "an unwonted and peculiar taste could be recognized," and other attendees shared his assessment.[38] Evidently, the "real taste of the meat" was "extremely disagreeable," had a "peculiar flavor and odor," caused "strong distaste," and ultimately, from the effect that it had on a "great many" of those present, diners were "led to the conclusion that it is not good wholesome food."[39] In fact, it was so bad that one of Buckland's correspondents insisted that it be served to jailed criminals as additional punishment: "Be assured these fellows who would garrot you, murder your wives and children or commit the most fearful crimes, would shudder at the thought of dining upon horseflesh. No! they or most of them would die of starvation rather than be reduced to this most dreadful necessity."[40]

The collective response to the eland, a spiral-horned African antelope, was of a much different tenor. On January 19, 1859, a "committee of taste," comprised of Richard Owen and "three brother naturalists" attended a dinner at the London Tavern, where a six-year-old male eland was the featured protein. According to the journal of Frank Buckland, "The savoury smell of the roasted beast seemed to have pervaded the naturalist world, for a goodly company were assembled, all eager for the experiment. At the head of the table sat Professor Owen himself, his scalpel turned into a carving knife, and his gustatory apparatus in full working order."[41] This "experiment" was quite the success, and Richard Owen gushed in an article for *The Times* the following day, that eland was "the finest, closest, most tender and masticable of any meat," and evidently, "the suggestion that it was mammalian meat, with a soupçon of pheasant flavor, was generally accepted."[42]

As with any new scientific findings, rival scientific groups often debated the flavor "facts" described by other exotic eaters. David Livingstone, a member of another dining club, reported to Owen that "the flesh of a fat eland has upset the whole party of about seventy persons," giving "rise to the feeling that [elands] may be better after domestication" and the decision that "a she-giraffe is very much better."[43] But while there may have been bickering between naturalists, there was little dispute among the public that science was the final arbiter of taste. An article in *Chambers's Journal of Popular Literature, Science, and Arts* portrayed the eland debate this way: "A new candidate has appeared for the suffrages of dinner-givers and dinner-eaters, and science has been called in to decide upon the claims of the aspirant to the honors of the cloth."[44] Purple prose aside, such "popular" articles make clear that taste was a fact, and only science could draw the final conclusion.

Exotic animal eating practices, then, fell into line with a joined scientific and social project. For Georgian and Victorian naturalists, one had to taste the world in order to know it fully, and the tongue was a valid scientific instrument. "Observation" extended not only to the eyes, but to all sensory experience, and there were certain facts about the world that could be discerned only through a methodical, scientific approach to taste. Exotic eaters' taxonomies of taste were not only the objects of idle speculation or theoretical science, though. Practical application of scientific knowledge was the order of the day, and as odd as it may seem, the fervor for eating hippo, puma, and antelope played a significant part in the larger social project of addressing food shortages. (Or, at least, that was the ostensible purpose.) Victorian naturalists witnessed a rapidly changing world: new animals, new technologies, rising populations, and growing misery. A scientific approach to food was their way of grappling with these changes and of finding solutions to the troubles of modern life. William Buckland perhaps put it best when he said, "The human mind has an appetite for truth of every kind, physical as well as moral, and the real utility of science is to afford gratification to this appetite."[45]

EPILOGUE

Seeing Is Not Believing

WILLIAM BUCKLAND AND nineteenth-century gastronomers may have thought that "the stomach ... rules the
world," but by and large, sensory historians have argued that it
is the eye that rules modern life.[1] The basic narrative centers on
something called the "Great Divide Theory," which originated
with Marshall McLuhan in the 1960s and was elaborated upon
by Walter Ong in the 1980s. These theorists saw modernity as the
culmination of a long historical process that led people to rely overwhelmingly on their eyesight. The long-ago shift from oral culture
to print culture meant that history became transmitted through
texts rather than oral traditions. By the fifteenth century, thanks
to the invention of the printing press, even more people gained
access to the printed word. As print culture spread, people placed
their trust in the authoritativeness of texts.

According to this theory, the eighteenth century was the divid-
ing point from previous centuries of slow development. During
this period, literacy boomed, a newfangled medium called the
newspaper was created, and letters circulated freely. Even the

name of the Enlightenment belied the period's trust in eyesight, with illumination serving as the culture's key metaphor for reason, understanding, and social progress. Moving forward, modern intellectual life, media, and culture was "ocularcentric," and throughout the nineteenth, twentieth, and twenty-first centuries, this reliance on vision has continued, if not grown. Not all historians agree with McLuhan and Ong's ideas about oral and literate cultures, but the basic idea that we rely on our eyes more than our other sensory organs is still prevalent.

This narrative has been adopted and adapted by a number of scholars of modernity. Martin Jay has written on the "scopic regimes of modernity," acknowledging, "It is difficult to deny that the visual has been dominant in modern Western culture in a variety of ways."[2] Guy Debord argued that we live in a society of spectacle; Michel Foucault explained how modern life has become permeated with surveillance; the psychologist Jacques Lacan introduced "the gaze" to explain the anxiety that develops when a person becomes aware that they are visible to others (e.g., when a child first recognizes herself in a mirror); Laura Mulvey turned "the gaze" into a symbol of power imbalances (e.g., the "male gaze"); and Fredric Jameson has described how the superficiality of postmodernism transforms reality into images. Sensory historians and anthropologists have also tended to adopt this perspective. Here's a characteristic example from Constance Classen, David Howes, and Anthony Synnott's book *Aroma:* "The devaluation of smell in the contemporary West is directly linked to the revaluation of the senses which took place during the eighteenth and nineteenth centuries. The philosophers and scientists of that period decided that, while sight was the preeminent sense of reason and civilization, smell was the sense of madness and savagery."[3]

On a basic level, these claims make a lot of sense. Literate societies do rely heavily on their eyesight, and with the proliferation of texting, blogs, and advertising, it seems clear that large parts of our world are constructed around the ability to see. To support the claim that the other senses have fallen victim to vision, one would only need to point to the modern obsession with deodorization, Americans' love of personal space, and the fact that museums no longer invite visitors to taste the exhibits. But by and large, I'm skeptical of the Great Divide Theory, as well as the claim that the other senses have been "lowered" because of eyesight's power. In this book, I have been advancing a different narrative, one that focuses more on the interconnection and mutual participation of the senses than on their battles with one another. In Chapter Seven, I focused on the harmonies of nature to show ways in which inventors from the fifteenth to the twentieth centuries explored the idea that sight, sound, smell, taste, and touch are interwoven. Similarly, in Chapter Nine, I showed how, even as "taste" became the central metaphor for refinement, gastronomers considered visuality, texture, odor, and other types of experiences to be essential to good taste. In Chapter Ten, I showed how scientific observation in the early nineteenth century relied, not only on the eyes, but also on odor and taste. And these examples only scratch the surface. The picture that I have tried to paint of the long eighteenth century is one that focuses not on sight's rise to prominence, but on a concept of the senses that would have been more popular in the eighteenth century itself: the idea that the senses are deeply interconnected. Perception is not just the sum total of separate, easily separable parts. It's constantly evolving, complex, and multifaceted, and we need to come up with a more holistic understanding of perception in order to come to grips with how our minds and bodies work.

While a number of Enlightenment writers praised eyesight, the sources simply don't bear out the claim that other senses were sidelined in this period. For a sense to be sidelined, it has to lose some cultural value; people have to think of it less and care about the other senses more. I would argue that the fact that we exercise more control on our sensory environments doesn't mean that we value our senses less. Take odor. Walking down the aisles of any grocery store, it's possible to find deodorants, deodorizers, and odor neutralizers, giving credence to the fact that we strive to exercise more, rather than less, control over odors. I determine what I want my clothes to smell like, what I want my carpet to smell like, even what I want my garbage bags to smell like. But this is a far cry from the argument that "smell is repressed in the modern West." In many cases, deodorized air is simply a "blank slate" for the odors that we do want to smell. Scented candles, wax burners, aromatic lotions, fragrant soaps, and other odor-oriented products are available in abundance. The vigilance with which we attend to odors shows that they still matter to us. In fact, I'd argue that smell might even have a heightened effect in a world in which scent is so strongly controlled, because if something violates our neutral sphere, we notice it even more. If I came home to a nauseating odor of rotting meat, that scent certainly wouldn't strike me as marginal. Indeed, scent might even take on new importance in the modern world, offering new opportunities for self-definition. In the premodern world, everyone would have smelled of musk, onion, or other strong odors, all oriented toward fighting off miasmatic air. In the modern world, where concepts of cleanliness and air have shifted, it's possible to decide whether the scent of carnation or sandalwood is more "me." Our frame of reference for odor has shifted significantly, but a change in meaning doesn't necessarily mean absence.

I'm not out to sweep away all the scholarship that's come before, deny that eyesight is important in modern life, or refute the claim that our sensory expectations have changed radically. The concept of sensory hiearchies, where certain senses dominate others, can be extremely helpful, and a great deal of excellent scholarship has been produced on the basis of these conclusions. But they shouldn't be the only way that we think about the relationship between the senses. The historian Leigh Eric Schmidt has made this case beautifully: "The modern sensorium remains more intricate and uneven . . . more diffuse and heterogeneous, than the discourses of Western visuality and ocularcentrism allow."[4] Hierarchies pit different aspects of ourselves against one another that, more often than not, work in tandem. For instance, eating a salty potato chip will certainly engage the sense of taste. But it also will engage the sense of hearing (the crunch when you bite down), the sense of touch (the crispy shards and greasy feel), the sense of smell (the glorious aroma that seems to emanate from all things fried), and the sense of sight (you may pick out the chips with black spots or decide which chip to eat first based on its pleasing shape). We have a unified perception of the experience, but it's reliant on the cooperation of many senses.

Why should you care if people hierarchize the senses? By questioning the notion of sensory hierarchies and the modern prioritization of vision, it might be easier to figure out how the other senses fit into our lives. Accepting the narrative of ocularcentrism means accepting that our lives are bereft of the rich, deep influence of the other senses. But by reorienting the way that we understand our processes of perception, we gain the power to learn something new about our lives today. Thinking about the relationship between different types of sensations can make you more aware of the food you eat, the fragrances you inhale, and the hugs you receive from the people you love. It's amazing how much your experience can change just by shifting your perspective a little bit.

I think this is a big part of why Classen, Howes, and Synnott wanted to bring attention to the question of deodorization in the first place. They wanted to show that the eye shouldn't control our lives and that there are other sensory experiences that greatly matter. While I may not fully agree with the idea of ocularcentrism and "sidelined" senses, I do think there is something to the claims of theorists who stress the modern obsession with sight. Many of them insist that modern life revolves too heavily around appearances and surfaces; we trust our sight, and don't tend to dig deeper. This reliance on appearances has subtly, yet pervasively, contributed to an intellectually superficial society. I hope this book has called awareness to the fact that we should move beyond basic appearances, since experience is often much more complex than we imagine. The things that we assume to be stable—like our five senses—often require rethinking. And the feelings that seem cut-and-dried are often the product of complicated, unconscious, long-standing cultural assumptions and historical developments. Quick information is a great thing, but it also requires processing and considered evaluation.

As a historian, I have another major reason for thinking that the Great Divide Theory matters. If you accept the narrative of ocularcentrism, you may very well end up with an idea of the Enlightenment that's false. I began this book by mentioning many of the common ideas that have been perpetuated about the Enlightenment: it was an era obsessed with reason; Enlightenment philosophy sought to wipe away misconceptions and superstitions; science and evidence triumphed over tradition and religion. The narrative of ocularcentrism, at least as sensory historians have used it thus far, supports this bullet-point version of the Enlightenment. The eighteenth century, so it goes, was the moment in which scientific values of objectivity and rationality came to the fore. Sight, as a distance sense that had long been identified with the higher powers of the mind, fit ideally with these values, and in the words of the historian Robert Jütte, "From this time onward, the sense of sight more or less assumed precedence over all the other senses."[5] The observant, philosophical Enlightenment created an ocularcentric world.

The above characterization of the Enlightenment might have been the norm a hundred, or even fifty, years ago, but eighteenth-century scholars have shown that these basic assumptions need to be revised. As early as 1939, the historian R. R. Palmer argued that Jesuit writers shared many of the same basic ideas about nature as the *philosophes,* and while they may have written with different purposes and conclusions, they shared an "enlightened" language.[6] More recently, Jessica Riskin has stressed the way that science developed through "sentimental empiricism," a method of inquiry that blended subjective and objective perspectives on the world.[7] Similarly, Anne C. Vila has claimed that it is impossible to understand eighteenth-century psychology, philosophy, aesthetics, and literature, without "re-somatizing" the way that we think about these various topics.[8] It is technically true that the Enlightenment was an age devoted to reason, that philosophers dominated the intellectual scene, and that naturalists cared a great deal about firsthand observation. But there's a lot more to these statements than meets the eye, and in this book, I have tried to show how the larger arc of sensory history ties into the updated, less schematic version of the Enlightenment that is more familiar to specialists of the period.

While the eighteenth century valued eyesight, it wasn't an overwhelmingly visual era. Certain groups of people worked in the depths of night, some pedagogues suggested learning without the aid of sight, and new social anxieties developed as a result of no longer having clear visual distinctions between groups of people. Denis Diderot wrote in 1751, "I found that, of all the senses, sight was the most superficial, hearing the most arrogant, smell the most voluptuous, taste the most superstitious and the least faithful, touch the most profound and the most philosophical."[9]

Also, as you've gathered from this book, *philosophes* followed the mantra of "reason," but their version of reason was embodied, and feeling formed a central part of their worldview. There was no dichotomy between the mind's logical ideas and the body's gut feelings. They all came from the senses, and as such, they all had a crucial place in understanding the world.

Finally, the Enlightenment was just as much a social and cultural movement as an intellectual one. Philosophy ruled the intellectual day, but it wasn't a detached philosophy in which theory was divorced from practice. Enlightenment *philosophes* argued about the nature of feeling, knowledge, and nature itself, all in the pursuit of making the world a better place. Social, political, and economic reform went hand in hand with sensationalism, materialism, and sentimentalism, and as such, Enlightenment knowledge had a significant effect on culture at large. The Enlightenment was far from a restricted, elite phenomenon, which is why it is necessary to look beyond Diderot to Le Camus, Rousseau to Haüy, and Voltaire to Buckland. People from all echelons of society borrowed and exchanged fashions, ideas, and objects, building new forms of identity and culture as they went.

The eighteenth century has a lot of lessons to offer us. For one, Enlightenment writings place such a huge emphasis on the senses that anyone reading them can't help but think about how much feeling matters in our daily lives. Obviously, on a day-to-day basis, we recognize just how much stress can affect us, how anger can make a bad day even worse, and how being loved can soften even the hardest dispositions. We're no strangers to emotions and to the prominent place that they play in our lives, but it's still all too easy to get into the routines of daily life without focusing on the experiences of the senses. *Philosophes* recognized the incredible importance of sensory experience, and they also believed that no experience was too small to matter. They remind us that it's worthwhile to pay attention to the small, physical moments in our lives.

Eighteenth-century philosophy also gives us a perspective in which the emotions are always mixed up with reason. The mind-body mutuality of the eighteenth century is one of the period's most interesting features, and I think that this model can give us a more complex way to think about how perception works. We already believe in psychosomatic medical conditions, where ideas can have a direct effect on the body. Why not take seriously the idea of embodied reason, where our physical feelings and judgment work in tandem?

What's more, the eighteenth-century notion of a conjoined body and mind teaches us that it's best to strive for balance in all things, so that all the parts of our being can be healthy. Don't eat too much cake, but don't deprive yourself. Don't read too many books, but don't ignore the world of ideas. Listen to the Marquis de Sade just enough to see his value, but don't try to model yourself after him. Enlightenment philosophy and medicine teaches that if you overdo any one element in life, something else will likely be misaligned. This seems like a pretty good rule of thumb.

Another good lesson to take from the eighteenth century is the idea that everyone has a role to play in society. While there were some people who stayed with the traditional exclusionary line, there were plenty of Enlightenment reformers who dreamed of a world in which everyone was included. Schools for the blind, deaf, and physically disabled arose after the mid eighteenth century. Philanthropic organizations grew rapidly both in number and in members, and in France, the Revolution brought with it the idea of universal public education, which continued to grow even after the Revolution had reached its end.[10] New democratic theories of government and sensationalist concepts of the "blank slate" mind upheld the notion that everyone had unique talents.

As long as these talents served the general good, reformers maintained, difference was to be accepted. Diversity has concrete benefits, but in order for those benefits to come to pass, it's necessary to accept, encourage, and approve of difference in the first place.

Finally, who can forget the benefits of Enlightenment optimism? Eighteenth-century reformers set out to change the world. Diderot and d'Alembert compiled their *Encyclopédie* with the idea that it would benefit generations to come. Louis-Sébastien Mercier wrote a utopian novel called *The Year 2440* that portrayed a world in which all the best Enlightenment reforms had come to pass. (Notably, this was a world in which slavery had been abolished, in which people wore comfortable, loose-fitting clothing, and in which there was no Catholic Church, although the idea of a Supreme Being still existed. That said, women were still excluded from public functions.) And who can forget Condorcet's belief that humanity was steadily moving toward the tenth, most perfect stage of development? You have to admire that these folks dreamed big and shot for the moon. We could learn from their passion for reform and their faith in a better future. If the perfect is the enemy of the good, so is complacency.

One of their best lessons, though, is that improvement doesn't always have to come in the form of large-scale, sweeping change. The Enlightenment teaches us that each experience, moment, and feeling matters. Nineteenth-century naturalists claimed that in order to form a true opinion of an object, a person needed to use all her senses, which collaborated to reveal the truth of the world. From this perspective, an informed opinion could only be the product of multisensory experience. I believe that it's the same with our lives today: we have to evaluate from multiple angles and experience the world in new ways in order to truly know ourselves. Our identities come from the things we think and do, but equally, they develop out of the things that we feel and experience.

I began this book with a quotation from Voltaire, and I think it's equally fitting that we leave off with him. "The senses are the doors of the understanding," he wrote. "Sensation envelops all our faculties. . . . Without [sensation] there cannot be life."[11] Voltaire liked to tell people what he thought, and equally, he liked to tell people what they should think. Modesty was not Voltaire's strong point, but as he drew his *Philosophical Dictionary* entry on sensation to a close, he acknowledged the immense uncertainty and possibility that accompanied a worldview in which sensation was crucial to human life. With fitting rhetorical flourish, he voiced a sentiment that I would like to second: "What are we to conclude from all this? You who read and think, conclude."[12]

ACKNOWLEDGMENTS

Thank you to my agent, Marcy Posner, and my editor, Amy Cherry, for wholeheartedly embracing such a quirky book from a first-time author. Both of you have worked generously to shape the narrative, humor, and arguments of this book, and I have been continually grateful to have two such brilliant women working by my side. To Remy Cawley, Fred Wiemer, and the rest of the team at Norton, I appreciate all the attention and care that you have put into this book. It is so much better, thanks to your support.

I am thankful for the generous financial support that I have received from the Jack Miller Center, John Templeton Foundation, Georges Lurcy Charitable and Educational Trust, Society for French Historical Studies, Huntington Library, and University of Chicago. I am also deeply indebted to the many libraries, museums, and archives whose holdings have made this book possible.

This book took on a life of its own, separate from my doctoral research, but I would be remiss if I didn't thank all the academic colleagues and supervisors who have dedicated their brainpower to my work. In graduate school, Jan Goldstein was the first person to ask me, "What is the common thread between these odd stories you're collecting?" Remarkably, she didn't bat an eye when I answered, "Sensation." In my first job, Chris Nippert-Eng encouraged me to think about how I could speak to a broader audience, and without her enthusiasm, this book would never have come into being. Countless thanks also go out to Paul Cheney, Fredrik Jonsson, Robert Morrissey, University of Chicago workshop participants, and the attendees of various conferences who have commented on my work over the years. Likewise, I owe my students a huge debt of gratitude. They have encouraged me to think more deeply about eighteenth-century smells and tastes than I ever thought possible, and they are experts at asking, "So what?"—a question that all historians should feel obligated to answer.

Ed Fee, thank you for being a sounding board, an endless source of laughter, and a comforting presence when the writing wasn't going well. Beth King, Catherine Clark, Ben Lynerd, Sébastien Greppo, and Ankit Srivastava were early readers of this book, and everyone should be grateful that they encouraged me to cut some of the first-draft jokes. Many thanks to Erika Honisch for her generous help with the music theory in Chapter Seven. I am also thankful to Kate Alfano, Annalise Ansell, Juliana Barr, Brandy Blue, Jaime Bobbitt, Amanda Cadogan, Richard Del Rio, Timm Dolley, Alex Dubé, the Fee family, Mark Fletcher, Jessica Fripp, Harold Gabel, Carrie Grinstead, Daniel Gullo, Jordana Heller, Randal Hendrickson, Jason and Inna Henry, Brian Jacobson, Todd Joiner, Tyson Leuchter, Eugénie Pascal, Jonathan Renshon, Michelle Schwarze, Will Shelton, Suzanne Taylor, Alexia Yates, FBC, OMC, and all my book club women for your contributions to my mind and spirit.

Above all, I am profoundly grateful to my family for supporting me, even when they couldn't fathom why a ranch girl would want to move to the city, become a French historian, and write on obscure topics. I love you beyond measure, and I promise that I will never make you eat horse.

NOTES

Introduction

1 Voltaire, "Sensation," *Dictionnaire philosophique IV, Oeuvres complètes de Voltaire* (Paris: Garnier Frères, 1879), 20:419.

2 I'm sensitive to the plight of the oyster, and I'm sure that there are other people who care deeply. But we can probably agree that your average person probably doesn't dedicate too much time to considering how many senses an oyster has.

3 Voltaire, "Sensation," 20:419.

4 Denis Diderot, "The Definition of an Encyclopedia," in *The Old Regime and the French Revolution,* ed. Keith Michael Baker, University of Chicago Readings in Western Civilization 7 (Chicago: University of Chicago, 1987), 71.

5 Jean le Rond d'Alembert, *Discours préliminaire des éditeurs (Juin 1751),* in *Encyclopédie, ou dictionnaire raisonné des sciences, des arts et des métiers, etc.,* ed. Denis Diderot and Jean le Rond d'Alembert, University of Chicago: ARTFL Encyclopédie Project (Spring 2013 Edition), ed. Robert Morrissey, http://encyclopedie.uchicago.edu/.

6 It's important to say a quick word about women. *Philosophes* were men, and by and large, the public faces of the Enlightenment were male, but that didn't mean that women didn't play an active part in the intellectual culture. Some well-respected women were in charge of the *philosophes'* salon gatherings, certain ladies were extremely well educated, and compared to the nineteenth century, elite women in the Enlightenment had some definite intellectual and social advantages. I will eventually say more about

women, from all social strata, but since I have primarily written about guys so far (and pretty famous ones at that), it bears mentioning that I'm not simply forgetting about the other half of the population.

7 Peter Gay, *The Enlightenment: The Rise of Modern Paganism* (1966; reis., New York: W. W. Norton, 1995), 3–4.

8 Enlightenment writers seem to have forgotten about the vibrant intellectual contributions of scholasticism, the innovativeness of Gothic architecture, the technological impact of the printing press, and the impressive cultural contributions of all those medieval writers and artists. Indeed, the term "Dark Ages" was coined by the fourteenth-century humanist Petrarch, who, oddly enough, would have been included in the period that eighteenth-century writers saw as being cloaked in intellectual shadow. So instead of taking Enlightenment writers at their word and thinking of the Middle Ages as "dark," just think of what a good PR team the *philosophes* made.

9 The seventeenth-century English diarist Samuel Pepys held an elaborate feast each year in celebration of his survival of a kidney stone removal. The procedure was a harrowing one, involving the insertion of a metal tube into the penis, a finger up the rectum, and an incision between the genitals and the anus. Given the lack of anesthesia, several people were required to hold the patient down until he passed out from the pain. Coupled with the fact that lithotomies had a meager success rate and numerous complications, one can see why Pepys had plenty of reason to celebrate.

10 Étienne Bonnot de Condillac, *Essay on the Origin of Human Knowledge*, ed. Hans Aarsleff (Cambridge: Cambridge University Press, 2001), 11.

Chapter One: The Self-Made Man

1 John Locke, *Second Treatise of Government* (Indianapolis: Hackett Publishing Co., 1980), 8.

2 Claude-Adrien Helvétius, *De l'esprit* (Paris: Durand, 1758), 10. Helvétius, and his wife Minette (and her famous troop of Angora cats), ran one of the most renowned salons in France. Minette, as the *salonnière*, would have been in charge of directing the conversation and keeping it civil—no mean task, given the hotheadedness of many Enlightenment men of letters. The attendee list of the Helvétius salon sounds like a who's who of eighteenth-century France. Benjamin Franklin, Thomas Jefferson, Napoleon Bonaparte, Diderot, and d'Alembert are prominent names you may recognize. For a nerd like me, this is the greatest dinner party imaginable.

3 Paul Henri Thiry, Baron d'Holbach, *The System of Nature*, trans. Samuel Wilkinson (England, 1820–21; reprint Whitefish, MT: Kessinger Publishing, 2004), 1:47–48.

4 Charles Bonnet, *Essai analytique sur les facultés de l'âme*, 2d ed. (Copenhagen and Geneva: Claude Philibert, 1769), 1:xxiv.

5 In many regards, sensationalism developed as a reaction to the famous claim of the seventeenth-century philosopher René Descartes, who announced, "I think, therefore I am," insisting that the mind and body were separate. Such a belief is called "Cartesian dualism," and in one of the nerdiest jokes I know, it gets Descartes into trouble: Descartes walks into a bar and begins to order a number of cocktails. A short while later, the bartender sees that Descartes is wasted. He cuts him off, saying, "I think you've had enough." Descartes, in a slurring voice, responds, "I think not!" Then he disappears.

6 John Locke, *An Essay Concerning Human Understanding,* ed. Peter H. Nidditch (Oxford: Oxford University Press, 1979), 6.

7 Locke, *Essay,* 43.

8 René Descartes, 1643 letter to Voetius, *Oeuvres de Descartes,* ed. Charles Adam and Paul Tannery (Paris: J. Vrin, 1904), 8b: 166–67, quoted in Lex Newman, "Descartes' Epistemology", *The Stanford Encyclopedia of Philosophy* (Winter 2014 Edition), ed. Edward N. Zalta, http://plato.stanford.edu/archives/win2014/entries/descartes-epistemology/.

9 Étienne Bonnot de Condillac, *Traité des sensations, Oeuvres complètes de Condillac* (Paris: Gratiot, Houel, Guillaume, Pougin & Gide, 1798) 3:14.

10 Ibid., 3:9.

11 Jean-Jacques Rousseau, *Confessions*, trans. Angela Scholar, ed. Patrick Coleman (Oxford: Oxford University Press, 2000), 261–63.

12 Ibid., 337–38.

13 Rousseau, *Émile*, trans. Barbara Foxley (London and North Clarendon, VT: Everyman, 1993), 32.

14 Ibid., 35.

15 Julia Douthwaite, *The Wild Girl, Natural Man, and the Monster: Dangerous Experiments in the Age of Enlightenment* (Chicago: University of Chicago Press, 2002), 137–38.

16 Paul-Victor de Sèze, *Recherches phisiologiques et philosophiques sur la sensibilité ou la vie animale* (Paris: Prault, 1786), 235.

17 Ibid., 200–201.

18 Benjamin Franklin, *Benjamin Franklin's The Art of Virtue: His Formula for Successful Living,* 3d. ed., ed. George L. Rogers (Eden Prairie, MN: Acorn Publishing, 1996), 185, 196.

19 Antoine Le Camus, *Médecine de l'esprit* (Paris: Ganeau, 1753), 1:180.

20 Charles-Louis de Secondat, Baron de La Brède et de Montesquieu, *The Spirit of Laws,* in *Great Books of the Western World* (Chicago: Encyclopædia Britannica, 1952), 38:107.

21 Le Camus, *Médecine de l'esprit,* 1:309.

22 The theory of nonnaturals was actually a holdover from the medical theory of the Greek physician Galen, but thanks to a growing emphasis on sensation, the nonnaturals played an increasingly important role in eighteenth-century medicine.

23 Le Camus, *Médecine de l'esprit,* 1:255–56.

24 Ibid., 2:111.

25 Ibid., 1:359–60.

26 Ibid., 2:311.

27 Helvétius, *De l'esprit,* 276.

28 Marie Jean Antoine Nicolas de Caritat, Marquis de Condorcet, *Esquisse d'un tableau historique des progrès de l'esprit humain,* 4th ed. (Paris: Agasse, 1798), 2.

29 Ibid., 372.

30 Samuel-Auguste Tissot, *De la Santé des gens de lettres* (Paris: Éditions de la Différence, 1991), 37.

31 Tissot, *De la Santé,* 46. Tissot's concerns about the academic life were not universally accepted, but Denis Diderot did admit that Tissot's ideas had some grounding in truth. Diderot wrote to his mistress Sophie Volland in 1762, "We aren't made for reading, meditation, letters, philosophy, and sedentary life. . . . I would be healthier if I had spent some of the time that I've hunched over my books stretched out over a woman instead." (Denis Diderot, letter to Sophie Volland, 7 Nov. 1762, *Oeuvres de Diderot,* ed. Laurent Versini [Paris: Robert Laffont, 1997], 5:470).

32 George Lakoff and Mark Johnson, *Philosophy in the Flesh: The Embodied Mind and its Challenge to Western Thought* (New York: Basic Books, 1999), 4.

Chapter Two: Drinking Your Way to a New You

1 Luc Bihl-Willette, *Des Tavernes aux bistrots: Histoire des cafés* (Lausanne: L'Age d'Homme, 1997), 35.

2 François Fosca, *Histoire des cafés de Paris* (Paris: Firmin-Didot & Compagnie, 1934), 30.

3 Bihl-Willette, *Des Tavernes aux bistrots,* 44.

4 As with any law, there were those who disobeyed. Court cases abound with stories of gamblers who scrambled to hide their cards in their hats when the police arrived and of shop owners brought up on charges of "bad commerce," the polite euphemism for prostitution. Judging only by its prevalence, I imagine that bad commerce made for good business.

5 Louis-Sébastien Mercier, *Tableau de Paris: Nouvelle édition, corigée et augmentée* (Amsterdam: n.p., 1789), 11:47.

6 The Armenian garb and ceremonial presentation was a reference to coffee's Middle Eastern origins and to Pascal, an Armenian street vendor who first publicly served the brew at the 1671 Saint-Germain Fair.

7 Daniel Roche, *Le Peuple de Paris: Essai sur la culture populaire au XVIIIe siècle* (Paris: Aubier Montaigne, 1981), 257.

8 Mercier, *Tableau de Paris,* 11:44.

9 Appropriately enough for someone invested in the spice trade, Pierre Poivre's name translates to "Peter Pepper," and scholars have speculated that he may have been the inspiration behind the eighteenth-century tongue twister, "Peter Piper picked a peck of pickled peppers."

10 Cissie Fairchilds, "The Production and Marketing of Populuxe Goods in Eighteenth-century Paris," in *Consumption and the World of Goods,* ed. John Brewer and Roy Porter (New York: Routledge, 1993), 236.

11 The comb-makers also laid claim to a number of popular eighteenth-century items, including snuffboxes, canes, fans, board games, crucifixes, rosaries, and musical instruments.

12 Nicolas Delamare, *Traité de la police* (Paris: Michel Brunet, 1719), 3:798.

13 Pierre Duplais, *Des Liqueurs et de la distillation des alcools, ou le liquoriste et le distillateur modernes* (Versailles : L'Auteur; Paris, 1855), 1:32.

14 "Par privilège exclusif, permission & lettres-patentes du Roi, enrégistrées au Parlement de Paris," *Mercure de France* (Feb. 1766): 212.

15 Jean-Elie Bertrand, *Descriptions des arts et métiers* (Neuchâtel: Imprimérie de la Société Typographique, 1780), 12:351.

16 "Causes jugées au Conseil de Police: infractions aux règlements des communautés d'artisans et de marchands, engagements forcés, commerce de livres prohibés, etc., 1748–1752," Archives nationales, Y9523^B 1749.

17 François-René-André Dubuisson, *L'Art du distillateur et marchand de liqueurs considérées comme Alimens médicamenteux* (Paris: L'Auteur, Dubuisson Fils, Cusin, 1779), v.

18 "Odontalgie," *L'Avantcoureur* 19 (26 May, 1761): 296; Fosca, *Histoire des cafés de Paris,* 11.

19 Jane Austen, *Sense and Sensibility*, The Cambridge Edition of the Works of Jane Austen, ed. Edward Copeland (Cambridge: Cambridge University Press, 2006), 7.

20 Ibid., 8.

21 *Encyclopédie, ou Dictionnaire raisonné des sciences, des arts et des métiers*, ed. Denis Diderot and Jean le Rond D'Alembert (University of Chicago: ARTFL Encyclopédie Project, Spring 2013 Edition, ed. Robert Morrissey), s.v. "Caffés," http://encyclopedie.uchicago.edu. (accessed May 20, 2013), 2:259.

22 Gabriel-François Venel, "Citronnier" in *Encyclopédie,* 3:493.

23 Philippe Sylvestre Dufour, *Traitez nouveaux et curieux du café, du thé, et du chocolate; Ouvrage également necessaire aux Medecins, et à tous ceux qui aiment leur santé* (La Haye: Adrian Moetjens, 1685), 70.

24 Joachim-Christophe Nemeitz, *Séjour de Paris, c'est à dire, Instructions fidéles, pour les Voiageurs de Condition* (Leiden, 1727), 110–11.

25 Voltaire, "Le Crocheteur borgne," in *Oeuvres complètes* (n.p.: Imprimerie de la Société Typographique, 1785), 45:423.

26 Charles-Antoine-Guillaume Pigault-Lebrun, *Les Empiriques* (Paris: Barba, Year III [1794–95]), 71.

27 Venel, "Oranger" in *Encyclopédie,* 11:558; Venel, "Romarin" in *Encyclopédie,* 14:346.

28 *Dictionnaire de l'Académie française*, 4th ed. (Paris, 1762), s.v. "hypocondre."

29 Moreau de Saint-Elier, *Traité de la communication des maladies,* 50.

30 Claude-Nicolas Le Cat, *Traité des sensations et des passions en général, et des sens en particulier* (Paris: Chez Vallat-la-Chapelle, 1767), 89–93, 206; Le Cat's claims about spontaneous combustion were, in large part, based on a 1725 court case. The wife of tavern owner Jean Millet was found smoldering on the kitchen floor, and the police arrested Mr. Millet, charging him with murder. Millet was released, but apparently, the *tavernier* had been driven crazy by the proceedings, and he spent the rest of his life in an insane asylum (Jan Bondeson, *A Cabinet of Medical Curiosities* [New York: W. W. Norton, 1999], 3). The belief in the spontaneous combustion of humans was prevalent well into the nineteenth century. For one notable literary example, see Charles Dickens's *Bleak House* (1852). In Chapter 32, the gin-addled Mr. Krook went up in a burst of greasy flames during an afternoon nap. When Mr. Snagsby and Mr. Guppy finally discovered him, Krook was little more than a lump of ashy coal.

31 "Autre [Chanson pour les preneurs de caffé]," *Chansons Nouvelles* (Troyes: P. Garnier, [1685–1738]), 24. This section is dated 1723.

32 Daniel Roche, *A History of Everyday Things: The Birth of Consumption in France, 1600–1800,* trans. Brian Pearce (Cambridge: Cambridge University Press, 2000), 246.

33 Andrew Stern, "Two-Thirds of Americans Perk Up with Coffee: Survey," Reuters, 24 Sep. 2011, http://www.rawstory.com/2011/09/two-thirds-of -americans-perk-up-with-coffee-survey/.

34 Sir James Mackintosh, quoted in Stephen Braun, *Buzz: The Science and Lore of Alcohol and Caffeine* (Oxford: Oxford University Press, 1996), 133.

35 Jules Michelet, *Pages choisies des grandes écrivains: Michelet,* 7th ed. (Paris: Librairie Armand Colin, 1902), 402.

36 Dufour, *Traitez nouveaux et curieux,* 85.

37 "Eloge du caffé," *Chansons nouvelles* (Troyes: P. Garnier, [1685–1738]), 1.

38 Fortunato Bartolomeo De Felice, *Encyclopédie, ou dictionnaire universel raisonné des connaissances humaines,* Supplément (Yverdon: n.p., 1775), s.v. "Cacao et chocolat," 2:407.

39 Robert James, *Dictionnaire universel de médecine,* ed. Julien Busson, trans. Diderot, Eidous, and Toussaint (Paris: Briasson, David, Durand, 1746), s.v. "Cacao," 2:1235.

40 Apparently, the aristocratic Marquis de Sévigné caught on early to the hot properties of chocolate, because over the course of 1671, she changed her tune about the beverage's benefits. Writing to her daughter, Sévigné first advised chocolate's use as a restorative, but soon thereafter, she warned against eating too much since it could "burn the blood." She relayed a precautionary tale about a pregnant woman who ate too much chocolate and consequently gave birth to a sickly, black baby (Bertram M. Gordon, "Chocolate in France: Evolution of a Luxury Product," in *Chocolate: History, Culture, and Heritage,* eds. Lewis Evan Grivetti and Howard-Yana Shapiro [Hoboken: John Wiley, 2009], 573).

41 James, *Dictionnaire universel,* 2:1231; "Suite de l'extrait des observations sur le Cacao et le Chocolat; seconde partie," *Journal Oeconomique* (April 1772): 166.

42 "Seconde Lettre de M. Parmentier, aux Auteurs du Journal," *Journal de Paris* 93 (3 April 1785), 380. Parmentier's chocolate tips were surely appreciated, but it's for his other culinary crusades that we should be even more grateful. He was responsible for convincing the French that the potato was edible. Parmentier was also responsible for establishing the first mandatory

smallpox vaccination, pioneering the extraction of sugar from beets, and founding a school for bread-making.

43 Wolfgang Schivelbusch, *Tastes of Paradise: A Social History of Spices, Stimulants, and Intoxicants,* trans. David Jacobson (New York: Pantheon, 1992), 92, 87.

44 James, *Dictionnaire universel,* 2:1228; "Suite de l'extrait . . . ," *Journal Oeconomique* (April 1772): 162, 167; Denis Diderot, "Chocolat" in *Encyclopédie,* 3:359. Reformers may have waxed poetic about the value of chocolate as a source of food for the poor, but at least in Europe, it wasn't until the end of the Napoleonic Wars and the rise of industrialization that chocolate was truly affordable for the masses. The trajectory of chocolate's shift from a luxury good to a common commodity closely resembles that of sugar, which has been described by the historian Sidney Mintz. Changing economic and technological conditions not only facilitated a drop in sugar's price, but the conditions of factory work also created the need for cheap, calorie-heavy "convenience foods," which appealed to working-class families with limited time. The "fast food" culture with which we are so familiar today, laden with sugar and fat, actually had its roots in the eighteenth century (Sidney Mintz, *Sweetness and Power: The Place of Sugar in Modern History* [New York: Penguin, 1986], 148).

45 Louis Evan Grivetti, "Medicinal Chocolate in New Spain, Western Europe, and North America," in *Chocolate: History, Culture, and Heritage,* ed. Louis Evan Grivetti and Howard-Yana Shapiro (Hoboken, NJ: John Wiley, 2009), 74.

46 D. de Quélus, *The Natural History of Chocolate,* trans. J. Roberts (London, 1730), 58, quoted in Grivetti, 74.

47 Nicolas Lémery, *Dictionnaire universel des drogues simples* (Paris: Houry, 1760), s.v. "Chocolatum," 210.

48 Review of *Hygiene, five ars sanitatem conservandi, Poema. Auctore* Stephano-Ludovico Geoffroy . . . , *Journal Oeconomique* (Feb. 1772), 83.

49 Lémery, *Dictionnaire,* 209.

50 "Suite de l'extrait . . . ," *Journal Oeconomique* (April 1772), 165; Diderot, *Encyclopédie,* s.v. "Chocolat" 3:360; "Seconde Lettre de M. Parmentier . . . ," *Journal de Paris* 93 (3 April 1785), 380.

51 "Suite de l'extrait . . . ," *Journal Oeconomique* (April 1772): 162–63.

52 "Les proprietez du chocolat," in *Chansons Nouvelles* (Troyes: P. Garnier, [1685–1738]), 18.

53 "Critique sur le café," in *Chansons Nouvelles* (Troyes: P. Garnier, [1685–1738]), 11.

Chapter Three: Living in a World of Sound

1 Louis-Sébastien Mercier, *Panorama of Paris: Selections* from Le Tableau de Paris, ed. Jeremy D. Popkin, trans. Helen Simpson (University Park, PA: Pennsylvania State University Press, 1999), 97.

2 Ibid.

3 Ibid., 93.

4 Ibid.

5 Ibid., 95.

6 Jean-Aymar Piganiol de La Force, *Description historique de la ville de Paris et de ses environs, nouvelle édition* (Paris: Humaire, 1770), 3:293.

7 Emile Zola, *The Belly of Paris*, trans. Mark Kurlansky (New York: Modern Library, 2009), 32.

8 Mercier, *Panorama*, 96.

9 Daniel Roche, *A History of Everyday Things: The Birth of Consumption in France, 1600–1800*, trans. Brian Pearce (Cambridge: Cambridge University Press, 2000), 114.

10 Mercier, *Panorama*, 71.

11 *Journal de voyage de deux jeunes Hollandais à Paris en 1656–1658* (Paris: A.P. Faugère, 1899), 87.

12 Rebecca L. Spang, *Stuff and Money in the Time of the French Revolution* (Cambridge: Harvard University Press, 2015), 45.

13 Ibid., 46.

14 Wolfgang Schivelbusch, *Disenchanted Night: The Industrialization of Light in the Nineteenth Century*, trans. Angela Davies (Berkeley: University of California Press, 1995), 86.

15 Mercier, *Panorama*, 43.

16 Ibid., 132–33.

17 Christian Morrisson and Wayne Snyder, "The Income Inequality of France in Historical Perspective," *European Review of Economic History* 4, no. 1 (2000): 66.

18 Mercier, *Panorama*, 41.

19 Pierre-Joseph Macquer, quoted in Schivelbusch, *Disenchanted Night*, 11.

20 Schivelbusch, *Disenchanted Night*, 138.

21 Ibid., 9.

22 Rachel Bowlby, *Just Looking: Consumer Culture in Dreiser, Gissing, and Zola* (New York: Routledge Revivals, 2009), 1.

23 Guy Debord, *Society of the Spectacle,* Deadface Media Group, 2013, ¶1.

24 Karl Marx, "Economic and Philosophic Manuscripts of 1844," in *The Marx-Engels Reader,* 2d. ed., ed. Robert C. Tucker (New York: W. W. Norton, 1978), 89.

25 Marta Dischinger, "The Non-Careful Sight," in *Blindness and the Multi-Sensorial City*, ed. Patrick Devlieger, Frank Renders, Hubert Froyen, and Kristel Wildiers (Antwerp: Garant, 2006), 161.

26 Alec Forshaw and Theo Bergstrom, *Smithfield: Past and Present* (London: William Heinemann Ltd., 1980), 59, quoted in Carolyn Steel, *Hungry City: How Food Shapes Our Lives* (London: Vintage, 2013), 132.

27 Piganiol de La Force, *Description historique de la ville de Paris,* 3:293.

28 Daniel Roche, *The People of Paris: An Essay in Popular Culture in the 18th Century,* trans. Marie Evans and Gwynne Lewis (Berkeley: University of California Press, 1987), 233.

29 Restif de La Bretonne's love of literature already seems to have been present during his teenage years, when he served as an apprentice printer. Around the age of fifteen, he made love to his master's wife while reading one of Voltaire's plays aloud, and he was so devoted to this woman that he became infatuated with every woman who resembled her. This must have been a great many women, since the amorous author claimed to have accumulated 700 affairs. Evidently, the nocturnal spectator was particularly taken with feet, and the word for a sexual shoe fetish—"retifism"—bears testimony to his legacy (Jacques Barzun, "Introduction: Restif de La Bretonne," in *Les Nuits de Paris, or The Nocturnal Spectator: A Selection,* by Restif de La Bretonne, trans. Linda Asher and Ellen Fertig [New York: Random House, 1964], vii).

30 Ibid., 19.

31 These on-the-ground observations contradicted, or at least complicated, the opinions of the many Enlightenment economic and social theorists who believed in *doux commerce*, or "sweet commerce." Proponents of this idea argued that commerce had the power to polish and refine the manners of anyone participating in commercial exchange. For example, Montesquieu wrote in *Spirit of the Laws* (1748), "Commerce . . . polishes and softens barbaric ways," and Thomas Paine declared in *Rights of Man* in 1792, "[Commerce] is a pacific system, operating to cordialize mankind, by rendering Nations, as well as individuals, useful to each other." From this perspective, commercial exchange could soften even the roughest of demeanors, making society sweeter and gentler with every passing day. But to hear folks talk, it seems that sweet commerce had little effect on the salty and sour vendors of Les Halles. (All quoted in Albert Hirschman, "Rival Interpretations of Market Society: Civilizing, Destructive, or Feeble?" *Journal of Economic Literature* 20 [December 1982]: 1464–65.)

32 *Journal de voyage*, 87.

33 Henry de Lécluse, *Le Déjeuné de la rapée, ou, Discours des Halles et des Ports; avec un extrait de l'inventaire des meubles & effets trouvés dans le magasin a une des harangères de la Halle, & une liste des plus rares curiosites trouvés dans le même magasin.* (Duchesne, Grenouillère, 1758), 37–41.

34 *Journal de voyage*, 87.

35 Louis-Sébastien Mercier, *Tableau de Paris: Nouvelle édition, corigée et augmentée* (Amsterdam: n.p., 1782), 4:152.

36 Mercier, *Panorama*, 45.

37 Ibid., 133.

38 Fernand Braudel, *The Wheels of Commerce,* vol. 2 of *Civilization and Capitalism, 15th–18th Century,* trans. Siân Reynolds (New York: Harper & Row, 1982), 36.

39 "Chanson Nouvelle, Des agrémens des Halles et marchez de Paris," *Nouveau recueil de chansons* (ARTFL Electronic Edition, 2009).

40 Jean-Jacques Rousseau, *Discours sur l'origine et les fondements de l'inégalité parmi les hommes* (Amsterdam: Marc Michel Rey, 1755), 79–80.

41 Braudel, *Wheels of Commerce,* 30.

42 Louis-Sébastien Mercier, *Tableau de Paris: Nouvelle édition, corigée et augmentée* (Amsterdam: n.p., 1783), 6:220-21.

43 George Orwell, *The Road to Wigan Pier* (Orlando: Harvest Books, 1958), 127–28.

44 Mark Catesby, *The Natural History of Carolina, Florida, and the Bahama Islands* (London: Printed for C. Marsh, 1754), 2:viii, quoted in Mark M. Smith, *How Race Is Made: Slavery, Segregation, and the Senses* (Chapel Hill: University of North Carolina Press, 2006), 14.

45 David Howes and Marc Lalonde, "The History of Sensibilities: Of the Standard of Taste in Mid-Eighteenth-century England and the Circulation of Smells in Post-Revolutionary France," *Dialectical Anthropology* 16 (1991): 125–35.

46 Zola, *Belly of Paris,* 35.

Chapter Four: Becoming Useful Citizens

1 [Pierre-Jean-Baptiste Nougaret], "Foire Saint Ovide," in *Almanach forain, ou les Différens spectacles des boulevards et des foires de Paris* (Paris: Valleyre l'aîné, 1773), n.p.

2 Joan Lane, *A Social History of Medicine: Health, Healing, and Disease in England, 1750–1950* (New York: Routledge, 2001), 151.

3 Ibid.

4 Nicolas-Edme Restif de La Bretonne, "Complainte du paysan et de la paysanne chantée dans leur pays," in *Paysanne Pervertie, ou Les Dangers de la Ville* (Brussels: J.-J. Gay, 1883), 3:247.

5 Susan P. Conner, "The Pox in Eighteenth-century France," in *The Secret Malady: Venereal Disease in Eighteenth-century Britain and France,* ed. Linda E. Merians (Lexington: University Press of Kentucky, 1996), 26.

6 Annie Murphy Paul, *Origins: How the Nine Months Before Birth Shape the Rest of Our Lives* (New York: Simon & Schuster, 2010), 32.

7 Lane, *A Social History of Medicine,* 136.

8 John Rhodes, *The End of Plagues: The Global Battle Against Infectious Disease* (New York: Palgrave MacMillan, 2013), 12.

9 Guenter B. Risse, "Medicine in the Age of Enlightenment," in *Medicine in Society: Historical Essays,* ed. Andrew Wear (Cambridge: Cambridge University Press, 1992), 191.

10 Zina Weygand, *The Blind in French Society from the Middle Ages to the Century of Louis Braille,* trans. Emily-Jane Cohen (Stanford, CA: Stanford University Press, 2009), 16.

11 Ibid., 18–19.

12 A test conducted at MIT between 2003 and 2010, called Project Prakash, put the Molyneux problem to the test. It seems that John Locke was right. Subjects had no innate ability to transfer their tactile knowledge to the visual objects.

13 For more on the Molyneux problem, see Marjolein Degenaar, *Molyneux's Problem: Three Centuries of Discussion on the Perception of Forms,* trans. Michael J. Collins (Dordrecht: Kluwer Academic Publishers, 1996). Julien Offray de La Mettrie was quite the character. He trained as a physician under some of the most prominent doctors in Europe, after which he joined the army of the Gardes Français as a medical officer. He was dismissed from his post for a controversial publication, *Natural History of the Soul*, which was condemned by the Parliament of Paris and publicly burned by the hangman. Having few allies, La Mettrie fled to Holland, a country known for its free press. In late 1747, he published an even more scandalous book called *Man a Machine*, which, aptly enough, claimed that man was nothing more than a machine. It covered all sorts of topics, like babies' erections, cannibalism, madness, and evolution (well before Lamarck and Darwin made this topic famous). Even the tolerant Dutch couldn't stomach La Mettrie's sacrilege, so, under the protection of Frederick the Great, the King of Prussia, La Mettrie left for Berlin in 1748. Frederick apparently

took to the bright-eyed jokester and even personally delivered the philosopher's eulogy.

14 Antoine Le Camus, *Médecine de l'esprit* (Paris: Ganeau, 1753), 2:94–95.

15 Denis Diderot, "Lettre sur les aveugles," in *Oeuvres de Diderot*, ed. Laurent Versini (Paris: Robert Laffont, 1997), 1:147.

16 Ibid., 1:166.

17 Jean-Bernard Mérian, *Mémoires sur le problème de Molyneux*, ed. Francine Markovits (Paris: Flammarion, 1984), 180.

18 Ibid., 182–83.

19 Ibid., 185–86.

20 Ibid., 186.

21 Ibid., 183–84.

22 Ibid., 187.

23 Jean-Jacques Rousseau, *Émile,* trans. Barbara Foxley (London: Everyman, 1993), 122.

24 Ibid., 116.

25 Gaspard Guillard de Beaurieu, *L'Elève de la nature* (Lille: C. G. J. Lehoucq, 1778), 1:2, quoted in Julia V. Douthwaite, *The Wild Girl, Natural Man, and the Monster: Dangerous Experiments in the Age of Enlightenment* (Chicago: University of Chicago Press, 2002), 119.

26 Douthwaite, *The Wild Girl*, 129.

27 The Abbé Dulaurens had a bizarre set of experiences himself. As punishment for his blasphemies, Dulaurens's Catholic superiors kept the impious preacher suspended in a wooden cage at a Trinitarian monastery for several months. While captive, the wayward *abbé* used a metal scrap to carve poetry into the bars. Later, in 1767, he was imprisoned for his unorthodox writings, and he spent nearly thirty years incarcerated in a "convent-prison" where he eventually went mad (Douthwaite, *The Wild Girl,* 126).

28 Valentin Haüy, "Précis historique de la Naissance, des Progrès, et de l'état actuel de l'Institution des Enfans-Aveugles," in *Essai sur l'éducation des aveugles* (Paris: Enfans-Aveugles, sous la direction de M. Clousier, 1786), 119.

29 Catherine Duprat, *"Pour l'amour de l'humanité": Le temps des philanthropes: La philanthropie parisienne des Lumières à la monarchie de Juillet* (Paris: Éditions du C.T.H.S., 1993), 68.

30 Ibid., 8.

31 Haüy, *Essai sur l'éducation des aveugles*, vi.

32 In the late 1740s, a series of famines drove starving vagrants to Paris, and the Paris police began to round up any inactive citizens and lock them up,

put them to work, exile them from the city, or send them to populate the colonies in Louisiana or the Caribbean. This might have been well and good, but in the spring of 1750, rumors began to circulate that the police were kidnapping not just vagrants, but also the children of poor Parisians. Things came to a head on May 1, when a constable arrested six children that he found playing in the street; soldiers stepped in to oppose the arrest, and residents of the neighborhood joined the skirmish. On May 22 and 23, revolts erupted, and a constable who was accused of taking an eleven-year-old girl was murdered. His corpse was dragged to the Lieutenant General's house, and Parisians gathered at the house of the dead man's mistress. In a mock religious ceremony, they "blessed" a cat with gutter water, slit its throat, and burned it as a warning that all police spies could end up like the feline in question. The violence ended relatively quickly after a series of public-order measures were implemented (Arlette Farge and Jacques Revel, *The Vanishing Children of Paris: Rumor and Politics Before the French Revolution,* trans. Claudia Miéville [Cambridge: Harvard University Press, 1991]).

33 "Bienfaisance. Aux Auteurs du Journal," *Journal de Paris* 260 (September 17, 1784): 1101.

34 Haüy, *Essai sur l'éducation des aveugles,* 109–10; Ibid., 82.

35 "Bienfaisance," *Journal de Paris* 8 (September 8, 1787): 31.

36 Maurice de la Sizeranne, *The Blind as Seen Through Blind Eyes,* trans. F. Park Lewis (New York: G. P. Putnam's Sons, 1893), 68–69.

37 Patricia Fara, *An Entertainment for Angels: Electricity in the Enlightenment,* Revolutions in Science, ed. Jon Turney (Cambridge, UK: Totem Books, 2002), 15.

38 *Les Livres de Hiérome Cardanus médecin milanois, intitulés de la subtilité et subtiles inventions, ensemble les causes occultes et raisons d'icelles,* trans. Richard Le Blanc (Paris: G. Le Noir, 1556), 324b, quoted in Weygand, *The Blind in French Society,* 32.

Chapter Five: Blowing Smoke up the Ass

1 Benjamin Franklin, "A Letter to a Royal Academy (1781)," in *Fart Proudly: Writings of Benjamin Franklin You Never Read in School,* ed. Carl Japiske (Berkeley, CA: Frog Books, 2003), 13–17.

2 Franklin would be pleased as punch to discover that a Frenchman, Christian Poincheval, made the dream a reality. In 2007, Poincheval created the

Pilule Pet ("Fart Pill"), which can make a person's gas smell like ginger, chocolate, violet, or rose. There's also a version for dogs.

3 Alain Corbin, *The Foul and the Fragrant: Odor and the French Social Imagination* (Cambridge: Harvard University Press, 1988), 123.

4 Franklin, "A Letter to a Royal Academy," 13–17.

5 See Constance Classen, David Howes, and Anthony Synnott, *Aroma: The Cultural History of Smell* (New York: Routledge, 1994).

6 Albrecht von Haller, quoted in Corbin, *Foul and Fragrant*, 6.

7 Louis de Jaucourt, "Odorat," in *Encyclopédie, ou Dictionnaire raisonné des sciences, des arts et des métiers*, ed. Denis Diderot and Jean le Rond d'Alembert, (University of Chicago: ARTFL Encyclopédie Project, Spring 2013 Edition, ed. Robert Morrissey), http://encyclopedie.uchicago.edu. (accessed May 20, 2013), 11:354.

8 Dr. J. Hill, *Cautions Against the Immoderate Use of Snuff* (London, 1761), quoted in Wolfgang Schivelbusch, *Tastes of Paradise: A Social History of Spices, Stimulants, and Intoxicants*, trans. David Jacobson (New York: Pantheon, 1992), 145–46.

9 Jean-Jacques Rousseau, *Émile*, trans. Barbara Foxley (London: Everyman, 1993), 116–22.

10 Nancy G. Siraisi, *Medieval and Early Renaissance Medicine: An Introduction to Knowledge and Practice* (Chicago: University of Chicago Press, 1990), 124.

11 Georges Vigarello, *Le Propre et le sale: L'Hygiène du corps depuis le Moyen Âge* (Paris: Éditions du Seuil, 1985).

12 Joan DeJean, *The Age of Comfort: When Paris Discovered Casual—and the Modern Home Began* (New York: Bloomsbury, 2009), 71.

13 Ibid., 81.

14 Corbin, *Foul and Fragrant*, 67.

15 Ibid., 72.

16 Elisabeth de Feydeau, *A Scented Palace: The Secret History of Marie Antoinette's Perfumer*, trans. Jane Lizop (New York: I. B. Tauris, 2006), 58.

17 Ibid., 47.

18 Ibid., 3.

19 Jean-Louis Fargeon, *L'Art du parfumeur, ou Traité complet de la préparation des parfums, cosmétiques, pommades, pastilles, odeurs, huiles antiques, essences, bains aromatiques et des gants de senteur, etc.* (Paris: Delalain fils, 1801), 1.

20 Fargeon was arrested during the Revolution because of his ties to the crown, and he narrowly escaped the guillotine. While in prison, he wrote bitterly of his plight, asking, "To prove my patriotism, should I create a

perfume based upon the odor of blood that permeates the air around the guillotine?" (Feydeau, *A Scented Palace,* 3–4).

21 Ibid., 59.

22 Corbin, *Foul and Fragrant,* 17.

23 Pierre Bertholon, *De l'électricité du corps humain dans l'état de santé et de maladie* (Lyon: Bernuset, 1780), 22.

24 Ibid., 22–23.

25 Pierre Bertholon, *De l'électricité du corps humain dans l'état de santé et de maladie* (Paris: Croulbois; Lyon: Bernuset, 1786), 2:25–26, quoted in François Zanetti, "L'électricité du corps humain chez l'abbé Bertholon et quelques contemporains," *Annales historiques de l'électricité,* no. 8 (Dec. 2010): 14.

26 Paola Bertucci, "Sparking Controversy: Jean Antoine Nollet and Medical Electricity South of the Alps," *Nuncius* 20, no. 1 (2005): 164.

27 Ibid., 165.

28 Ibid., 154.

29 Ibid., 179.

30 François Zanetti, "L'électricité médicale dans la France des Lumières; Histoire culturelle d'un nouveau remède," Ph.D. dissertation (University of Paris X, 2011), 1:37.

31 "Registres contenant le jugement de la Société royale de médecine sur les remèdes et les différentes préparations qui lui ont été présentés, 1780–1783," Académie nationale de médecine, Société royale de médecine MS 14, 117.

32 Susan P. Conner, "The Pox in Eighteenth-century France," in *The Secret Malady: Venereal Disease in Eighteenth-century Britain and France,* ed. Linda E. Merians (Lexington: University Press of Kentucky, 1996), 24.

33 Nicolas André, *Dissertation sur les maladies de l'urèthre, qui ont besoin de bougies* (Paris: Pecquet, 1751), 186.

34 Ghislaine Lawrence, "Tools of the Trade: Tobacco Smoke Enemas," *Lancet* 359 (April 20, 2002): 1442.

35 Apparently, the French did not catch on to the bellows method as quickly, and as late as 1790, the Royal Society of Medicine was still receiving applications for "a machine for drowned people" that involved "a flexible tube made of supple leather, which ends in a nozzle that can be inserted in the anus for the injection of tobacco smoke." At least the leather was supple ("Registres contenant le jugement de la Société royale de médecine sur les remèdes et les différentes préparations qui lui ont été présentés," vol. 2, Académie nationale de médecine, Société royale de médecine, MS15, 300).

36 Roy Porter, *Flesh in the Age of Reason* (New York: W. W. Norton, 2003), 214.

37 Lawrence, "Tools of the Trade," 1442.

38 It is possible that the concept of the tobacco enema actually originated with Native Americans, who developed an impressive array of tobacco consumption methods (Jason Hughes, *Learning to Smoke: Tobacco Use in the West* [Chicago: University of Chicago Press, 2003], 21).

39 Falconet, Archives Nationales M852.

40 Académie royale des sciences procès verbaux 67 (1748), 101.

41 In ancient Greek medicine, there were four humors (black bile, yellow bile, blood, and phlegm), which were thought to have different properties: dry, moist, cold, or hot. Each of these also was thought to correspond to different temperaments—sanguine, melancholic, phlegmatic, or choleric—although it was possible for a person to have a mixed temperament. According to Louis XV's doctor, François Quesnay, you should really want to be bilious-melancholic-choleric, because people with this temperament have a brain that is soft enough to have a lively imagination, a relatively good memory, and only moderately melancholy tendencies.

42 Claude Brunet, *Le Bon usage du Tabac en Poudre* (Paris, 1700), quoted in Schivelbusch, *Tastes of Paradise,* 103.

43 Ibid.

44 *Collection Académique, composée des mémoires, actes ou journaux des plus Célébres Académies et Sociétés Littéraires, des Extraits des meilleurs Ouvrages Périodiques, des Traités particuliers et des Piéces Fugitives les plus rares, Concernant L'histoire naturelle et la botanique, la physique expérimentale et la chymie, la médecine et l'anatomie* (Dijon and Paris: François Desventes and Michel Lambert, 1766), 7:625.

45 Brunet, *Le Bon usage*, quoted in Schivelbusch, *Tastes of Paradise,* 103.

46 Gabriel-François Venel, "Odorant, Principe," in *Encyclopédie,* 11:353.

47 Ibid.; Henri Rousseau, *Préservatifs et remèdes universels tirés des animaux, des végétaux et des minéraux* (Paris: Claude Cellier, 1706), 107, quoted in Annick Le Guérer, *Le parfum: Des origines à nos jours* (Paris: Odile Jacob, 2005), 147.

48 Venel, "Odorant," 11:354.

49 Jean-Claude de La Métherie, *Vues physiologiques sur l'organisation animale et végétale* (Amsterdam and Paris: P. F. Didot, 1780), 311. Emphasis mine.

50 Inge Depoortere, "Taste Receptors of the Gut: Emerging Roles in Health and Disease," *Gut* 63, no. 1 (Jan. 2014): 179–90.

Chapter Six: What Is a Sense?

1   Joanna Cole and Bruce Degen, *The Magic School Bus Explores the Senses* (New York: Scholastic, 2001), 6.

2   Ian Ritchie, "Fusion of the Faculties: A Study of the Language of the Senses in Hausaland," in *The Varieties of Sensory Experience: A Sourcebook in the Anthropology of the Senses,* ed. David Howes (Toronto: University of Toronto Press, 1991), 194.

3   David Howes, "Introduction: The Revolving Sensorium," in *The Sixth Sense Reader*, ed. David Howes (Oxford, UK: Berg, 2009), 2.

4   Ibid., 24.

5   Aristotle, "On Sense and the Sensible," trans. J. I. Beare, in *The Works of Aristotle, Vol. 1, Great Books of the Western World* Series, ed. Robert Maynard Hutchins (Chicago: Encyclopædia Britannica, 1952), 8:673.

6   *Encyclopédie, ou Dictionnaire raisonné des sciences, des arts et des métiers*, ed. Denis Diderot and Jean le Rond D'Alembert, (University of Chicago: ARTFL Encyclopédie Project, Spring 2013 Edition, ed. Robert Morrissey), s.v. "Sens," http://encyclopedie.uchicago.edu. (accessed May 20, 2013), 15:24.

7   Étienne Bonnot de Condillac, *Traité des sensations*, in *Oeuvres complètes de Condillac* (Paris: Gratiot, Houel, Guillaume, Pougin & Gide, 1798), 3:51.

8   Bernard Mandeville, "Remark R," *The Fable of the Bees; or, Private Vices, Publick Benefits* (Adelaide: University of Adelaide Press, 2015), https://ebooks.adelaide.edu.au/m/mandeville/bernard/bees/index.html.

9   A materialist philosopher refers to someone who maintains that matter is the most fundamental substance in nature. Materialists held that everything, including thought, can be reduced to processes of material interactions. Almost all Enlightenment materialists were sensationalists but not all sensationalists were materialists. A number of sensationalist philosophers still stuck to the Christian line, and while they argued that the senses are our only means of learning about the world, they still left plenty of room for the soul or God. Materialists like Helvétius and his equally notorious friend the Baron d'Holbach maintained that the universe was nothing more than matter in motion, based on consistent laws of cause and effect.

10   Claude-Adrien Helvétius, *De l'esprit* (Paris: Durand, 1758), 238.

11   Emanuel Swedenborg, *The Delights of Wisdom Concerning Conjugial Love* (London: R. Hindmarsh, 1794), 165.

12   Leigh Eric Schmidt, "Swedenborg's Celestial Sensorium: Angelic Author-

ity, Religious Authority, and the American New Church Movement," in *The Sixth Sense Reader*, ed. David Howes (Oxford, UK: Berg, 2009), 162.

13 Georges-Louis Leclerc, Comte de Buffon, "Des sens en général," *Oeuvres complètes de Buffon,* ed. H. R. Duthilloeul (Douai: Tarlier, 1822), 3:263.

14 Ibid., 3:264.

15 Paul-Victor de Sèze, *Recherches phisiologiques et philosophiques sur la sensibilité ou la vie animale* (Paris: Prault, 1786), 151–52.

16 Jean Anthelme Brillat-Savarin, *The Physiology of Taste, or Meditations on Transcendental Gastronomy* (1925; reprint, Mineola, NY: Dover Publications, 2002), 3–4.

17 Ibid., 15–16.

18 Ibid., 16.

19 Ibid., 17.

20 Condillac, *Traité des sensations,* 52.

21 Immanuel Kant, *Lectures on Ethics,* ed. J. B. Schneewind; ed. and trans. Peter Heath (Cambridge: Cambridge University Press, 2001), 155; Immanuel Kant, *Anthropology from a Pragmatic Point of View,* ed. Robert B. Loudon (Cambridge: Cambridge University Press, 2006), 51.

22 Voltaire, *Philosophical Dictionary*, ed. and trans. Theodore Besterman (New York: Penguin, 2004), 29–31.

23 Ibid., 30.

24 Edmund Burke, "On the Sublime and Beautiful," *The Harvard Classics, Volume 24: Edmund Burke,* ed. Charles W. Eliot (New York: P. F. Collier & Son, 1909), 36.

25 Ibid., 38, 37.

26 Ibid., 30.

27 Ibid., 37.

28 Paul Henri Thiry, Baron d'Holbach, *The System of Nature,* trans. Samuel Wilkinson (1820–21; reprint, Whitefish, MT: Kessinger Publishing, 2004), 1:58.

29 Ibid., 1:19–20.

30 William Pattison, "A Tale" (1728), quoted in Aine Collier, *The Humble Little Condom: A History* (Amherst, NY: Prometheus Books, 2007), 77. A woman might feel as if she were choosing between Scylla and Charybdis when given the choice between a condom and another contraceptive method mentioned in Casanova's memoirs. One of the chevalier's particularly brazen lovers used part of a lemon as a cervical cap during their lovemaking (Giacomo Casanova, *The Memoirs of Giacomo Casanova di Seingalt,* trans. Arthur Machen [London: Casanova Society, 1922], 7:53).

31 Daniel Turner, *Syphilis: A Practical Dissertation on the Venereal Disease* (London: Bonwicke, Goodwin, Walthoe, Wotton, Manship, Wilkin, Tooke, Smith & Ward, 1717), 74.

32 Carol Blum, *Strength in Numbers: Population, Reproduction, and Power in Eighteenth-century France* (Baltimore: Johns Hopkins University Press, 2002), 3.

33 Ibid., 2.

34 Although his books were filthier than most, Sade certainly was not alone in writing philosophical pornography. In fact, as the historian Robert Darnton has beautifully shown, philosophical and political pornography were popular literary genres in the eighteenth century, and works falling into these categories were not simply dismissed as mindless smut.

35 Marquis de Sade, "Dialogue Between a Priest and a Dying Man (1782)," in *Justine, Philosophy in the Bedroom, and Other Writings*, ed. and trans. Richard Seaver and Austryn Wainhouse (New York: Grove Press, 1965), 165.

36 Caroline Warman, *Sade: From Materialism to Pornography, Studies in Voltaire and the Eighteenth Century* 1 (Oxford, UK: Voltaire Foundation, 2002), 69.

37 Ibid., 27.

38 Burke, "On the Sublime and Beautiful," 57.

39 Marquis de Sade, *Juliette,* trans. Austryn Wainhouse (New York: Grove Press, 1968), 232.

40 Ibid., 340–41.

41 Sade may not have been on many people's "best-loved" list, but his appreciation for shock resonated with the concerns of sociologists and psychologists that emerged a century later. In 1903, Georg Simmel argued that modern life—with its traffic, noise, crowds, and thrilling entertainments (like films and amusement parks)—was nothing more than a barrage of stimuli. Modern humans were hyperstimulated, and their sensory worlds were fundamentally different from those of the people who had come before them. Freud argued that humans develop a psychological mechanism to cope with these stimuli—the stimulus shield—but as the shield gets thicker, it takes ever-more stimulation to get through to a person. In other words, theorists at the turn of the twentieth century worried that the shocks of modern life created a psychological need for even greater shocks, and with industrialization, the rise of consumerism, and mass culture, humans grew increasingly desensitized to the world around them.

42 Warman, *Sade,* 81.

43 Marquis de Sade, *Philosophy in the Bedroom*, in *Justine, Philosophy in the*

Bedroom, and Other Writings, trans. Richard Seaver and Austryn Wainhouse (New York: Grove Press, 1965), 237–38.

44 Ibid., 238.

45 Ibid.

46 Warman, *Sade,* 81.

47 Emma Spary, *Utopia's Garden: French Natural History from Old Regime to Revolution* (Chicago: University of Chicago Press, 2000), 113–14.

Chapter Seven: Harmonious Nature

1 J.-B. Weckerlin, *Musiciana* (Paris: Garnier Frères, 1877), 348.

2 Ibid.

3 Pierre Bayle, *Historical and Critical Dictionary,* 2nd edition (London, 1736), 3:803.

4 Jacques Christophe Valmont de Bomare, *Dictionnaire raisonné universel d'histoire naturelle* (Paris: Lacombe, 1768), s.v. "chat," 2:50–51.

5 Harrison Weir, *Our Cats and All About Them: Their Varieties, Habits, and Management; and for Show, the Standard of Excellence and Beauty* (Boston and New York: Houghton, Mifflin & Co., 1889), 214.

6 Robert J. Richards, "Rhapsodies on a Cat-Piano, or Johann Christian Reil and the Foundations of Romantic Psychiatry," *Critical Inquiry* 24, no. 3 (Spring 1998): 702. His translation.

7 Ibid., 721–22.

8 Robert Darnton, *The Great Cat Massacre and Other Episodes in French Cultural History* (New York: Basic Books, 1984), 83.

9 Ibid., 76–77.

10 Ibid., 90–91.

11 Ibid., 95.

12 Athanasius Kircher, *Musurgia universalis* (Rome: Francesco Corbelletti, 1650), 1:37. Translation by Raymond J. Clark, in Suzannah Clark and Alexander Rehding, "Introduction," in *Music Theory and Natural Order from the Renaissance to the Early Twentieth Century,* ed. Suzannah Clark and Alexander Rehding (Cambridge: Cambridge University Press, 2001), 4.

13 Gaspar Schott, *Magia universalis naturae et artis, sive recondita naturalium et artificialium rerum scientia* (Würzburg: H. Pigrin, 1657–59), 2:371–73.

14 Louis-Bertrand Castel, "Clavecin pour les yeux, avec l'art de Peindre les sons, et toutes sortes de Pièces de Musique," *Mercure de France* (November 1725), 2559.

15 Louis-Bertrand Castel, "Suite et sixième Partie de Nouvelles Experiences d'Optique et d'Acoustique: adressées à M. le Président de Montesquieu, par le Pere Castel Jesuite," *Journal de Trévoux* (December 1735, Part 2), 2651.

16 Louis-Bertrand Castel, *L'optique des couleurs, Fondée sur les simples Observations, et tournée sur-tout à la pratique de la Peinture, de la Teinture et des autres Arts Coloristes* (Paris: Briasson, 1740), 298–300.

17 Ibid., 301.

18 Louis-Bertrand Castel, "Lettres du P. C[astel] J[ésuite] à Mr. L[e] C[omte] D[e] M[aillebois] L[ieutenant] G[énéral] des arm[ées] de S[a] M[ajesté]," 1752, Bibliothèque royale de Belgique/ Koninklijke bibliotheek van België [hereafter KBR], MS 20753-56, 50v°.

19 Kevin T. Dann, *Bright Colors Falsely Seen: Synaesthesia and the Search for Transcendental Knowledge* (New Haven: Yale University Press, 1998), 21.

20 Louis-Bertrand Castel, "Demonstration Geometrique du Clavecin pour les yeux et pour tous les sens, avec l'éclaircissement de quelques difficultez, et deux nouvelles Observations, par le R. P. Castel, Jesuite," *Mercure de France* (February 1726), 281.

21 Ibid., 279–80, 290.

22 Ibid., 286.

23 Castel, "Suite et sixième," 2731.

24 A number of cultures believe that red is a protective hue, and in 1910, the American physician James M. Phelan decided to put those powers to the test. He ran an experiment on 500 white soldiers in the Philippines to whom he supplied orange-red underwear. Phelan believed that these skivvies had the power to ward off ultraviolet rays. But when Phelan compared the well-being of his subjects with that of their compatriots, he was dismayed to find that those who wore the crimson undies fared worse. In fact, many complained of itchiness and discarded the briefs before the experiment ended (Warwick Anderson, *The Cultivation of Whiteness: Science, Health, and Racial Destiny in Australia,* [Durham, NC: Duke University Press, 2006], 153).

25 Louis-Bertrand Castel, "Suite et seconde partie des nouvelles expériences d'Optique et d'Acoustique, adressées à M. le Président de Montesquieu, Par le P. Castel, Jesuite," *Journal de Trévoux* (August 1735, part 2), 1625.

26 Louis-Bertrand Castel, "Lettres du P. C[astel] J[ésuite] à Mr. le C[omte] de M[aillebois]. Démonstration, théorico-pratique du clavecin oculaire," January 1753, KBR, MS 15746, 14r°, 23v°.

27 Louis-Bertrand Castel, "Lettres du P. C[astel] J[ésuite]," 1752, KBR, MS 20753-56, 47r°.

28 Descazeaux, "Stances sur le merveilleux Clavecin Oculaire," *Mercure de France* (April 1739), 769.

29 *Explanation of the Ocular Harpsichord, upon Shew to the Public* (London: Hooper & Morley, 1757), 2.

30 Castel, "Suite et sixième," 2645; Louis-Bertrand Castel, "Lettre D.P.C.I.A.M.L.P.D.M." *Journal de Trévoux* (August 1739), 1677.

31 Castel, "Lettres du P. C[astel] J[ésuite]," MS 15746, 17r°.

32 Louis-Bertrand Castel, "Lettre du Pere Castel, à M. Rondet, Mathématicien, sur sa Réponse au P.L.J. au sujet du Clavecin des couleurs," *Mercure de France* (July 1755), 144.

33 Castel, "Lettres du P. C[astel] J[ésuite]," MS 15746, 40v°-40r° [sic].

34 Ibid., 4v°.

35 Antoine Le Camus, *Médecine de l'esprit* (Paris: Ganeau, 1753), 2:82–83.

36 Polycarpe Poncelet, *Chimie du gout et de l'odorat, ou principes pour composer facilement, et à peu de frais, les Liquers à boire, et les Eaux de senteurs* (Paris: Imprimerie de P. G. Le Mercier, 1755), viii–ix.

37 Polycarpe Poncelet, *Nouvelle chymie du goût et de l'odorat, ou l'Art de composer facilement et à peu de frais les Liqueurs à boire et les Eaux de Senteurs, nouvelle édition* (Paris: Pissot, 1774), xl.

38 Joris-Karl Huysmans, *Against the Grain,* trans. John Howard (Project Gutenberg, 2004), Chapter 5, http://www.gutenberg.org/files/12341/12341-h/12341-h.htm.

39 Félix Fénéon, (1886), quoted in Dann, *Bright Colors Falsely Seen,* 27.

40 Charles Baudelaire, *Les Fleurs du mal* (Paris: Poulet-Malassis & de Broise, 1857), 20.

41 Jules Millet, *Audition colorée* (Paris: Octave Doin, 1892), quoted in Dann, *Bright Colors,* 29.

42 George Field, *Chromatics; Or, the Analogy, Harmony, and Philosophy of Colours,* 2nd ed. (London: David Bogue, 1845), 76.

43 S. Piesse, *Histoire des parfums et hygiène de la toilette* (Paris: J.-B. Baillière & fils, 1905), 29.

44 Antoine Louis Claude Destutt, comte de Tracy, *Élémens d'idéologie* (Brussels: August Wahlen, 1826), 1:24–25.

45 George Field, *Ethics, or the Analogy of the Moral Sciences Indicated: Comprehending Morals, Politics, and Theology* (London, 1824), 458.

46 Ibid., 474.

47 Castel, "Lettres du P. C[astel] J[ésuite] à Mr. L[e] C[omte] D[e] M[aillbeois]," MS 20753-56, 47v°.

Chapter Eight: Calling It Macaroni

1   Stella Blum, "Introduction," in *Eighteenth-century French Fashions in Full Color: 64 Engravings from the "Galerie des Modes," 1778–1787* (New York: Dover, 1982), viii.

2   Joan DeJean, *The Age of Comfort: When Paris Discovered Casual—and the Modern Home Began* (New York: Bloomsbury, 2009), 207.

3   Patrick Baty, "The History of Paint and the Birth of DIY," *Country Life Online,* August 2010, http://www.countrylife.co.uk/articles/the-history-of-paint-and-the-birth-of-diy-21348.

4   Daniel Roche, *The Culture of Clothing: Dress and Fashion in the Ancien Régime* (Cambridge: Cambridge University Press, 1996), 383.

5   Patrick Baty, "The Hierarchy of Colour in Eighteenth-century Decoration," *Patrick Baty* 2011, http://patrickbaty.co.uk/2011/11/13/hierarchy-of-colours/.

6   Mitchell Owens, "Monticello's Bright Past," *Elle Décor,* July/August 2010, 48.

7   Baty, "The Hierarchy of Colour."

8   Patrick Baty, "The Methods and Materials of the House-Painter in England: An Analysis of House-Painting Literature, 1660–1850," (B.A. thesis, University of East London, 1993), 91.

9   Blum, "Introduction," vii.

10 Ibid.

11 DeJean, *Age of Comfort,* 152.

12 Daniel Roche, *A History of Everyday Things: The Birth of Consumption in France, 1600–1800* (Cambridge: Cambridge University Press, 2000), 117.

13 Edmund Burke, *Burke's Philosophical Inquiry into the Origin of Our Ideas of the Sublime and Beautiful: With an Introductory Discourse Concerning Taste* (Baltimore: William and Joseph Neal, 1833), 134.

14 Caroline Weber, *Queen of Fashion: What Marie Antoinette Wore to the Revolution* (New York: Picador, 2007), 149.

15 DeJean, *Age of Comfort,* 153.

16 Jean-Jacques Rousseau, *Émile,* trans. Barbara Foxley (London and North Clarendon, VT: Everyman, 1993), 140.

17 Rebecca L. Spang, *The Invention of the Restaurant: Paris and Modern Gastronomic Culture* (Cambridge: Harvard University Press, 2001), 54.

18 One of the most famous cases of "maternal impressions" was that of Mary Toft, an eighteenth-century Englishwoman who was reputed to give birth to rabbits after being startled in the fields by one of the creatures during

her pregnancy. The theory had a remarkably long life, and even as late as 1794, it was commonly accepted in France. The mother of an infant born with a birthmark that resembled the Phrygian cap, a French Revolutionary symbol, was awarded an annual pension by the government as thanks for her patriotism (Jan Bondeson, *A Cabinet of Medical Curiosities* [New York: W. W. Norton, 1997], 122–55).

19 Spang, *Invention of the Restaurant*, 55.

20 Kathleen M. Brown, *Foul Bodies: Cleanliness in America* (New Haven: Yale University Press, 2011), 98–117.

21 Ibid., 111.

22 Ibid., 108.

23 David Batchelor, *Chromophobia* (London: Reaktion Books, 2000), 22.

24 Michael Taussig, *What Color Is the Sacred?* (Chicago: University of Chicago Press, 2009), 136.

25 Johann Wolfgang von Goethe, *Theory of Colors,* trans. C. L. Eastlake (Cambridge: MIT Press, 1970), 55, quoted in Batchelor, *Chromophobia,* 112.

26 Batchelor, *Chromophobia,* 23.

27 Ibid., 22.

28 Georges-Louis Leclerc, Comte de Buffon, *Histoire naturelle, générale et particulière avec la description du cabinet du roi* (Paris: Imprimerie royale, 1766), 14:314.

29 Kimberly Chrisman-Campbell, *Fashion Victims: Dress at the Court of Louis XVI and Marie-Antoinette* (New Haven: Yale University Press, 2015), 25.

30 Ibid., 10, 17.

31 Ibid., 41.

32 Weber, *Queen of Fashion,* 117.

33 Ibid., 158.

34 William Doyle, *The Oxford History of the French Revolution,* 2nd ed. (Oxford: Oxford University Press, 2003), 86.

35 A quick sketch of the French Revolution:

1789: The Estates-General, a legislative assembly, was called. The members got into a fight about representation, and the representatives of the Third Estate declared themselves the "National Assembly." The National Assembly announced on August 4 that all feudal rights were to be abolished, and later that month they accepted the "Declaration of the Rights of Man and Citizen," which outlined a series of natural rights. In September, they put limits on the king's powers.

1790: The National Assembly issued the "Civil Constitution of the Clergy," which required priests to take an oath of loyalty to the state above the pope. Political clubs like the Cordeliers and Jacobins grew in importance.

1791: Louis XVI and Marie-Antoinette were caught trying to escape. This episode was called "the Flight to Varennes" in honor of the city where they were caught. Public opinion turned against them, and they were seen as uncooperative with the new political changes. In September, Louis XVI reluctantly accepted the French Constitution of 1791, which set up a constitutional monarchy in which the king still had power but was ultimately beholden to a bicameral parliament. The National Assembly was dissolved, and the Legislative Assembly formed to build a new set of laws.

1792: The Legislative Assembly was split between moderate members who favored the constitutional monarchy and the more radical Jacobins who viewed the king as a traitor and called for more radical reform. In August, Louis XVI and the rest of the royal family were arrested. In September, the Legislative Assembly called for the provisional suspension of Louis XVI. A body called the National Convention, elected by universal male suffrage, came together to create a new constitution. Louis was brought to trial, and the politician Robespierre argued, "Louis must die so that the country may live."

1793: Louis XVI was beheaded, and the Committee of Public Safety was formed. It became the *de facto* executive government during the Reign of Terror, the period of violence for which the French Revolution is so well known. The Terror continued into 1794, many people were beheaded, and a number of new political measures were passed.

1794: Robespierre, the head of the Committee of Public Safety, was guillotined, and the Terror ended.

1795: The 1795 Constitution was ratified, and it set up an executive directory of five members. They remained in power until 1799, when Napoleon became the First Consul of the Republic, and the Revolution is generally considered to have ended.

36 *The Encyclopedia Britannica*, 11th ed., s.v. "Foullon, Joseph-François."

37 Weber, *Queen of Fashion,* 238.

38 Ibid., 242.

39 *Encyclopaedia Americana*, ed. Francis Lieber, E. Wigglesworth, and T. G. Bradford (Philadelphia, Carey & Lea, 1832), s.v. "tricolore."

40 Doyle, *French Revolution,* 121.

41 Rebecca L. Spang, *Stuff and Money in the Time of the French Revolution* (Cambridge: Harvard University Press, 2015), 142.

42 Ibid., 143.

43 *Encyclopaedia Americana,* s.v. "tricolore."

44 Ibid.

Chapter Nine; The Gourmand's Gaze

1 Giles MacDonogh, *A Palate in Revolution: Grimod de La Reynière and the* Almanach des Gourmands (London: Robin Clark, 1987), 7, 20.

2 Ibid., 22.

3 Phyllis P. Bober, "The Black or Hell Banquet," in *Oxford Symposium on Food and Cookery: Feasting and* Fasting, ed. Harlan Walker (London: Prospect Books, 1991), 55.

4 MacDonogh, *Palate in Revolution,* 24.

5 Ibid., 102–3.

6 Grimod's feast did have some precedents. The Roman emperor Domitian threw a "Hell Banquet" intended to terrify his political enemies. The dinner featured all-black food on black dishes, and the slave boys who served the food were painted black. Domitian refused to entertain any conversation that wasn't about death. (Actually, it seems that no one talked because all the guests were too horrified, so Domitian had a solo, death-themed soapbox that evening.) Macabre feasts also took place in the Renaissance at Carnival and the beginning of Lent. One feast from 1511 offered guests food in the shapes of lizards, scorpions, serpents, and other "devilish" creatures. Around the room, various tortures were staged, spotlighted at different points by the "flames of Hell" (Bober, 56).

7 Daniel Roche, *The Culture of Clothing: Dress and Fashion in the Ancien Régime* (Cambridge: Cambridge University Press, 1996), 58.

8 Jean-Paul Aron, *The Art of Eating in France: Manners and Menus in the Nineteenth Century,* trans. Nina Rootes (New York: Harper & Row, 1975), 24.

9 MacDonogh, *Palate in Revolution,* 49.

10 Ibid., 108.

11 Jean-Anthelme Brillat-Savarin, *The Physiology of Taste, or Meditations on Transcendental Gastronomy* (1925; reprint, Mineola, NY: Dover Publications, 2002), 35.

12 Alexandre Balthazar Laurent Grimod de la Reynière, "From *The Gourmand's Almanac* (1803–12)," in *Gusto: Essential Writings in Nineteenth-Century Gastronomy,* ed. Denise Gigante, trans. Michael Garval (New York: Routledge, 2005), 7.

13 Launcelot Sturgeon, *Essays, Moral, Philosophical, and Stomachical, on the Important Science of Good-Living,* 2nd ed. (London: G. and W. B. Whittaker, 1823), 39.

14 William Kitchiner, "From *Peptic Precepts* (1821)," in *Gusto,* 72.

15 The Alderman (pseudonym), "From *The Knife and Fork* (1849)," in *Gusto,* 239–40.

16 William Blanchard Jerrold, "From *The Epicure's Year Book and Table Companion* (1868)," in *Gusto,* 259.

17 Sturgeon, *Essays,* 162.

18 Grimod de la Reynière, "From *The Gourmand's Almanac,*" 28.

19 David Howes and Marc Lalonde, "The History of Sensibilities: Of the Standard of Taste in Mid-Eighteenth-century England and the Circulation of Smells in Post-Revolutionary France," *Dialectical Anthropology* 16 (1991): 130.

20 In India, the metaphor of "taste" for aesthetic capacities had been used since at least the third century C.E., but in Europe, the term "taste" as an aesthetic indicator came into use much later. Some historians date its first appearance to the fifteenth century, while others cite the following quotation by the seventeenth-century Spanish writer Baltasar Gracián y Morales as its first use: "Just as large morsels are suited to big mouths, so are high matters to high minds." The common use of the term really caught on in the eighteenth century (Carolyn Korsmeyer, "Part V: Preface," in *The Taste Culture Reader: Experiencing Food and Drink,* ed. Carolyn Korsmeyer [Oxford, UK: Berg, 2007]; Denise Gigante, *Taste: A Literary History* [New Haven: Yale University Press, 2005], 17).

21 David Hume, "Of the Standard of Taste," in *The Taste Culture Reader: Experiencing Food and Drink,* ed. Carolyn Korsmeyer (Oxford, UK: Berg, 2007), 202.

22 Ibid., 203.

23 Sturgeon, *Essays,* 4–5.

24 Grimod de la Reynière, "From *The Gourmand's Almanac,*" 12.

25 Ibid., 34.

26 Ibid.

27 Grimod de la Reynière, "From *The Gourmand's Almanac,*" 35.

28 Sturgeon, *Essays,* 36.

29 Hermits seemed to fascinate the well-to-do in this period. If a person had ample means and sprawling grounds in the long eighteenth century, he might succumb to the trend to hire an "ornamental hermit" to live in his garden. The hermit would reside in an on-premises hermitage and

make routine appearances to the home owner and his guests, given the gentry's conviction that "nothing . . . could give such delight to the eye, as the spectacle of an aged person, with a long grey beard, and a goatish rough robe, doddering about amongst the discomforts and pleasures of Nature" (Edith Sitwell, *English Eccentrics* [London: Faber & Faber, 1933], 48).

30 Ian Kelly, *Cooking for Kings: The Life of Antonin Carême, the First Celebrity Chef* (New York: Walker & Co., 2003), 38.

31 Paul Metzner, *Crescendo of the Virtuoso: Spectacle, Skill, and Self-Promotion in Paris During the Age of Revolution* (Berkeley: University of California Press, 1998), 73.

32 Maria Rundell, *New System of Domestic Cookery* (Exeter, Norris & Sawyer, 1807), 322–23, quoted in C. Anne Wilson, *Luncheon, Nuncheon, and Other Meals: Eating with the Victorians* (Dover, NH: Alan Sutton Publishing, 1994), 150.

33 Tiffany K. Wayne, *Women's Roles in Nineteenth-Century America* (Westport, CT: Greenwood Press, 2007), 29; Kiyoshi Shintani, "Cooking Up Modernity: Culinary Reformers and the Making of Consumer Culture, 1876–1916" (Ph.D. diss., University of Oregon, 2008), 152.

34 Andrea Broomfield, *Food and Cooking in Victorian England: A History* (Westport, CT: Praeger, 2007), 27.

35 Ibid., 21.

36 Sarah Freeman, *Mutton and Oysters: The Victorians and Their Food* (London: V. Gollancz, 1989), 69.

37 Russell Thacher Trall, *The New Hydropathic Cook-Book; with Recipes for Cooking on Hygienic Principles* (New York: Samuel R. Wells, 1873), v–vi.

38 *Our Own Book: A Victorian Guide to Life; Homespun Cuisine, Health, Romance, Etiquette, Raising Children and Farm Animals,* ed. Diane Janowski (Elmira, NY: New York History Review Press, 2008), 24, 29.

39 Dena Attar, "Keeping Up Appearances: The Genteel Art of Dining in Middle-Class Victorian Britain," in *The Appetite and the Eye: Visual Aspects of Food and Its Presentation Within Their Historic Context*, ed. C. Anne Wilson (Edinburgh: Edinburgh University Press, 1991), 132.

40 Ibid., 140.

41 I want to stress that this is the norm for modern America, with the caveat that certain populations like hunters or farmers might be well versed in the biological realities of meat. In other countries, the food traditions are different, and seeing fish with heads or ducks with feathers may not be considered shocking.

42 Norbert Elias, *The Civilizing Process: Sociogenetic and Psychogenetic Investigations* (Oxford, UK: Blackwell, 2000), 102.

43 Freeman, *Mutton and Oysters,* 92.

44 "Dirty Father Thames," *Punch* 378 (7 Oct. 1848): 151.

45 Denise Gigante, "Introduction," in *Gusto,* xxxv.

46 Joris-Karl Huysmans, *Against the Grain,* trans. John Howard (Project Gutenberg, 2004), Chapter 2, http://www.gutenberg.org/files/12341/12341-h/12341-h.htm.

47 Ibid., Chapter 1.

48 Joris-Karl Huysmans, "Préface," in *À rebours* (Paris: Gallimard Folio, 1977), quoted in Dean de la Motte, "Writing Against the Grain: *À rebours,* Revolution, and the Modernist Novel," in *Modernity and Revolution in Late Nineteenth-Century France,* ed. Barbara T. Cooper and Mary Donaldson-Evans (Newark: University of Delaware Press, 1992), 24.

Chapter Ten: Digesting Nature

1 Elizabeth Oke Gordon, *The Life and Correspondence of William Buckland, D.D., F.R.S., Sometime Dean of Westminster, Twice President of the Geological Society, and First President of the British Association* (London: J. Murray, 1894), 35.

2 Ibid., 31.

3 Augustus J. C. Hare, *The Story of My Life,* (London: George Allen, 1900), 5:358.

4 Ibid., 104.

5 When Frank heard that a panther at the Surrey Zoological Gardens had died, he wrote the curator asking for a couple of panther chops. The panther had been buried a couple of days earlier, but Frank insisted that it be dug up and butchered. Unsurprisingly, he decided that the panther was "not very good" (Harriet Ritvo, *The Animal Estate*: *The English and Other Creatures in the Victorian Age* [Cambridge: Harvard University Press, 1987], 238).

6 Peter Lund Simmonds, *The Curiosities of Food; Or, the Dainties and Delicacies of Different Nations Obtained from the Animal Kingdom* (London: R. Bentley, 1859), 52.

7 Ian Cameron, *To the Farthest Ends of the Earth: 150 Years of World Exploration by the Royal Geographical Society* (New York: E. P. Dutton, 1980), 16.

8   Clements Robert Markham, *Fifty Years' Work of the Royal Geographical Society* (London: J. Murray, 1881), 17.

9   Sofia Åkerberg, *Knowledge and Pleasure at Regent's Park: The Gardens of the Zoological Society of London During the Nineteenth Century* (Umeå, SWE: Department of Historical Studies, Umeå University, 2001), 194.

10 A. D. Bartlett, a superintendent of the Regent's Park Zoo, recorded the difficulty of disposing of great quantities of elephant meat. After the Royal College of Surgeons took the "useful" parts of a dead elephant, Bartlett sold the remains to a cat-meat vendor. Apparently, the vendor found it difficult to use so much meat as well, and he was obliged to salt great quantities to keep it from rotting. Consequently, he nearly lost all of his customers because the cats refused to eat the salty elephant (A. D. Bartlett, *Wild Animals in Captivity: Being an Account of the Habits, Food, Management and Treatment of the Beasts and Birds at the 'Zoo,'* ed. Edward Bartlett [London: Chapman & Hall, 1899], 54).

11 *Hints for the Table: Or the Economy of Good Living* (London: George Routledge & Sons, 1866), 58, quoted in Harriet Ritvo, *The Platypus and the Mermaid, and Other Figments of the Classifying Imagination* (Cambridge: Harvard University Press, 1997), 194; Simmonds, *The Curiosities of Food,* 5.

12 Walter Arnold, *The Life and Death of the Sublime Society of Beef Steaks* (London: Bradbury, Evans & Co., 1871), 2.

13 Simmonds, *Curiosities of Food,* 2.

14 Sarah Freeman, *Mutton and Oysters: The Victorians and Their Food* (London: V. Gollancz, 1989), 27.

15 Francis Buckland, "Acclimatisation of Animals," *Journal of the Society of Arts* 9 (Nov. 30, 1860): 19–30.

16 George Bompas, *Life of Frank Buckland,* 6th ed. (London: Smith, Elder & Co., 1885), 102–3.

17 A similar movement is gaining traction in the United States today. The activist Daniella Martin (author of the blog Girl Meets Bug and the book *Edible: An Adventure into the World of Eating Insects and the Last Great Hope to Save the Planet*) argues that entomophagy is a practical ecological alternative to our current food practices, and a number of start-ups like Bitty Foods and Exo began marketing cricket flour, hoping that it would gain traction as the next big protein. David Gracer, a writing professor and ardent entomophagist, has boldly declared, "Cows and pigs are the S.U.V.s; bugs are the bicycles" (Sam Nejame, "Man Bites Insect," *New York Times,* 10 Feb., 2008).

18 Simmonds, *Curiosities of Food,* 9, 70.

19 Louis Fraser, *Catalogue of the Knowsley Collections* (Knowsley, 1850), iii, quoted in Ritvo, *Animal Estate*, 239.

20 Bompas, *Life of Frank Buckland,* 116–21.

21 G. H. O. Burgess, *The Eccentric Ark: The Curious World of Frank Buckland* (New York: Horizon Press, 1967), 91–92.

22 Similar attempts were taking place in France as well. The French Imperial Acclimatization Society was founded in 1854, thanks to the efforts of the biologist Geoffroy Saint-Hilaire. By 1860, the French society had over 2,000 members, which included the King of Siam and the Emperor of Brazil.

23 Burgess, *Eccentric Ark,* 92.

24 Constance Classen, "Museum Manners: The Sensory Life of the Early Museum," *Journal of Social History* 40, no. 4 (Summer 2007): 895–914.

25 Hare, *Story of My Life,* 5:358.

26 William Tuckwell, *Reminiscences of Oxford* (New York: E. P. Dutton, 1908), 41.

27 Bompas, *Life of Frank Buckland,* 432.

28 Ibid., 28.

29 Ibid., 432.

30 *The Mummy!* described England in 2126, which was prospering under the reign of a female monarch. In addition to the Internet, espresso machines, and air-conditioning, the novel foreshadowed the invention of the steam plow, a technological insight that attracted the attention of John Claudius Loudon, a botanist, landscape enthusiast, and cemetery designer. His interest piqued, he made Jane's acquaintance, and one thing led to another, such that they were married seven months later.

31 Jane Loudon, *Mrs. Loudon's Entertaining Naturalist, Being Popular Descriptions, Tales, and Anecdotes of More than Five Hundred Animals* (London: Bell & Daldy, 1867), 39, 45, 64.

32 A 2006 scientific report has shown that an extract taken from the Chilean starfish *Stichaster striatus* could act as a deterrent to alcohol consumption. Supposedly, in rats with a "genetically established excessive appetite for alcohol," the extract effectively quashed their desire for alcohol. In case you're wondering how the scientists even thought to try this, they were basing their initial research on an oral tradition handed down from the seventeenth and eighteenth centuries. According to the story, laborers who worked on Jesuit-owned properties during the Spanish conquest of America were given a liquid made from boiled starfish, which would keep them from becoming alcoholics. (M. Font, N. Bilbeny, S. Contreras, C. Paeile, H. Garcia, "Effect of ME-3451-106, an Aqueous Extract of Stichaster stri-

atus with Inhibitory Activity of Voluntary Alcohol Intake, in Genetically Drinker Rats: Isolation and Identification of the Active Fraction," *Journal of Ethnopharmacology* 105, no. 1-2 [21 April 2006]: 26–33.)

33 "The Crystal Palace, at Sydenham," *Illustrated London News* (7 Jan. 1854): 22.

34 "Fun in a Fossil," *Punch, or the London Charivari,* vol. 26 (1854): 24.

35 "Bill of Fare at a Dinner Given at the Crystal Palace," Benjamin Waterhouse Hawkins Album Images, The Academy of Natural Sciences of Drexel University, Archives Collection 803.

36 Loudon, *Entertaining Naturalist,* 91, 75.

37 "The Dinner Question. Discussed by an Eight Hundred a Year Man," in *Bentley's Miscellany* 45 (1859): 166.

38 Frank Buckland, *Log-book of a Fisherman and Zoologist* (London: Chapman & Hall, 1876), 73.

39 Burgess, *Eccentric Ark,* 137.

40 Dab (pseudonym), *Land and Water* 8 (30 Oct. 1869), quoted in Burgess, *Eccentric Ark,* 138.

41 Bompas, *Life of Frank Buckland,* 99–100.

42 Richard Owen, *The Times* (21 Jan. 1859), quoted in Burgess, *Eccentric Ark,* 90.

43 Richard Owen, *The Life of Richard Owen* (New York: AMS Press, 1975), 1:114. A she-giraffe would have actually been one of the most expensive exotic animals at this time. The Zoological Society paid anywhere between £250 and £500 for a single giraffe, although at one point they considered paying £2,000 for a well-acclimated giraffe from Spain (Henry Scherren, *The Zoological Society of London: A Sketch of its Foundation and Development and the Story of Its Farm, Gardens, Menagerie, and Library* [London: Cassell & Co., 1905], 61–64).

44 "The Eland," in *Chambers's Journal of Popular Literature, Science, and Arts* 272 (March 1859): 183.

45 Gordon, *Life and Correspondence of William Buckland,* 25.

Epilogue: Seeing Is Not Believing

1 Elizabeth Oke Gordon, *The Life and Correspondence of William Buckland, D.D., F.R.S., Sometime Dean of Westminster, Twice President of the Geological Society, and First President of the British Association* (London: J. Murray, 1894), 31.

2 Martin Jay, *Force Fields: Between Intellectual History and Cultural Critique* (New York: Routledge, 1992), 114.

3 Constance Classen, David Howes, and Anthony Synnott; *Aroma: The Cultural History of Smell* (New York: Routledge, 1994), 4. Even though this is the dominant narrative, that's not to say that it has gone unquestioned. Mark M. Smith makes this clear in his book *Sensing the Past:* "If we take seriously the argument that the Enlightenment was more sensate and less overpoweringly visual than the great divide theory suggests, we open up theoretical crawlspace to understand how the non-visual senses remained important even as vision became more muscular." But by and large, the basic narrative has remained standing, as you can even see in Smith's concluding statement that "vision became more muscular" (Mark M. Smith, *Sensing the Past: Seeing, Hearing, Smelling, Tasting, and Touching in History* [Berkeley: University of California Press, 2008], 32).

4 Leigh Eric Schmidt, *Hearing Things: Religion, Illusion, and the American Enlightenment* (Cambridge: Harvard University Press, 2000), 22.

5 Robert Jütte, *A History of the Senses: From Antiquity to Cyberspace* (Cambridge, UK: Polity, 2005), 186.

6 R. R. Palmer, *Catholics and Unbelievers in Eighteenth-century France* (Princeton: Princeton University Press, 1939).

7 Jessica Riskin, *Science in the Age of Sensibility: The Sentimental Empiricists of the French Enlightenment* (Chicago: University of Chicago Press, 2002).

8 Anne C. Vila, *Enlightenment and Pathology: Sensibility in the Literature and Medicine of Eighteenth-century France* (Baltimore: Johns Hopkins University Press, 1998), 5.

9 Denis Diderot, "Letter on the Deaf and Dumb," in *Diderot's Early Philosophical Works,* ed. and trans. Margaret Jourdain (Chicago: Open Court Publishing, 1916), 165.

10 Isser Woloch, *The New Regime: Tranformations of the French Civic Order, 1789–1820s* (New York: W. W. Norton, 1994), 173–207.

11 Voltaire, *A Philosophical Dictionary,* in *The Works of Voltaire: A Contemporary Version,* ed. Tobias Smollett, trans. William F. Fleming (Akron, Ohio: Werner Co., 1904), 11:137.

12 Voltaire, *Philosophical Dictionary*, ed. and trans. Theodore Besterman (New York: Penguin, 2004), 379–80.

IMAGE CREDITS

35   Claude-Nicolas Le Cat, *Oeuvres physiologiques,* vol. 1, *Traité des sensations et des passions en générale et des sens en particulier* (Paris: Vallat-la-Chapelle, 1767). Courtesy of University of Chicago Special Collections Research Center.

36   Claude-Nicolas Le Cat, *Oeuvres physiologiques,* vol. 1, *Traité des sensations et des passions en générale et des sens en particulier* (Paris: Vallat-la-Chapelle, 1767). Courtesy of University of Chicago Special Collections Research Center.

88   "Grand concert extraordinaire exécuté par un détachement des quinze Vingts au Caffé des Aveugles, Foire Saint Ovide au Mois de Septembre 1771." Engraving. Paris: Mondare, rue St. Jacques. Reprinted, with permission, courtesy of Bibliothèque nationale de France.

135   Giacomo Casanova, *Mémoires, écrits par lui-même,* vol. 4 (Brussels, 1872). Courtesy of the Library of Congress, LC-USZ62-48784.

145   Johann Theodor de Bry, "Auriculus Midae Non Musica Gratior Ulla Est," *Emblemata saecularia* (1611; repr. Berlin: J. A. Stargardt, 1894). Courtesy of University of Chicago Special Collections Research Center.

INDEX

Page numbers in *italics* refer to illustrations.